D0563576

1

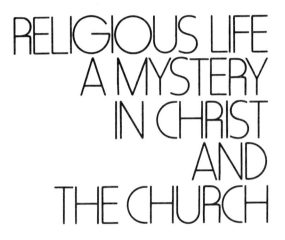

RELIGIOUS LIFE
A MYSTERY
IN CHRIST
AND
THE CHURCH

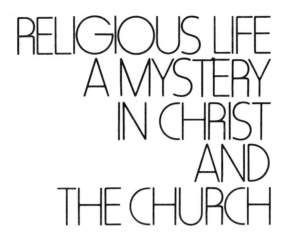

RELIGIOUS LIFE A MYSTERY IN CHRIST AND THE CHURCH

A Collated Study According to
Vatican Council II and Subsequent
Papal and Ecclesial Documents

Edited by

Sister M. Rose Eileen Masterman C.S.C.

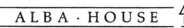 ALBA · HOUSE 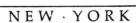 NEW · YORK

SOCIETY OF ST. PAUL, 2187 VICTORY BLVD., STATEN ISLAND, NEW YORK 10314

ACKNOWLEDGMENTS

U.S.C.C. for selections from *Ecclesiae Sanctae, Renovationis Causam, Venite Seorsum, Mysterium Fidei, Provida Mater Ecclesia, Primo Feliciter,* and *Cum Sanctissimus.*

America Press Inc., *Documents of Vatican II* (1966), Walter M. Abbott, S.J., Ed., for selections from *Lumen Gentium, Perfectae Caritatis, Christus Dominus,* and *Ad Gentes.*

Consortium Perfectae Caritatis, Inc. for the text of *Evangelica Testificatio.*

Library of Congress Cataloging
in Publication Data

Vatican Council. 2d, 1962-1965.
Religious life—a mystery in Christ
and the Church.

1. Monastic and religious life—Collected works.
I.   Masterman, Rose Eileen. II. Title.
BX2435.V37   1975   255   75-8729
ISBN 0-8189-0303-1

*Designed, printed and bound in the United States of
America by the Fathers and Brothers of the Society of St. Paul,
2187 Victory Boulevard, Staten Island, New York, 10314,
as part of their communications apostolate.*

1 2 3 4 5 6 7 8 9 (Current Printing: first digit).

AUTHOR'S FOREWORD

Contemporary concern for the present state of religious life is profound and momentous. The radical cause generally cited by perceptive observers is misunderstanding, or ignorance, or what is more disturbing, an unwillingness to accept principles and directives of the MAGISTERIUM of the Church expressed in II Vatican Council and subsequent papal and ecclesial documents concerning authentic religious life. How else may one account for the steadily mounting trends toward its secularization and attendant errors? To bring to primacy the perspective of religious life according to the teachings of the MAGISTERIUM, and, therefore according to the mind and will of Christ, is the essential purpose of this collated study.

The history of the past several years since the promulgation of these documents has witnessed many sincere but frequently ineffective efforts directed to the *"aggiornamento"* of religious life, which failed objectively through primacy placed on "adaptation" rather than on deep interior "renewal," both individual and communal, among many religious. Moreover, while in such efforts much has been said, written and attempted by way of implementation concerning "openness to the Spirit," there has been often an obvious omission of the primary and essential element in the process of authentic discernment upon which such "openness" rests, namely the expressed mind of the Church regarding religious life in the documents of her MAGISTERIUM.

Pope Paul VI speaking as Supreme Pontiff when proclaiming EVANGELICA TESTIFICATIO, his "Apostolic Exhortation to the Members of Every Religious Family in the Catholic World," was deeply aware that "in the process of dynamic excitement" (*aggiornamento*) "there is always danger that the spirit of the world becomes mixed in with the action of the Holy Spirit" (cf. ET, no. 6). He then asks the questions: "How can We help you make the right discernment as is necessary? How can the experience of past ages, joined with the result of present day reflection, be turned to appropriate practice, in order to strengthen the form of evangelical life?"

His answer is emphatically decisive: "According to the singular office and responsibility which God has laid upon us in His Church —that we must strengthen our brethren (Lk 22:32)—We want to have you proceed with greater security of mind and more joyful confidence along the way you have chosen. In the 'pursuit of perfect charity' (cf. *Decree on the Appropriate Renewal of Religious Life*) by which your life is ruled, how should you act otherwise than to be completely responsive to the Holy Spirit who, *working in the Church*, is calling you to the liberty of the children of God." (Gal 5:13; 2 Cor 3:17)

In this era of history, the Holy Spirit has called religious to attend to and discern His movements toward perfect charity, not *essentially* through psychology, sociology, anthropology, but rather through His words promulgated through the MAGISTERIUM of the Body of Christ, the Church. The present collated study of such teachings makes easily available all that the Holy Spirit has spoken at this time and in conformity with the authentic traditional teaching on religious life through the ages. Not subjective norms, effects of private discernment divorced from the objective reality of the voice of the Holy Spirit spoken through the Church, but those principles, norms and directives communicated to and through the living MAGISTERIUM which will safeguard the efficacy of authentic renewal of those who follow the path of evangelical, ecclesial religious life, the "divine gift to the Church" which she treasures, supports, and guides in the name and power of Christ Himself.

May the Holy Spirit, Soul of Christ's Body, the Church, bring to the fullness of "perfect charity" all who like Mary "ponder these things" in their heart, and seek to discern and implement in their lives what He has spoken through these conciliar, papal and ecclesial documents.   Sister M. Rose Eileen Masterman, C.S.C.

PREFACE

Religious life is radical. Freely to choose to live as pilgrims in a frugal and virginal dedication is so drastic that many men and women can scarcely grasp it even after one gives an adequate explanation. To surrender property, position and married love for the sake of a kingdom yet fully to come is so drastic that few "can take it."

The vision of religious life presented in these pages is exciting because it is real. It is the undiluted vision of the New Testament articulated for us in modern terms by the teaching Church. It is radical because it presents religious life as very different indeed from other vocations in the midst of God's people. It is prophetic because it declares the holy will of the Lord without debilitating compromise. It is new both because it calls for crucial adaptations and growth and because revealed truth is always new: "Jesus Christ is the same today as he was yesterday and as he will be for ever" (Heb 13:8).

A vision of religious life that leaves it indistinguishable from lay life is obviously neither radical nor prophetic. It is dull and uninteresting precisely because it is a least common denominator. The secular world itself is supremely uninterested in religious who live like everyone else. There is nothing to learn from them that the world does not already better know. They lack credibility.

Will Herberg has rightly pointed out that no lasting reform movement in the Catholic Church has ever succeeded without or against the Papacy. Contemporary history bears him out. Religious congregations that are following the guidelines of the teaching Church are usually coming through the difficulties of adaptation far more successfully than those who are rejecting those guidelines. The former tend to attract young people in considerable numbers, the latter do not. The former are united, the latter are polarized. Good theology works.

This volume presents the mind of the contemporary teaching Church on religious life. Sister M. Rose Eileen is to be commended for the diligent competency she has brought to this work of editing and collating these magisterial statements. May these pages aid formation personnel, general chapters and individual religious in achieving what St. Cyprian had in mind when back about 250 A.D. he characterized the early virgins as "the most illustrious portion of the flock of Christ."   —Thomas Dubay, S.M.

INTRODUCTION

Two recent developments, among several others, augment hope that the message of Vatican Council II, with all its rich potential for spiritual renewal and religious maturity, may be having a new birth of vigor and effective realization.

The first is the appearance of new translations, more carefully considered and competently weighed, of the documents of the Council. Inevitably, the first translations to appear immediately in the wake of the Council suffered from inescapable limitations. They were perforce hasty and even, on occasion tentative, even tendentious. The style of the translations was often journalistic rather than academic and scientific. Impromptu "reactions" were frequently appended to documents which, following on translations already suffering from lack of final clarity, complicated yet further the understanding of what the Council actually said and obscured the spirit of what the Council actually sought.

Accordingly, the message of the Council suffered in both letter and spirit, with consequent reduced impact and orderly, not to say enthusiastic implementation. If it be true, as it is, that the tendency of the letter of the law is to *inhibit* while that of the spirit is to *vivify*, it is not less true that unless one knows what the law is, all talk about its spirit, purpose and content becomes diffuse, counterproductive and in due course futile.

Hence the opportune nature of the new and restudied translations which are beginning to appear to replace with permanently valid texts the somewhat tentative, if for the moment necessary, first rapid versions. Hence, too, and not at all less useful, the value of a new development: the appearance of specialized, pin-pointed collections of precisely and only what was said on specific major points on which the Council pronounced and competent post-Conciliar agencies provided clarification and application of what was said.

Comes now Sister M. Rose Eileen Masterman, C.S.C., of St. Mary's, Notre Dame, with a veritable treasury of such specialized and organized ready-reference Council material on the Mystery of the Religious Life. The title might be misleading; Sister M. Rose Eileen Masterman obviously intends that her work spark meditation, but her dominant purpose is to provide, systematically and completely, the *exact letter* and *every letter* of Vatican Council teaching on religious life so that those who have the *spirit* or are open to the *spirit* may be helped to achieve sound renewal, authentic adaptation of selves and communities through holy and needed experimentation in the pursuit of that perfect charity which has always been, is now and will remain the heart's core of religious life.

There is no form of religious life and no aspect of its potential for good or possibility of problematic that is not somewhere touched upon and illumined in Vatican Council II. Nor is any of the mystery of religious life marginal to the mystery of the Church. Quite the contrary: the present writer for years before the Council was insisting in writing, retreats and public conferences that Catholic religious life was the "secret strength" of the Church wherever in the world the Church is found and whatever the work it is doing. Never a student in the Sisters' schools nor otherwise brought into contact with the religious in his formative years, he came to discover with maturing years that a major part of his fascination and love for the mystery of the Church was increasingly bound up with reflection on and marvel at the Religious Life as a supreme attempt to live out, literally and totally, everything that the Church is and should be.

There may be some among the disenchanted or battle-weary who question whether this projection of the spiritual splendor of the Church through the mystery of the Religious Life will radiate again in our day or the near future. The time schedule of such a renaissance or of any other renewal in the Church is not ours to guess; it is in the hands of God and therefore in good hands.

What is certain is that come it *must*, for the mystery of the Church demands as *essential* unique values proper to the Religious Life, just as salvation history and the human condition demand the presence among us at all times of those who are unashamedly seeking the *greater* perfection, making the *greater* sacrifice and bearing the *greater* witness. Such are those who pursue the Religious Life.

One other thing is certain: the great return and needed renewal will be hastened by the letter and spirit of Vatican Council II honestly understood, and therefore by Sister M. Rose Eileen Masterman's masterful, patient and lucid presentation of these in this indispensable book. God prosper it! *The coming of His Kingdom is at issue!*

John Cardinal Wright
Vatican City, October, 1974

CONTENTS

LIST OF ABBREVIATIONS

AG   *Ad Gentes,* Decree on the Church's Missionary Activity

AI   *Ad Instituenda,* June 4, 1970

BM   *Behold Your Mother—Woman of Faith,* U.S.A. National Conference of Bishops

CD   *Christus Dominus,* Decree on Bishops' Pastoral Office in the Church

CS   *Cum Sanctimissimus,* Secular Institutes, 1948

DC   *Dum Canonicarum,* December 8, 1970

DV   *Dei Verbum,* Dogmatic Constitution on Divine Revelation

ECRR   Decree, *Experimenta circa Regiminis Rationem,* February 2, 1972

ES   *Ecclesiae Sanctae,* Norms for the Implementation of *Christus Dominus, Presbyterorum Ordinis, Perfectae Caritatis,* and *Ad Gentes,* August 6, 1966

ET   *Evangelica Testificatio,* Apostolic Exhortation of the Supreme Pontiff, Paul VI, to the Members of Every Religious Family in the Catholic World, June 29, 1971

GE   *Gravissimum Educationis,* Decree on Christian Education

GS   *Gaudium et Spes,* Pastoral Constitution on the Church in the Modern World

IC   *Immensiae Caritatis,* Holy Eucharist, 1973

ID   *Indulgentiarum Doctrina,* Apostolic Constitution, On Indulgences, Pope Paul VI, June 1, 1967

LG   *Lumen Gentium,* Dogmatic Constitution on the Church

MC   *Marialis Cultis,* Pope Paul VI's Apostolic Constitution on Right Ordering and Development of Devotion to the Blessed Virgin Mary, February 2, 1974

ME	*Mysterium Ecclesiae*, Declaration in Defence of the Catholic Doctrine on the Church against Certain Errors of the Present Day, June 24, 1973
MF	*Mysterium Fidei*, The Mystery of Faith, Pope Paul VI, September 3, 1965
OT	*Optatam Totius*, Decree on Priestly Formation
OP	Ordo Paenitentiae, 1974
PC	*Perfectae Caritatis*, Decree on Appropriate Renewal of Religious Life
PF	*Primo Feliciter*, Secular Institutes, 1948
PM	*Pastorale Munus*, *Motu Proprio* of Paul VI granting special faculties and privileges to Local Ordinaries on a Permanent Basis, November 30, 1963
PME	*Provido Mater Ecclesia*, Secular Institutes 1947
RC	*Renovationis Causam*, Religious Formation, January 7, 1969
RL	*Religionum Laicalum*, Laicization of Religious, May 5, 1966
SC	*Sacrosanctum Concilium*, Pastoral Constitution on the Liturgy
SS	*Sedes Sapientiae*, Seat of Wisdom
SUI	Sacram Unctionem Infirmorum, Anointing of the Sick, 1972
SV	*Sacra Virginitate*, Sacred Virginity, March 25, 1954
UR	*Unitatis Redintegratio*, Decree on Ecumenism
VS	*Venite Seorsum*, Instruction on the Contemplative Life and on the Enclosure of Nuns, August 15, 1969
SCRSI	*Sacred Congregation for Religious and Secular Institutes*, Documents

PART ONE

THE MYSTERY OF THE CHURCH IN THE
MYSTERY OF CHRIST

TRINITARIAN—CHRISTOLOGICAL—SPIRIT-FILLED

THE CHURCH AS THE PRIMARY
AND PERENNIAL FONT OF ALL HOLINESS

THE CALL OF THE BODY OF CHRIST TO HOLINESS—
THE HOLINESS OF THE TRINITY, SOURCE, CAUSE,
AND END OF THE ONE SAME HOLINESS IN THE CHURCH

CHAPTER 1

THE CHURCH IN THE MYSTERY OF CHRIST

For the doctrinal basis of the Decree on the Appropriate Renewal of the Religious Life one must look to the foundational text of the Council, the *Constitution on the Church*. The Constitution declares that *everyone* in the Church is called to holiness in his own state of life, not merely certain Christians who have been set apart in monasteries and convents.

(Cf. LG, nos. 1-8)

LG 1. Christ is the light of all nations. Hence this most sacred Synod, which has been gathered in the Holy Spirit, eagerly desires to shed on all men that radiance of His which brightens the countenance of the Church. This it will do by proclaiming the gospel to every creature (cf. Mk 16:15).

By her relationship with Christ, the Church is a kind of sacrament or sign of intimate union with God, and of the unity of all mankind. She is also an instrument for the achievement of such union and unity. For this reason, following in the path laid out by its predecessors, this Council wishes to set forth more precisely to the faithful and to the entire world the nature and encompassing mission of the Church. The conditions of this age lend special urgency to the Church's task of bringing all men to full union with Christ, since mankind today is joined together more closely than ever before by social, technical, and cultural bonds.

LG 2. By an utterly free and mysterious decree of His own wisdom and goodness, the eternal Father created the whole world. His plan was to dignify men with a participation in His own divine life. He did not abandon men after they had fallen in Adam, but ceaselessly offered them helps to salvation, in anticipation of Christ the Redeemer, "who is the image of the invisible God, the firstborn of every creature" (Col 1:15). All the elect, before time began, the Father "foreknew and predestined to become conformed to the image of his Son, that he should be the firstborn among many brethren" (Rm 8:29).

He planned to assemble in the holy Church all those who would believe in Christ. Already from the beginning of the world the foreshadowing of the Church took place. She was prepared for in a remarkable way throughout the history of the people of Israel and by means of the Old Covenant. Established in the present era of time, the Church was made manifest by the outpouring of the Spirit. At the end of time she will achieve her glorious fulfillment. Then, as may be read in the holy Fathers, all just men from the time of Adam "from Abel, the just one, to the last of the elect," will be gathered together with the Father in the universal Church.

LG 3. The Son, therefore, came on mission from His Father. It was in Him, before the foundation of the world, that the Father chose us and predestined us to become adopted sons, for in Him it has pleased the Father to re-establish all things (cf. Ep 1:4-5, 10). To carry out the will of the Father, Christ inaugurated the kingdom of heaven on earth and revealed to us the mystery of the Father. By His obedience He brought about redemption. The Church, or, in other words, the kingdom of Christ now present in mystery, grows visibly in the world through the power of God.

This inauguration and this growth are both symbolized by the blood and water which flowed from the open side of the crucified Jesus (cf. Jn 19:34), and are foretold in the Lord's words concerning His death on the cross: "And I, if I be lifted up from the earth, will draw all men to myself" (Jn 12:32, Greek text). As often as the sacrifice of the cross in which "Christ, our passover, has been sacrificed" (1 Cor 5:7) is celebrated on an altar, the work of our redemption is carried on. At the same time, in the sacrament of the Eucharistic bread the unity of all believers who form one body in Christ (cf. 1 Cor 10:17) is both expressed and brought about. All men are called to this union with Christ, who is the light of the world, from whom we go forth, through whom we live, and toward whom our journey leads us.

LG 4. When the work which the Father had given the Son to do on earth (cf. Jn 17:4) was accomplished, the Holy Spirit was sent on the day of Pentecost in order that He might forever sanctify the Church, and thus all believers would have access to the Father through Christ in the one Spirit (cf. Ep 2:18). He is the Spirit of life, a fountain of water springing up to life eternal (cf. Jn 4:14; 7:38-39). Through Him the Father gives life to men who are dead from sin, till at last He revives in Christ even their mortal bodies (cf. Rm 8:10-11).

The Spirit dwells in the Church and in the hearts of the faithful as in a temple (cf. 1 Cor 3:16; 6:19). In them He prays and bears witness to the fact that they are adopted sons (cf. Gal 4:6; Rm 8: 15-16, 26). The Spirit guides the Church into the fullness of truth (cf. Jn 16:13) and gives her a unity of fellowship and service. He furnishes and directs her with various gifts, both hierarchical and charismatic, and adorns her with the fruits of His grace (cf. Ep 4:11-12; 1 Cor 12:4; Gal 5:22). By the power of the gospel He makes the Church grow, perpetually renews her, and leads her to perfect union with her Spouse. The Spirit and the Bride both say to the Lord Jesus, "Come!" (cf. Rv. 22:17).

Thus, the Church shines forth as "a people made one with the unity of the Father, the Son, and the Holy Spirit."

LG 5. The mystery of the holy Church is manifest in her very foundation, for the Lord Jesus inaugurated her by preaching the good news, that is, the coming of God's Kingdom, which, for centuries, had been promised in the Scriptures: "The time is fulfilled, and the kingdom of God is at hand" (Mk 1:15; cf. Mt 4:17). In Christ's word, in His works, and in His presence this kingdom reveals itself to men. The word of the Lord is like a seed sown in a field (Mk 4:14). Those who hear the word with faith and become part of the little flock of Christ (Lk 12:32) have received the kingdom itself. Then, by its own power the seed sprouts and ripens until harvest time (cf. Mk 4:26-29).

The miracles of Jesus also confirm that the kingdom has already arrived on earth: "If I cast out devils by the finger of God, then the kingdom of God has come upon you" (Lk 11:20; cf. Mt 12:28).

Before all things, however, the kingdom is clearly visible in the very person of Christ, Son of God and Son of Man, who came "to serve, and to give his life as a ransom for many" (Mk 10:45).

When Jesus rose up again after suffering death on the cross for mankind, He manifested that He had been appointed Lord, Messiah, and Priest forever (cf. Ac 2:36; Heb 5:6; 7:17-21), and He poured out on His disciples the Spirit promised by the Father (cf. Ac 2:33). The Church, consequently, equipped with the gifts of her Founder and faithfully guarding His precepts of charity, humility, and self-sacrifice, receives the mission to proclaim and to establish among all peoples the kingdom of Christ and of God. She becomes on earth the initial budding forth of that kingdom. While she slowly grows, the Church strains toward the consummation of the kingdom and, with all her strength, hopes and desires to be united in glory with her King.

LG 6. In the Old Testament the revelation of the kingdom had often been conveyed by figures of speech. In the same way the inner nature of the Church was now to be made known to us through various images. Drawn from pastoral life, agriculture, building construction, and even from family and married life, these images served a preparatory role in the writings of the prophets.

Thus, the Church is a sheepfold whose one and necessary door is Christ (Jn 10:1-10). She is a flock of which God Himself foretold that He would be the Shepherd (cf. Is 40:11; Ez 34:11 ff.). Although guided by human shepherds, her sheep are nevertheless ceaselessly led and nourished by Christ Himself, the Good Shepherd and the Prince of Shepherds (cf. Jn 10:11; 1 P 5:4), who gave His life for the sheep (cf. Jn 10:11-15).

The Church is a tract of land to be cultivated, the field of God (1 Cor 3:9). On that land grows the ancient olive tree whose holy roots were the patriarchs and in which the reconciliation of Jew and Gentile has been brought about and will be brought about (Rm 11:13-26). The Church has been cultivated by the heavenly Vinedresser as His choice vineyard (Mt 21:33-43 par.; cf. Is 5:1 ff.).

The true Vine is Christ who gives life and fruitfulness to the branches, that is, to us. Through the Church, we abide in Christ, without whom we can do nothing (Jn 15:1-5).

The Church has more often been called the edifice of God (1 Cor 3:9). Even the Lord likened Himself to the stone which the builders rejected, but which became the cornerstone (Mt 21:42 par.; cf. Ac 4:11; 1 P 2:7; Ps 117:22). On this foundation the Church is built by the apostles (cf. 1 Cor 3:11), and from it the Church receives durability and solidity. This edifice is adorned by various names: the house of God (1 Tm 3:15) in which dwells His family; the household of God in the Spirit (Ep 2:19-22); the dwelling place of God among men (Rv 21:3); and, especially, the holy temple. This temple, symbolized by places of worship built out of stone, is praised by the holy Fathers and, not without reason, is compared in the liturgy to the Holy City, the New Jerusalem. As living stones we here on earth are being built up along with this City (1 P 2:5). John contemplates this Holy City, coming down out of heaven from God when the world is made anew, and prepared like a bride adorned for her husband (Rv 21:1 f.).

The Church, "that Jerusalem which is above," is also called "our Mother" (Gal 4:26; cf. Rv 12:17). She is described as the spotless spouse of the spotless Lamb (Rv 19:7; 21:2, 9; 22:17). She it was whom Christ "loved and delivered himself up for her that he might sanctify her" (Ep 5:26), whom He unites to Himself by an unbreakable covenant, and whom He unceasingly "nourishes" and cherishes" (Ep 5:29). Once she had been purified, He willed her to be joined unto Himself and to be subject to Him in love and fidelity (cf. Ep 5:24). Finally, He filled her with heavenly gifts for all eternity, in order that we might know the love of God and of Christ for us, a love which surpasses all knowledge (cf. Ep 3:19). The Church on earth, while journeying in a foreign land away from her Lord (cf. 2 Cor 5:6), regards herself as an exile. Hence she seeks and experiences those things which are above, where Christ is seated at the right hand of God, where the life of the Church is hidden with Christ in God until she appears in glory with her Spouse (cf. Col 3:1-4).

LG 7. In the human nature which He united to Himself, the Son of God redeemed man and transformed him into a new creature (cf. Gal 6:15; 2 Cor 5:17) by overcoming death through His own death and resurrection. By communicating His Spirit to His brothers, called together from all peoples, Christ made them mystically into His own body.

In that body, the life of Christ is poured into the believers, who, through the sacraments, are united in a hidden and real way to Christ who suffered and was glorified. Through baptism we are formed in the likeness of Christ: "For in one Spirit we were all baptized into one body" (1 Cor 12:13). In this sacred rite, a union with Christ's death and resurrection is both symbolized and brought about: "For we were buried with him by means of Baptism into death." And if "we have been united with him in the likeness of his death, we shall be so in the likeness of his resurrection also" (Rm 6: 4-5).

Truly partaking of the body of the Lord in the breaking of the Eucharistic bread, we are taken up into communion with Him and with one another. "Because the bread is one, we though many, are one body, all of us who partake of the one bread" (1 Cor 10:17). In this way all of us are made members of His body (cf. 1 Cor 12:27), "but severally members one of another" (Rm 12:5).

As all the members of the human body, though they are many, form one body, so also are the faithful in Christ (cf. 1 Cor 12:12). Also, in the building up of Christ's body there is a flourishing variety of members and functions. There is only one Spirit who, according to His own richness and the needs of the ministries, distributes His different gifts for the welfare of the Church (cf. 1 Cor 12:1-11). Among these gifts stands out the grace given to the apostles. To their authority, the Spirit Himself subjected even those who were endowed with charisms (cf. 1 Cor 14). Giving the body unity through Himself and through His power and through the internal cohesion of its members, this same Spirit produces and urges love among the believers. Consequently, if one member suffers anything, all the members suffer it too, and if one member is honored, all the members rejoice together (cf. 1 Cor 12:26).

The Head of this body is Christ. He is the image of the invisible God and in Him all things came into being. He has priority over everyone and in Him all things hold together. He is the Head of that body which is the Church. He is the beginning, the firstborn from the dead, so that in all things He might have the first place (cf. Col 1:15-18). By the greatness of His power He rules the things of heaven and the things of earth, and with His all-surpassing perfection and activity He fills the whole body with the riches of His glory (cf. Ep 1:18-23).

All the members ought to be molded into Christ's image until He is formed in them (cf. Gal 4:19). For this reason we who have been made like unto Him, who have died with Him and been raised up with Him, are taken up into the mysteries of His life, until we reign together with Him (cf. Ph 3:21; 2 Tm 2:11; Ep 2:6; Col 2:12; etc.). Still in pilgrimage upon the earth, we trace in trial and under oppression the paths He trod. Made one with His sufferings as the body is one with the head, we endure with Him, that with Him we may be glorified (cf. Rm 8:17).

From Him, "the whole body, supplied and built up by joints and ligaments, attains a growth that is of God" (Col 2:19). He continually distributes in His body, that is, in the Church, gifts of ministries through which, by His own power, we serve each other unto salvation so that, carrying out the truth in love, we may through all things grow up into Him who is our head (cf. Ep 4:11-16, Greek text).

In order that we may be unceasingly renewed in Him (cf. Ep 4:23), He has shared with us His Spirit who, existing as one and the same being in the head and in the members, vivifies, unifies, and moves the whole body. This He does in such a way that His work could be compared by the holy Fathers with the function which the soul fulfills in the human body, whose principle of life the soul is.

Having become the model of a man loving his wife as his own body, Christ loves the Church as His bride (cf. Ep 5:25-28). For her part, the Church is subject to her Head (cf. Ep 5:22-23). "For in him dwells all the fullness of the Godhead bodily" (Col

2:9). He fills the Church, which is His Body and His fullness, with His divine gifts (cf. Ep 1:22-23) so that she may grow and reach all the fullness of God (cf. Ep 3:19).

LG 8. Christ, the one Mediator, established and ceaselessly sustains here on earth His holy Church, the community of faith, hope, and charity, as a visible structure. Through her He communicates truth and grace to all. But the society furnished with hierarchical agencies and the Mystical Body of Christ are not to be considered as two realities, nor are the visible assembly and the spiritual community, nor the earthly Church and the Church enriched with heavenly things. Rather they form one interlocked reality which is comprised of a divine and a human element. For this reason, by an excellent analogy, this reality is compared to the mystery of the incarnate Word. Just as the assumed nature inseparably united to the divine Word serves Him as a living instrument of salvation, so, in a similar way, does the communal structure of the Church serve Christ's Spirit, who vivifies it by way of building up the body (cf. Ep 4:16).

This is the unique Church of Christ which in the Creed we avow as one, holy, catholic, and apostolic. After His Resurrection our Savior handed her over to Peter to be shepherded (Jn 21:17), commissioning him and the other apostles to propagate and govern her (cf. Mt 28:18 ff.). Her He erected for all ages as "the pillar and mainstay of the truth" (1 Tm 3:15). This Church, constituted and organized in the world as a society, subsists in the Catholic Church, which is governed by the successor of Peter and by the bishops in union with that successor, although many elements of sanctification and of truth can be found outside of her visible structure. These elements, however, as gifts properly belonging to the Church of Christ, possess an inner dynamism toward Catholic unity.

Just as Christ carried out the work of redemption in poverty and under oppression, so the Church is called to follow the same path in communicating to men the fruits of salvation. Christ Jesus, "though He was by nature God . . . emptied himself, taking the nature of a slave" (Ph 2:6), and "being rich, he became poor" (2 Cor 8:9) for our sakes. Thus although the Church needs human resources to carry out her mission, she is not set up to seek earthly glory, but to proclaim humility and self-sacrifice, even by her own example.

Christ was sent by the Father "to bring good news to the poor, to heal the contrite of heart" (Lk 4:18), "to seek and to save what was lost" (Lk 19:10). Similarly, the Church encompasses with love all those who are afflicted with human weakness. Indeed, she recognizes in the poor and the suffering the likeness of her poor and suffering Founder. She does all she can to relieve their need and in them she strives to serve Christ. While Christ, "holy, innocent, undefiled" (Heb 7:26) knew nothing of sin (2 Cor 5:21), but came to expiate only the sins of the people (cf. Heb 2:17), the Church, embracing sinners in her bosom, is at the same time holy and always in need of being purified, and incessantly pursues the path of penance and renewal.

The Church, "like a pilgrim in a foreign land, presses forward amid the persecutions of the world and the consolations of God," announcing the cross and death of the Lord until He comes (cf. 1 Cor 11:26). By the power of the risen Lord, she is given strength to overcome patiently and lovingly the afflictions and hardships which assail her from within and without, and to show forth in the world the mystery of the Lord in a faithful though shadowed way, until at the last it will be revealed in total splendor.

Cf. *Mysterium Ecclesiae*—The Mystery of the Church—Congregation for the Faith, June 24, 1973.

Cf. *Indulgentiarum Doctrina*—Apostolic Constitution on Indulgences, January 1, 1967.

CHAPTER 2

THE MYSTERY OF HOLINESS

THE CALL OF THE BODY OF CHRIST TO HOLINESS—
THE HOLINESS OF THE TRINITY—
THE SOURCE, CAUSE, AND END OF THE ONE,
SAME HOLINESS IN CHRIST'S BODY, THE CHURCH

Holiness is primarily an attribute of God, "He alone is holy"; therefore all human holiness can only be a share in, or a participation through the *grace of God*, in God's holiness in Christ and in His Body, the Church.

LG 39. Faith teaches that the Church, whose mystery is being set forth by this sacred Synod, is holy in a way which can never fail. For Christ, the Son of God, who with the Father and the Spirit is praised as being "alone holy," loved the Church as His Bride, delivering Himself up for her. This He did that He might sanctify her (cf. Ep 5:25-26). He united her to Himself as His own body and crowned her with the gift of the Holy Spirit, for God's glory. Therefore in the Church, everyone belonging to the hierarchy, or being cared for by it, is called to holiness, according to the saying of the Apostle: "For this is the will of God, your sanctification" (1 Th 4:3; cf. Ep 1:4).

Now, this holiness of the Church is unceasingly manifested, as it ought to be, through those fruits of grace that the Spirit produces in the faithful. It is expressed in multiple ways by those individuals who, in their walk of life, strive for the perfection of charity, and thereby help others to grow. In a particularly appropriate way this holiness shines out in the practice of the counsels

customarily called "evangelical." Under the influence of the Holy
Spirit, the practice of these counsels is undertaken by many Christians, either privately or in some Church-approved situation or state,
and produces in the world, as produce it should, a shining witness
and model of holiness.

[Holiness is from Christ and His Paschal Mystery—His Passion,
Death, Resurrection, Glorification by the Father—through the Church
and her mystery, to persons who compose the People of God in
Christ. Holiness, which is essentially God's loving presence through
grace and the infused virtues of faith, hope, and charity, is the
very life of the Church communicated to all who are incorporated
in Christ through Baptism.—Ed.]

LG 40. The Lord Jesus, the divine Teacher and Model of all
perfection, preached holiness of life to each and every one of His
disciples, regardless of their situation: "You therefore are to be
perfect, even as your heavenly Father is perfect" (Mt 5:48). He
Himself stands as the Author and Finisher of this holiness of life.
For He sent the Holy Spirit upon all men that He might inspire
them from within to love God with their whole heart and their
whole soul, with all their mind and all their strength (cf. Mk
12:30) and that they might love one another as Christ loved them
(cf. Jn 13:34; 15:12).

The followers of Christ are called by God, not according to
their accomplishments, but according to His own purpose and grace.
They are justified in the Lord Jesus, and through baptism sought
in faith they truly become sons of God and sharers in the divine
nature. In this way they are really made holy. Then, too, by God's
gifts they must hold on to and complete in their lives this holiness
which they have received. They are warned by the Apostle to live
"as becomes saints" (Ep 5:3), and to put on "as God's chosen
ones, holy and beloved, a heart of mercy, kindness, humility, meekness, patience" (Col 3:12), and to possess the fruits of the Spirit
unto holiness (cf. Gal 5:22; Rom 6:22). Since we all truly offend
in many things (cf. Jm 3:2), we all need God's mercy continuously
and must daily pray: "Forgive us our debts" (Mt 6:12).

Thus it is evident to everyone that all the faithful of Christ of whatever rank or status are called to the fullness of the Christian life and to the perfection of charity. By this holiness a more human way of life is promoted even in this earthly society. In order that the faithful may reach this perfection, they must use their strength according as they have received it, as a gift from Christ. In this way they can follow in His footsteps and mold themselves in His image, seeking the will of the Father in all things, devoting themselves with all their being to the glory of God and the service of their neighbor. In this way too, the holiness of the People of God will grow into an abundant harvest of good, as is brilliantly proved by the lives of so many saints in Church history.

[Holiness is one, but the forms and tasks of life through which it is pursued are many; "many forms of the one life in Christ." In each and all Christian holiness is a mystery of death and resurrection. The cross is central to the mystery of holiness. The self-denial and self-emptying are positive functions, not negative, not frustrating, but a stage in the total life-giving process of being conformed to the image of the risen Christ; the positive substance of sanctification.—Ed.]

LG 41. In the various types and duties of life, one and the same holiness is cultivated by all who are moved by the Spirit of God, and who obey the voice of the Father, worshipping God the Father in spirit and in truth. These souls follow the poor Christ, the humble and cross-bearing Christ, in order to be made worthy of being partakers in His glory. Every person should walk unhesitatingly according to his own personal gifts and duties in the path of a living faith which arouses hopes and works through charity.

In the first place, the shepherds of Christ's flock ought to carry out their ministry with holiness, eagerness, humility, and courage, in imitation of the eternal High Priest, the Shepherd and Guardian of our souls. They will thereby make this ministry the principal means of their own sanctification. Those chosen for the fullness of the priesthood are gifted with sacramental grace enabling them to exercise a perfect role of pastoral charity through prayer, sacrifice, and preaching, as through every form of a bishop's care and service. They are enabled to lay down their life for their sheep fearlessly, and, made a model for their flock (cf. 1 P 5:3), can lead the Church to ever-increasing holiness through their own example.

Thanks to Christ, the eternal and sole Mediator, priests share in the grace of the bishop's rank and form his spiritual crown. Like bishops, priests should grow in love for God and neighbor through the daily exercise of their duty. They should preserve the bond of priestly fraternity, abound in every spiritual good, and give living evidence of God to all men. Let their heroes be those priests who have lived during the course of the centuries, often in lowly and hidden service, and have left behind them a bright pattern of holiness. Their praise lives on in the Church.

A priest's task is to pray and offer sacrifice for his own people and indeed the entire People of God, realizing what he does and reproducing in himself the holiness of the things he handles. Let him not be undone by his apostolic cares, dangers, and toils, but rather led by them to higher sanctity. His activities should be fed and fostered by a wealth of meditation, to the delight of the whole Church of God. All priests, especially those who are called diocesan in view of the particular title of their ordination, should bear in mind how much their sanctity profits from loyal attachment to the bishop and generous collaboration with him.

In their own special way, ministers of lesser rank also share in the mission and grace of the supreme priest. First among these are deacons. Since they are servants of the mysteries of Christ and the Church, they should keep themselves free from every fault, be pleasing to God, and be a source of all goodness in the sight of men (cf. 1 Tm 3:8-10, 12-13).

Called by the Lord and set aside as His portion, other clerics prepare themselves for various ministerial offices under the watchful eye of pastors. They are bound to bring their hearts and minds into accord with the splendid calling which is theirs, and will do so by constancy in prayer, burning love, and attention to whatever is true, just, and of good repute, all for the glory and honor of God. In addition, there are laymen chosen by God and called by the bishop to devote themselves exclusively to apostolic labors, working with great fruitfulness in the Lord's field.

Married couples and Christian parents should follow their own proper path to holiness by faithful love, sustaining one another in grace throughout the entire length of their lives. They should imbue their offspring, lovingly welcomed from God, with Christian truths and evangelical virtues. For thus they can offer all men an example of unwearying and generous love, build up the brotherhood of charity, and stand as witnesses to and cooperators in the fruitfulness of Holy Mother Church. By such lives, they signify and share in that very love with which Christ loved His Bride and because of which He delivered Himself up on her behalf. A like example, but one given in a different way, is that offered by widows and single people, who are able to make great contributions toward holiness and apostolic endeavor in the Church.

Finally, laborers, whose work is often toilsome, should by their human exertions try to perfect themselves, aid their fellow citizens, and raise all of society, and even creation itself, to a better mode of existence. By their lively charity, joyous hope, and sharing of one another's burdens, let them also truly imitate Christ, who roughened His hands with carpenter's tools, and who in union with His Father is always at work for the salvation of all men. By their daily work itself laborers can achieve greater apostolic sanctity.

Those who are oppressed by poverty, infirmity, sickness, or various other hardships, as well as those who suffer persecution for justice' sake—may they all know that in a special way they are united with the suffering Christ for the salvation of the world. The Lord called them blessed in His gospel. They are those whom "the God of all grace, who has called us unto his eternal glory in Christ Jesus, will himself, after we have suffered a little while, perfect, strengthen, and establish" (1 P 5:10).

All of Christ's faithful, therefore, whatever be the conditions, duties, and circumstances of their lives, will grow in holiness day by day through these very situations, if they accept all of them with faith from the hand of their heavenly Father, and if they cooperate with the divine will by showing every man through their earthly activities the love with which God has loved the world.

[The holy man is in the world, not of it. Holiness is of God and is centered in God, like the Church herself, to whose mystery it belongs. Holiness transcends the world even in loving and serving it.

The Church's teaching on holiness in the Church and on the calling of all men to share in it is practical and contemporary. It is likewise pastoral, since it seeks to awaken Christians to a sense of their ultimate, *mystical* vocation, that vocation which calls them to conformity to and identification with the Mystery of Christ.—His Paschal Mystery.—Ed.]

LG 42. "God is love, and he who abides in love abides in God, and God in him" (1 Jn 4:16). God pours out His love into our hearts through the Holy Spirit, who has been given to us (cf. Rm 5:5). Thus the first and most necessary gift is that charity by which we love God above all things and our neighbor because of God. If that love, as good seed, is to grow and bring forth fruit in the soul, each one of the faithful must willingly hear the Word of God and with the help of His grace act to fulfill His will.

Each must share frequently in the sacraments, the Eucharist especially, and in liturgical rites. Each must apply himself constantly to prayer, self-denial, active brotherly service, and the exercise of all the virtues. For charity, as the bond of perfection and the fulfillment of the law (cf. Col 3:14; Rm 13:10), rules over all the means of attaining holiness, gives life to them, and makes them work. Hence it is the love of God and of neighbor which points out the true disciple of Christ.

Since Jesus, the Son of God, manifested His charity by laying down His life for us, no one has greater love than he who lays down his life for Christ and his brothers (cf. 1 Jn 3:16; Jn 15:13). From the earliest times, then, some Christians have been called upon—and some will always be called upon—to give this supreme testimony of love to all men, but especially to persecutors. The Church, therefore, considers martyrdom as an exceptional gift and as the highest proof of love.

By martyrdom a disciple is transformed into an image of his

Master, who freely accepted death on behalf of the world's salvation; he perfects that image even to the shedding of blood. Though few are presented with such an opportunity, nevertheless all must be prepared to confess Christ before men, and to follow Him along the way of the cross through the persecutions which the Church will never fail to suffer.

[The evangelical counsels already mentioned in art. 39 are now developed more fully as:
1. expressions of love of God;
2. expressions of the holy freedom of the children of God to choose always the most perfect good;
3. witness to the charity and humility of the self-emptying Christ (Ph 2:7). The Paschal Mystery of death and resurrection gives the evangelical counsels their meaning and power and makes them a *sign* showing forth Christ to the world.—Ed.]

The holiness of the Church is also fostered in a special way by the observance of the manifold counsels proposed in the gospel by our Lord to His disciples. Outstanding among them is that precious gift of divine grace which the Father gives to some men (cf. Mt 19:11; 1 Cor 7:7) so that by virginity, or celibacy, they can more easily devote their entire selves to God alone with undivided heart (cf. 1 Cor 7:32-34). This total continence embraced on behalf of the kingdom of heaven has always been held in particular honor by the Church as being a sign of charity and stimulus towards it, as well as a unique fountain of spiritual fertility in the world.

The Church also keeps in mind the advice of the Apostle, who summoned the faithful to charity by exhorting them to share the mind of Christ Jesus—He who "emptied himself, taking the nature of a slave . . . becoming obedient to death" (Ph 2:7-8), and, because of us, "being rich, he became poor" (2 Cor 8:9).

Since the disciples must always imitate and give witness to this charity and humility of Christ, Mother Church rejoices at finding within her bosom men and women who more closely follow and more clearly demonstrate the Savior's self-giving by embracing poverty with the free choice of God's sons, and by renouncing their own wills. They subject the latter to another person on God's behalf, in pursuit of an excellence surpassing what is commanded. Thus they liken themselves more thoroughly to Christ in His obedience.

[Chapter V ends by insisting on the eschatological nature of all holiness, for holiness, like the Church herself "to which we are called in Christ Jesus and in which we attain holiness, will be consummated only in the glory of heaven" (Rv. 3:21).—Ed.]

LG 47. Let all who have been called to the profession of the vows take painstaking care to persevere and excel increasingly in the vocation to which God has summoned them. Let their purpose be a more vigorous flowering of the Church's holiness and the greater glory of the one and undivided Trinity, which in Christ and through Christ is the fountain and the wellspring of all holiness.

LG 48. All of Christ's followers, therefore, are invited and bound to pursue holiness and the perfect fulfillment of their proper state. Hence, let them all see that they guide their affections rightly. Otherwise, they will be thwarted in the search for perfect charity by the way they use earthly possessions and by a fondness for riches which goes against the gospel spirit of poverty. The Apostle has sounded the warning: let those who make use of this world not get bogged down in it, for the structure of this world is passing away (cf. 1 Cor 7:31, Greek text).

Part Two

THE MYSTERY OF RELIGIOUS LIFE IN THE MYSTERY OF CHRIST

THE RADICAL FOLLOWING OF CHRIST IN THE PASCHAL MYSTERY IN PUBLICLY VOWED CONSECRATED CHASTITY, POVERTY, AND OBEDIENCE IN PURSUIT OF THE PERFECTION OF CHARITY, IN TOTAL SURRENDER TO GOD, AND IN SACRAMENTAL ENCOUNTER WITH CHRIST

CHAPTER 3

MYSTERY OF RELIGIOUS LIFE IN CHRIST

Chapter VI is a logical continuation and development of Chapter V on "The Call of the Whole Church to Holiness." The theme of the evangelical counsels is the direct transition from *Lumen Gentium's* consideration of holiness in general in Chapter V, and of holiness in religious life specifically in Chapter VI. Article 42 of the former considers the nature of the evangelical counsels as practiced privately and unofficially and is the introduction, so to speak, to Chapter VI which presents the nature of ecclesial religious life lived under publicly professed vows accepted formally by the Church.

But religious life publicly organized and officially approved in the Church is a way of "life apart" to facilitate as fully and effectively as possible the radical practice of the complete Gospel life. Chapter IV of *Lumen Gentium*, in art. 31 specifically states: "The term 'laity' is here understood to mean all the faithful *except* those in holy orders and those in a religious state sanctioned by the Church." "Religious are not a third state in addition to clergy and laity, but they are clerics or laity who have dedicated themselves to a life according to the evangelical counsels, and thus differ from those pursuing the secular form of life discussed in Chapter IV." (cf. note on art. 43)

The Church sets up for religious "stable forms of living" embodying the vowed practice of the counsels (art. 43). This fact separates religious from the general and ordinary ways of life followed by human society as such, including the general society of the Church,

and even from the Christian way of life of those who practice
the counsels "privately." But such separation is intended to lead
religious to a *deeper* union with the Church and her mystery and
a *deeper union* with human society likewise (arts. 44,46).

Throughout Chapter VI, this double aspect and purpose of religious life dominates its theology as presented by Vatican Council II:

    a. the evangelical purpose to practice radically the counsels
       of the Gospel.

    b. its ecclesial aspect as a form of life in Christ's Body, the
       Church, to create communities ordered to the primary pursuit
       of the "perfection of Charity" thereby participating in the
       mission of the Church for the redemptive sanctification of
       the world.

Articles 43-47 present the doctrine of religious life in the mystery
of Christ and the Church solemnly proclaimed to the whole world
by Vatican Council II—the teaching of the supreme magisterial
authority of the Church on religious life.

NATURE OF RELIGIOUS LIFE

LG 43. The evangelical counsels of chastity dedicated to God,
poverty, and obedience are based upon the words and example
of the Lord. They were further commended by the apostles and
the Fathers, and other teachers and shepherds of the Church. The
counsels are a divine gift, which the Church has received from
her Lord and which she ever preserves with the help of His grace.
Church authority has the duty, under the inspiration of the Holy
Spirit, of interpreting these evangelical counsels, of regulating their
practice, and finally of establishing stable forms of living according
to them.

Thus it has come about that various forms of solitary and
community life, as well as different religious families have grown
up. Advancing the progress of their members and the welfare of
the whole body of Christ, these groups have been like branches
sprouting out wondrously and abundantly from a tree growing
in the field of the Lord from a seed divinely planted.

These religious families give their members the support of greater stability in their way of life, a proven method of acquiring perfection, fraternal association in the militia of Christ, and liberty strengthened by obedience. Thus these religious can securely fulfill and faithfully observe their religious profession, and rejoicing in spirit make progress on the road of charity.

From the point of view of the divine and hierarchical structure of the Church, the religious state of life is not an intermediate one between the clerical and lay states. Rather, the faithful of Christ are called by God from both these latter states of life so that they may enjoy this particular gift in the life of the Church and thus each in his own way can forward the saving mission of the Church.

Cf. the following related article of II Vatican Council's Decree *Perfectae Caritatis*: Decree on the Appropriate Renewal of the Religious Life.

PC 1. In its Constitution which begins, "The Light of the World," this most sacred Synod has already pointed out how the teaching and example of the Divine Master laid the foundation for a pursuit of perfect charity through the exercise of the evangelical counsels, and how such a pursuit serves as a blazing emblem of the heavenly kingdom. In this present document, the Synod intends to deal with the life and rules of those institutes whose members profess chastity, poverty, and obedience, and to make provisions for their needs as the tenor of the times indicates.

From the very infancy of the Church, there have existed men and women who strove to follow Christ more freely and imitate Him more nearly by the practice of the evangelical counsels. Each in his own way, these souls have led a life dedicated to God. Under the influence of the Holy Spirit, many of them pursued a solitary life, or founded religious families to which the Church willingly gave the welcome and approval of her authority.

And so it happened by divine plan that a wonderful variety of religious communities grew up. This variety contributed mightily toward making the Church experienced in every good deed (cf. 2 Tm 3:17) and ready for a ministry of service in building up Christ's body (cf. Ep 4:12). Not only this, but adorned by the various gifts of her children, the Church became radiant like a bride made beautiful for her spouse (cf. Rv 21:2); and through her God's manifold wisdom could reveal itself (cf. Ep 3:10).

But whatever the diversity of their spiritual endowments, all who are called by God to practice the evangelical counsels, and who do so faithfully, devote themselves in a special way to the Lord. They imitate Christ the virgin and the poor man (cf. Mt 8:20; Lk 9:58), who, by an obedience which carried Him even to death on the cross (cf. Ph 2:8), redeemed men and made them holy. As a consequence, impelled by a love which the Holy Spirit has poured into their hearts (cf. Rm 5:5), these Christians spend themselves ever increasingly for Christ, and for His body the Church (cf. Col 1:24).

Hence the more ardently they unite themselves to Christ through a self-surrender involving their entire lives, the more vigorous becomes the life of the Church and the more abundantly her apostolate bears fruit.

A life consecrated by a profession of the counsels is of surpassing value. Such a life has a necessary role to play in the circumstances of the present age. That this kind of life and its contemporary role may achieve greater good for the Church, this sacred Synod issues the following decrees. They concern only the general principles which must underlie an appropriate renewal of the life and rules of religious communities. These principles apply also to societies living a community life without the exercise of vows, and to secular institutes, though the special character of both groups is to be maintained. After the Council, the competent authority will be obliged to enact particular laws opportunely spelling out and applying what is legislated here.

Cf. the following related articles of Pope Paul VI's Papal Exhortation, *Evangelica Testificatio,* to nuns and consecrated virgins of the whole Catholic world.

RELIGIOUS LIFE: A DIVINE GIFT TO PRESERVE

The Gospel Witness

ET 1. The Gospel witness of the religious life clearly manifests to mankind the primacy attributed to the love of God. It does this with such intensity that we have the Holy Spirit to thank for it. In all simplicity—following the example of our venerated predecessor, John XXIII, on the eve of the ecumenical Second Vatican Council, We would like to declare to you how much hope is stirred up in us, as well as in all the pastors and faithful of the Church, by the spiritual generosity of those men and women who have consecrated their life to the Lord, by preserving the spirit and practice of the evangelical counsels. We also desire so to assist you that, by adhering to the doctrine of the Second Vatican Council, you may continue on the path of the followers of Christ, which you have undertaken.

Teaching of the Second Vatican Council

ET 2. In doing this, our intention is to meet the anxiety, uncertain state of mind, and instability shown by some. We also wish to strengthen those who are seeking a true renewal of the religious life. For there have been certain changes, very boldly and arbitrarily induced, an extreme distrust of times past, even when they witness to the wisdom and vigor of ecclesial traditions, and a habit of mind which wrongly claims that a person should rashly conform to the profound transformations by which our age is being violently shaken. All these reasons, no doubt, have led some people to decide that the distinctive elements of the religious life are destined to die. Have not some even gone so far that, contrary to human and divine law, they appealed to the Council with the purpose of calling into doubt the very foundation of the religious life? It is absolutely certain, however, that the Council recognized that this "distinct gift" has a unique place in the life of the Church. The reason is that those who received it are, by its power, more conformed "to that kind of life of virginity and poverty which Christ the Lord chose

for Himself and which His Virgin Mother also embraced."[1] Moreover, the Council has shown the ways by which the same gift should
be renewed according to the prescriptions of the Gospel.[2]

Proven Doctrine for Acquiring Perfection

ET 37. The Council considers "a proven doctrine for acquiring
perfection" as a patrimony of the institutes and one of the greatest
benefits they are expected to confer upon you. But since this perfection consists in an ever increasing love of God and our brethren,
that doctrine must be understood in a settled and specific way,
namely as a doctrine of life to be actually put into practice. It follows,
then, that such inquiries as institutes are undertaking, cannot revolve
only around certain adjustments occasioned by reason of changed
circumstances in the world. They must rather serve to rediscover
such profitable forms of support as are absolutely necessary to
lead a life deeply animated by the love of God and one's fellowmen.

Testimony of the Church's Constant Tradition

ET 3. The tradition of the Church from her first beginnings
must we recall it to mind?—offers this exceptional testimony of a
steady firmness in seeking for God, of an exclusive and undivided
love for Christ, and of zeal which irrevocably vows itself to the
extension of His kingdom. Without this visibly manifest sign,
there is danger that the very charity by which the universal Church
is nourished would grow cold; that the marvelous salvific message
of the Gospel, which is contrary to popular opinion, would be
dimmed and that the salt of faith would be lost in a world which
in our days is becoming secularized.

The Holy Spirit from the first centuries has stirred up the
marvelous courage of disciples and virgins as well as hermits,
side by side with the martyrs who gave heroic profession of Christ.
There was already then a certain outline of the religious life which

---

1. Second Vatican Council, Dogmatic Constitution **Lumen Gentium**,
VI, 46, A.A.S. 57, 1965, p. 52.
2. Second Vatican Council, Decree **Perfectae Caritatis** 2.

constantly developed. It grew progressively and took on different forms of communal or solitary life in response to the pressing invitation of Christ: "There is no one who has left house, wife, brothers, parents or children for the sake of the kingdom of God who will not be given repayment many times over in this present time, and, in the world to come, eternal life." (Lk 18:29-30)

Who would dare claim that such a calling no longer has the same strength and vitality? That the Church can do without these outstanding witnesses of a love of Christ which surpasses the powers of nature? Or that the world could allow these lights to be extinguished without suffering harm? They are luminaries which announce the kingdom of God with a liberty that is not burdened with obstacles and is practiced by thousands of sons and daughters of the Church in their daily lives.

"Therefore, it has seemed good to Us to recall here the priceless importance and necessary function of religious life; for this state of life which receives its distinctive character from profession of the evangelical vows is a perfect way of living according to the example and teaching of Jesus Christ, especially since it is a state of life which keeps in view the constant growth of charity, leading to final perfection. In other ways of life the specific ends, advantages, and functions, though legitimate in themselves, are of a temporal character."

CHAPTER 4

TOTAL SURRENDER TO GOD IN LOVE

THE MANY-SPLENDORED WITNESS

(Cf. LG, nos. 43, 44, 13)

Gift of Self through Voluntary Profession

ET 7. Beloved sons and daughters, having freely responded to the invitation of the Holy Spirit you have decided to follow Christ, devoting yourselves totally to Him. The evangelical counsels of chastity consecrated to God, of poverty, and obedience have become the laws of your life. Moreover, as the Council reminds us, "the authority of the Church, under the guidance of the Holy Spirit, ha~ the duty to interpret these evangelical counsels, to regulate their practice, and finally to build on them stable forms of life." Thus, the Church recognizes the counsels and renders authentic that state of life which comes into existence by the profession of the evangelical counsels: "The Christian believer binds himself to the three afore-mentioned counsels, either by vows, or by other sacred bonds which are essentially like the vows. In this way, a person is totally surrendered to God, loved beyond all things. It is true that through baptism he dies to sin and is consecrated to God. But that he might be able to derive more abundant fruit from this baptismal grace, he intends, by the profession of the evangelical counsels in the Church, to free himself from those obstacles which could draw him away from the fervor of charity and the perfection of divine worship. Thus he is more intimately consecrated to the divine service. This consecration will be the more perfect, to the extent to which the indissoluble union of Christ with His Spouse, the Church is expressed by more firm and stable bonds." (LG, nos. 43, 44)

This doctrine of the Council places in clear light the grandeur of this gift, which you have freely decided to give of yourselves—after the pattern of Christ's self-giving to the Church—and therefore, like His, yours is most absolute and irrevocable. It was precisely for the kingdom of heaven that you have generously and with no reservation vowed to Christ that power of loving, that desire of possessing, and that faculty of independently regulating your own life, all of which gifts are so precious to man. Such is your consecration which is made in the Church and through her ministry, both the ministry of those who act in the name of the Church and receive the religious profession, as well as of the Christian community. It is this Christian community which lovingly acknowledges, welcomes, fosters and sustains those who, in its bosom, freely expend themselves as a living sign "which can and ought to effectively attract all the members of the Church to a diligent fulfillment of the duties of their Christian vocation . . . since the religious state manifests to all believers the possession of heavenly goods already present in this world."

Life Wholly Dedicated to God

ET 4. Beloved sons and daughters, who practice the evangelical counsels, you have wished to follow Christ more freely and imitate Him more closely. You have dedicated your whole life to God by a distinctive consecration, which is rooted in and more fully expresses the consecration of baptism. Could you but realize the high esteem and loving affection that We have for you in the name of Christ Jesus! We commend you to our most dear brothers in the episcopate who, together with their collaborators in the priesthood, recognize their responsibility in conscience toward the religious life. We also ask all the laity to whom "secular duties and activities belong properly, though not exclusively," to understand how strongly they are urged by you to strive for that holiness to which they also are called by their baptism in Christ to the glory of the Father.

Joyful and Balanced Austerity

ET 30. We must confess, sons and daughters in Christ Jesus, that in these days it is hard to find a way of leading one's life that agrees with this necessity. Too many contrary incentives, in fact, pressure you to seek before everything else an effectiveness in your work based on human calculation. But is it not precisely your responsibility to give an example of joyful and balanced austerity, while you embrace the difficulties inherent in work and the demands of society and bear the hardships of life with all its anxiety and uncertainty as so many renunciations simply required for the fulness of the Christian life? After all, religious are striving for "holiness by a more narrow path." Therefore in the midst of these cares and trials, great or small, your interior fervor of spirit enables you to find the cross of Christ and helps you to accept it with faith and love.

CONSECRATED CHASTITY

(Cf. LG, no. 44)

PC 12. That chastity which is practiced "on behalf of the heavenly Kingdom" (Mt 19:12), and which religious profess, deserves to be esteemed as a surpassing gift of grace. For it liberates the human heart in a unique way (cf. 1 Cor 7:32-35) and causes it to burn with greater love for God and all mankind. It is therefore an outstanding token of heavenly riches, and also a most suitable way for religious to spend themselves readily in God's service and in works of the apostolate. Religious thereby give witness to all Christ's faithful of that wondrous marriage between the Church and Christ her only spouse, a union which has been established by God and will be fully manifested in the world to come.

Hence, as they strive to live their profession faithfully, religious do well to lodge their faith in the words of the Lord; trusting in God's help rather than presuming on their own resources, let them practice mortification and custody of the senses. They should take advantage of those natural helps which favor mental and bodily health. As a result they will not be influenced by those erroneous claims which present complete continence as impossible or as harmful to human development. In addition a certain spiritual instinct should lead them to spurn everything likely to imperil chastity. Above all, everyone should remember—superiors especially —that chastity has stronger safeguards in a community when true fraternal love thrives among its members.

Since the observance of total continence intimately involves the deeper inclinations of human nature, candidates should not undertake the profession of chastity nor be admitted to its profession except after a truly adequate testing period and only if they have the needed degree of psychological and emotional maturity. They should not only be warned of the dangers confronting chastity, but be trained to make a celibate life consecrated to God part of the richness of their whole personality.

THE THREE-FOLD SURRENDER TO GOD

Love of God, Motive for Consecrated Chastity

ET 13. Only the love of God—it must be repeated—with the strongest motivation impels people to embrace chastity. This love makes such an uncompromising demand for fraternal charity that a religious should thereby live with his peers more deeply in the heart of Christ. Provided this condition is satisfied, the gift of self, by which a person devotes himself to God and to others, will be the source of a tranquil peace. There is no question of despising human love or marriage. Is it not, according to faith, the image and sharing of that love of effective unity by which Christ is joined to His Church? Chastity consecrated to God evokes this unity more directly and brings to perfection that conquest of self which every human love must strive to attain. Consequently in our age, when "destructive eroticism" is more rampant than ever before, chastity must now be as perfectly as possible understood and put into living practice with generosity and the right kind of attitude. Chastity, an emphatically positive virtue, witnesses to that love by which God is preferred to all other things. It symbolizes in a most prominent and definitive way the mystery of the union of the Mystical Body with its Head and of the Spouse with her eternal Bridegroom. Finally it influences a person, transforms and pervades him in reaching to the depths of his being through a mysterious assimilation with Christ.

Mystical Influence of Consecrated Chastity in the World

ET 14. You, therefore, have the duty, beloved sons and daughters, to revive the full efficacy of the Christian spiritual teaching of chastity consecrated to God. For this virtue when it is really preserved in living out one's life for the kingdom of heaven, liberates the heart of man and thus becomes "a sign and incentive of charity, in fact, a unique source of spiritual fruitfulness in the world."[1] Although the world does not always recognize it, yet consecrated chastity continues to exert its own mystical influence in the world.

Religious Celibacy Founded on Christian Revelation

ET 15. Our responsibility, then, is to make sure that our conviction of mind remains steadfast and certain on the following: the excellence and fruitfulness of purity, preserved in religious celibacy for the love of God, has its ultimate foundation in the Word of God, in the doctrine of Christ, in the life of His Virgin Mother, and in the apostolic tradition constantly maintained by the Church. For there is question here of a precious gift which the Father lavishly bestows on certain people. This gift is indeed fragile and easily vulnerable, since it is subject to human weakness and the contradiction of mere reason. Moreover, it cannot be comprehended by those to whom it has not been revealed by the light of the Word incarnate how the person who "loses his life" for His sake, "will find it."[2]

SCRSI, July 10, 1972:

The term *virginity* has a specific meaning and should not be substituted for the word *chastity*.

---

1. Cf. **Lumen Gentium**, 42.
2. Cf. **Mt** 10, 39; 16, 25; **Mk** 8, 35; **Lk** 9,24; **Jn** 12,25.

CONSECRATED POVERTY

(Cf. LG, no. 44)

PC 13. Poverty voluntarily embraced in imitation of Christ provides a witness which is highly esteemed, especially today. Let religious painstakingly cultivate such poverty, and give it new expressions if need be. By it a man shares in the poverty of Christ, who became poor for our sake when before He had been rich, that we might be enriched by His poverty (cf. 2 Cor 8:9; Mt 8:20).

Religious poverty requires more than limiting the use of possessions to the consent of superiors; members of a community ought to be poor in both fact and spirit, and have their treasures in heaven (cf. Mt 6:20).

In discharging his duty, each religious should regard himself as subject to the common law of labor. While making necessary provisions for their livelihood and undertakings, religious should brush aside all undue concern and entrust themselves to the providence of the heavenly Father (cf. Mt 6:25).

In their constitutions, religious communities can allow their members to renounce any inheritance which they have acquired or are due to acquire.

Depending on the circumstances of their location, communities as such should aim at giving a kind of corporate witness to their own poverty. Let them willingly contribute something from their own resources to the other needs of the Church, and to the support of the poor, whom religious should love with the tenderness of Christ (cf. Mt 19:21; 25:34-46; Jm 2:15-16; 1 Jn 3:17). Provinces and houses of a religious community should share their resources with one another, those which are better supplied assisting those which suffer need.

To the degree that their rules and constitutions permit, religious communities can rightly possess whatever is necessary for their temporal life and their mission. Still, let them avoid every appearance of luxury, of excessive wealth, and accumulation of possessions.

Grave Responsibility of Consecrated Poverty

ET 16. As chaste followers of Christ, you also intend to pass your life in poverty according to His example in the use of such goods of this world as are necessary for daily sustenance. On this issue, in fact, our contemporaries are pressing hard upon you with embarrassing questions. Undoubtedly, religious institutes have a grave responsibility to fulfill in works of mercy, of giving help to those in need, and of social justice. In the exercise of such ministries, these institutes should always keep in mind what the Gospel demands, that they consciously adjust themselves to present necessities.

Fraternal Sharing and Dependence

ET 21. The need of fraternal sharing so strongly asserted today must retain its Gospel vigor. As it is written in *The Teaching of the Twelve Apostles* : . . . "if you are sharers in the goods of immortality, how much more in mortal things?" Poverty, so lived, in being truly reduced to practice that possessions, not excluding salary, are brought together in common—testifies to the spiritual communion by which you are joined. Such poverty is a strong exhortation which is offered to all the rich and also brings relief to your brothers and sisters who are suffering want. The eagerness with which everyone is rightly endowed to accept duties on his own initiative is manifested not by enjoying one's own income but by sharing the common goods in a fraternal spirit. The forms of poverty of individuals and of each community will depend on the nature of the institute and the form of obedience which is practiced there. Thus according to each one's special vocation, the character of dependence which inheres in all poverty is put into effect.

The Cry of the Poor

ET 17. "The cry of the poor,"[3] which was never more insistent, you hear uttered by those who are personally in need and by those who are oppressed by collective misery. Did Christ not come in answer to their appeal as God's children enjoying a certain privi-

---

3. Cf. **Ps** 9, 13; **Job** 34, 28; **Pr** 21, 13.

leged claim[4] and did He not go so far as to become identified with them?[5] In a world that is making extraordinary progress, these multitudes and pitiful individuals still persist and plead with a pressing cry for "a conversion of mind and custom."[6] This pertains especially to you who are following Christ more closely in His earthly state of emptying Himself.[7] This invitation—as We are not unaware—echoes in your hearts so strongly and so insistently that some of you are at times incited even to take violent action. However, as followers of Christ, how can you walk another path than the one which He trod? For His way, as you know, is not some kind of political or transitory theory and movement; but a call for conversion of heart, for deliverance from every earthly encumbrance, for love.

Material Progress and the Duty of Religious

ET 19. In a human civilization and a world which reflects a prodigious movement of almost infinite material progress, what witness does a religious give, who lets himself be carried away by a concern for his own ease and for whom it appears to be perfectly normal to take everything offered him without discernment or moderation? Consequently, at a time when many are living in great danger of being entrapped by the alluring security of possession, knowledge and power, God's invitation places you as it were at the highest pinnacle of Christian conscience. For it is your duty to warn men that their true and unqualified progress consists in responding to their vocation, "to participate as sons in the life of the living God, the Father of all mankind."[8]

Submission to the Law of Labor

ET 20. You also understand the complaint of so many human lives which are involved as it were in a relentless whirlpool of labor for

---

4. Cf. **Lk** 4, 18; 6, 20.
5. Cf. **Mt** 25, 35-40.
6. **Gaudium et Spes**, 63, A.A.S. 58, 1966, p. 1085.
7. Cf. **Mt** 19, 21; 2 **Cor** 8, 9.
8. Paul VI, Encyclical Letter **Populorum Progressio**, 21, A.A.S. 59, 1967, p. 268.

making money, of profit for ensuring pleasure, and of consumer goods which, in turn, sometimes demand an inhuman exertion of strength. One of the primary purposes of your poverty, therefore, will be the witness of that human attitude proper to labor, which should be undertaken with liberty of spirit and restored to its true nature, by which it becomes a source and service for sustaining life. Has not the Council very opportunely declared your necessary submission to "the common law of labor"? This then is the duty by which you are bound: you must be concerned with your own livelihood and that of the brethren or sisters, and, by your labor, alleviate the lot of the poor. But your activity may not contradict the vocation of your various institutes, nor should you undertake such labors, as a matter of custom, as would substitute for the specific tasks proper to these institutes. For, otherwise, it will necessarily happen that you will be somehow led to a secular way of life with harm to the religious life. Be watchful, therefore, of the spirit that moves you; what disaster would certainly befall you if you considered yourselves commended solely by the profit derived from secular pursuits!

Re-Assessment of Religious Poverty

ET 18. How then will you respond to the cry of the poor in your life? That cry must, above all, keep you from practicing even the least semblance of social injustice. Moreover, it obliges you in duty to have the conscience of people aroused by the extreme condition of misery and confronting demands of social justice as the Gospel and Church teach. That cry moves some of you to join in their lot as poor people and to share their anguish and sorrows. Again, it calls not a few of your institutes to so modify some of their tasks as to benefit the poor; as, in fact, many have already generously done. Finally, it enjoins on you the use of goods determined by the circumstances required for the fulfillment of your duties. In your daily life you must give evidence, even externally, of authentic poverty.

SCRSI—July 10, 1972:

The matter of the vow of poverty and its practice should be

accurately specified by the chapter. Religious must recognize the importance and dignity of work in earning their livelihood. Their life style, characterized as it should be by simplicity, will result in genuine fraternal sharing, an intrinsic part of both poverty and common life. A correct sense of dependence must be included not only in legislation but also in actual living. Chapter decisions which tend to dispense with any kind of dependence or accountability are not acceptable.

CONSECRATED OBEDIENCE

(Cf. LG, nos. 44, 46)

PC 14. Through the *profession of obedience*, religious offer to God a total dedication of their own wills as a sacrifice of themselves; they thereby unite themselves with greater steadiness and security to the saving will of God. In this way they follow the pattern of Jesus Christ, who came to do the Father's will (cf. Jn 4:34; 5:30; Heb 10:7; Ps 39:9). "Taking the nature of a slave" (Ph 2:7), He learned obedience from His sufferings (cf. Heb 5:8). Under the influence of the Holy Spirit, religious submit themselves to their superiors, whom faith presents as God's representatives, and through whom they are guided into the service of all their brothers in Christ. Thus did Christ Himself out of submission to the Father minister to the brethren and surrender His life as a ransom for many (cf. Mt 20:28; Jn 10:14-18). In this way, too, religious assume a firmer commitment to the ministry of the Church and labor to achieve the mature measure of the fullness of Christ (cf. Ep 4:13).

Therefore, in a spirit of faith and of love for God's will, let religious show humble obedience to their superiors in accord with the norms of rule and constitution. Realizing that they are giving service to the upbuilding of Christ's body according to God's design, let them bring to the execution of commands and to the discharge of assignments entrusted to them the resources of their minds and wills, and their gifts of nature and grace. Lived in this manner, religious obedience will not diminish the dignity of the human person but will rather lead it to maturity in consequence of that enlarged freedom which belongs to the sons of God.

For his part, as one who will render an account for the souls entrusted to him (cf. Heb 13:17), each superior should himself be docile to God's will in the exercise of his office. Let him use his authority in a spirit of service for the brethren, and manifest thereby the charity with which God loves them. Governing his subjects as God's own sons, and with regard for their human personality, a superior will make it easier for them to obey gladly. Therefore he must make a special point of leaving them appropriately free with respect to the sacrament of penance and direction of conscience. Let him give the kind of leadership which will encourage religious to bring an active and responsible obedience to the offices they shoulder and the activities they undertake. Therefore a superior should listen willingly to his subjects and encourage them to make a personal contribution to the welfare of the community and of the Church. Not to be weakened, however, is the superior's authority to decide what must be done and to require the doing of it.

Let chapters and councils faithfully acquit themselves of the governing role given to them; each should express in its own way the fact that all members of the community have a share in the welfare of the whole community and a responsibility for it.

Obedience Patterned after Christ

ET 23. Does not the same fidelity inspire your profession of obedience, in the light of faith and according to the same impelling power of the charity of Christ? By this profession, in fact, you immolate your will entirely and enter more certainly and securely into His plan of salvation. Following the example of Christ, who came to do the will of His Father, and joined with Him, who "learned obedience from the things which He suffered and ministered to His brethren," you "have bound yourselves more closely to the service of the Church" and your brethren.[9]

The Gospel Longing for Fraternity

ET 24. The Gospel longing for fraternity was signally expressed

---

9. Cf. PC, 14; Jn 4, 34; 5, 30; 10, 15-18; Heb 5, 8; 10, 7; Ps 40 (39), 8-9.

by the Council, inasmuch as the Church has defined herself as the
People of God, in which the hierarchy zealously serve the members
of Christ and are conjoined among themselves by the same charity.[10]
In the religious state, just as in the whole Church, the same paschal
mystery of Christ is honored by being lived out. The deepest meaning
of obedience is expressed in the fullness of this mystery of death
and resurrection, where man's supernatural destiny is admirably
and utterly fulfilled; since man reaches the true life by sacrifice,
suffering and death.

Exercising authority among your brethren, therefore, is the
same as ministering to them[11] after the example of Him, who "gave
His life as a ransom."[12]

Authority and Obedience, Sharing the Oblation of Christ

ET 25. Authority, therefore, and obedience, serving the common
good, are exercised as two complementary aspects of the same act
of sharing in the oblation of Christ. Those who act endowed with
authority should comply with the Father's most loving design in
their brethren; while religious, by accepting their precepts, follow
the example of our Master and are joined to His work of salvation.
Thus authority and each person's liberty need not be in opposition.
Together they result in fulfilling the will of God, which is sought
fraternally through a trustful dialogue between superior and brother
when the matter in question is personal, or through agreement of
a general nature when the matter affects the whole community.
In this quest, a religious should avoid both needless agitation of
spirit and the desire to allow the seductive power of current opinion
to prevail over the deepest concept of the religious life. Everyone,
but especially superiors and those who exercise any responsibilities
among their brethren or sisters are in duty bound to revive in the
communities that certitude of faith by which they should be governed. The aim of the foregoing quest is to have this certitude more

---

10. Cf. **Lumen Gentium**, Chaps. I-III, A.A.S. 57, 1965, pp. 5-36.
11. Cf. **Lk** 22, 26-27; **Jn** 13, 14.
12. **Mt** 20, 28; cf. **Ph** 2, 8.

clearly perceived and carried into the practice of daily life—as occasion demands, but under no circumstances may it lead to controversy. This task of communal discernment must end, if disaster threatens, by the judgment and will of superiors whose presence, acknowledged as such, is indispensably necessary for any kind of community.

Obedience in Harmony with the Institute

ET 26. Today's conditions of life have their influence, as is evident, on the way in which you exercise obedience. Thus many among you perform some of their tasks outside of religious houses and engage in activities for which they are suited by reason of special skill. Others again are led to unite themselves in groups devoted to a certain specialized work and subject to the groups' control. Does not the danger which is imminent in such situations advise that the sense of obedience be strengthened and more diligently cultivated? Certain conditions, however, must be observed to insure that the danger be brought to true profit. In the first place, then, it is necessary to investigate whether a work undertaken corresponds with the vocation of the institute. Also the respective spheres of action should be accurately defined. But above all there has to be transition from external action to the demands of community life. In this matter care must be exercised to safeguard the full efficacy of such features as are essentials of a religious life which is properly and truly so called. For one of the principal duties by which superiors are bound is to see to it that those conditions are provided for the brethren or sisters in religion as are necessary for their spiritual life. But how can they do this unless the whole community trustfully cooperates?

Liberty Strengthened through Obedience

ET 27. This, too, it is well to add: the more you contribute portions of your service, the more necessary it is for you to renew, in the fullness of its meaning, the gift of yourself. The Lord commands each one to "lose his life" if he wishes to come after Him.[13] You

---

13. Cf. *ibid.* 9, 23-24.

will observe this precept if you receive the norms of your superiors like a bulwark of your religious profession, which is "the total dedication of one's will as a sacrifice of oneself offered to God."[14] Christian obedience is the absolute and blind submission of every contingency to the divine will. Your obedience, however, is more demanding because through it you have given yourselves in a special way to God, and your faculty of choosing is bound, as by limits, by the obligations which you have yourselves assumed. Your situation, therefore, in which you are now living, draws its origin from a complete act of your own freedom. Consequently, you should always strive to make that act more vital, both by your own initiative as well as by the assent you give to the prescriptions of your superiors. Among the benefits of the religious state, the Council includes "liberty strengthened through obedience";[15] and, in stressing these words, teaches that "religious obedience not only does not lessen the dignity of the human person but brings it to maturity through that greater freedom of the children of God."[16]

Resolving Conflicts

ET 28. Nevertheless, is it not possible for a conflict to arise between the authority of a superior and the conscience of a religious, which is that "sacred chamber of man where he is alone with God whose voice echoes in his depths"?[17] This We must repeat: conscience is not the one and only judge of the moral character of the actions which it prompts, since it must itself be subject to objective norms and, when necessary, be corrected and duly straightened out.

The foregoing is apart from circumstances when something is enjoined which clearly contradicts the divine laws or the constitutions of the institute, or which brings with it a serious and sure evil; for then the obligation to obey ceases. A superior's directives affect an area in which the calculation of the greater good can vary, depending

---

14. Cf. **Perfectae Caritatis**, 14, A.A.S. 58, 1966, p. 708.
15. **Lumen Gentium**, 43, A.A.S. 57, 1965, p. 49.
16. **Perfectae Caritatis**, 14, A.A.S. 58, 1966, p. 709.
17. **Gaudium et Spes**, 16, A.A.S. 58, 1966, p. 1037.

on how a given situation is viewed. To conclude, however, that because an order truly seems to be less good therefore it is wrong and opposed to conscience, would mean a failure to understand— or at least show a lack of realistic judgment—that not a few human situations are unclear and have valid reasons on either side of an issue. Moreover, a refusal of obedience often brings serious harm to the common good. A religious must not, then, easily claim that a superior's directives contradict the judgment of his conscience. Admittedly such an exceptional case will sometimes cause a veritable agony of soul, according to Christ's own example, "who learned obedience from the things that He suffered."[18]

Self-Denial a Part of Obedience

ET 29. This is being said, therefore, to make it plainly understood how much self-denial the exercise of religious obedience demands. Accordingly you should experience something of the burden by which the Lord was drawn to the cross, namely to that "baptism by which He had to be baptized," where that fire would be kindled which also inflames you;[19] something, too, of that "folly," which St. Paul wishes for all of us and which alone can make us wise.[20] Let the cross, then, be for you what it was for Christ: the approval of the highest love. Does not a certain mysterious necessity exist between renunciation and joy, between sacrifice and greatness of soul, between discipline and spiritual liberty?

(Cf. PC, nos. 5-6)

Happiness through Sacrifice and Religious Vocations

ET 55. The joy which comes from your belonging at all times to the Lord is an incomparable fruit of the Holy Spirit, a joy you have already been given to experience. Filled with this gladness, which Christ will sustain in you even amidst trials, look forward confidently to what is to come. The manner in which this gladness

---

18. **Heb** 5, 8.
19. Cf Lk 12, 49-50.
20. Cf. 1 Cor 3, 18-19.

radiates from your communities is a proof to all that the state of life you have chosen helps you, by the triple renunciation imbedded in your religious profession, to expand immeasurably your life in Christ. Seeing you and your life, the young will be able to understand well the appeal that Jesus always insures is being sounded among them. The Council, in fact, warns you on this very issue: "Religious should keep in mind that the best recommendation of their institute and invitation to undertake the religious life is the example of their own personal life." (cf. PC, 24)

There is no doubt moreover that, out of their deep respect and great sense of love, bishops, priests, parents and Christian educators will kindle in many the desire of joining you as companions. They will thus be answering to the invitation of Christ which He does not cease to make heard in the hearts of His followers.

SCRSI, August, 1971

... it is necessary to have clear ideas and sound principles on obedience which is based on the doctrine of Christ 'obedient unto death,' and which reinforces the fraternal bonds among the members and the superiors....

You have the responsibility of your life; but you have freely committed it to God in the hands of your superiors....

SCRSI, December, 1971

Fellowship (in Government)—authority detrimental to true authority and practice of religious obedience.

SCRSI, July 10, 1972

The necessity for consultation and collaboration should be included but the obligation and the right of the superior to exercise prudently the role of personal authority should be respected.

SCRSI DECREE:
EXPERIMENTA CIRCA REGIMINIS RATIONEM

On the form of ordinary government and the eligibility of secularized religious men for ecclesiastical offices and benefices.

Experiments in forms of government have given rise to a

number of problems and questions especially with regard to the personal authority of the superior.

Furthermore, it has seemed opportune to reexamine at this time the prohibitions of canon 642 affecting secularized religious men.

After preliminary study by consultors, the members of this Sacred Congregation, in the plenary assembly of September 24 and 25, 1971, carefully considered the following questions:

1. Whether, contrary to the prescriptions of canon 516, an exclusively collegial form of ordinary government may be admitted for a whole religious institute, for a province, or for individual houses, in such a way that the superior, if there is one, is merely an executive.

2. Whether canon 642 may be suspended so as to permit religious men who have been properly dispensed from their vows to be eligible for and to hold ecclesiastical offices or benefices without the special permission of the Holy See.

After due consideration, the aforesaid assembly adopted unanimously the following decisions:

Answer to Question 1: Negative; according to the mind of Vatican Council II (in the decree *Perfectae caritatis,* no. 14 and the pontifical exhortation *Evangelica testificatio,* no. 25,) superiors must have personal authority, without prejudice to the practice of legitimate consultation and to the limits placed by common or partial law.

Answer to Question 2: Affirmative.

His Holiness Pope Paul VI in the audience granted to the Secretary of this Sacred Congregation for Religious and for Secular Institutes on November 18, 1971, approved the conclusions of the plenary assembly.

By this decree, the Sacred Congregation promulgates the above decisions and declares them immediately effective without executory clause. They will remain in force until superseded by the revised Code of Canon Law.

Given at Rome, February 2, 1972.

I. Card. ANTONIUTTI
Prefect

AUTHORITY IN RELIGIOUS INSTITUTES

Jurisdiction of Roman Pontiff, (Mt 16:18-19; Jn 21:15ff.)
   (Cf. LG, no. 22; CD, no. 2)

Jurisdiction of College of Bishops
   (Cf. LG, no. 22; CD, no. 2-6)

Jurisdiction of Individual Bishops
   (Cf. LG, no. 23; CD, no. 8)

Subjection of Religious to the Church
   Cf. LG, nos. 43, 45; ES, I, nos. 22-40)

No Change in Governmental Structure nor in Authority of
Religious Superiors
   (Cf. PC, no. 14; ET, no. 25)

   Decree, SCRSI, February 2, 1972, *Experimenta circa Regiminis Rationem*

New Emphasis on Obedience
   (Cf. PC, no. 14; ES, I, no. 4; ET, nos. 23, 28

Source of Authority
   (Cf. CC, nos. 501-502)

   "Chapter elects but does not confer authority; superiors
   and chapter have dominative authority according to their constitutions; dominative authority is the power to rule an imperfect
   society; authority is of the same origin as that of the society
   itself."

CHAPTER 5

IN SACRAMENTAL ENCOUNTER WITH CHRIST

MYSTERIUM FIDEI, POPE PAUL VI, 1966
ON THE DOCTRINE AND WORSHIP OF
THE HOLY EUCHARIST

Paul VI, by Divine Providence Pope, to our venerable brothers, the patriarchs, primates, archbishops, bishops and other local ordinaries in peace and communion with the Holy See, and to all the clergy and faithful of the world: On the doctrine and worship of the Holy Eucharist. Venerable Brothers and Dear Sons: Health and Apostolic Benediction.

The Catholic Church has always devoutly guarded as a most precious treasure the mystery of Faith, that is, the ineffable gift of the Eucharist which she received from Christ her spouse as a pledge of His immense love, and during the Second Vatican Council in a new and solemn demonstration she professed her faith and veneration for this mystery. When dealing with the restoration of the Sacred Liturgy, the Fathers of the council, by reason of their pastoral concern for the whole Church, considered it of the highest importance to exhort the faithful to participate actively with sound faith and with the utmost devotion in the celebration of this most Holy Mystery, to offer it with the priest to God as a sacrifice for their own salvation and for that of the whole world, and to find in it spiritual nourishment.

For if the sacred liturgy holds the first place in the life of the Church, the Eucharistic Mystery stands at the heart and center of the liturgy, since it is the font of life by which we are cleansed and

strengthened to live not for ourselves but for God, and to be united
in love among ourselves.

To make evident the indissoluble bond which exists between
Faith and devotion, the Fathers of the council, confirming the
doctrine which the Church has always held and taught and which
was solemnly defined by the Council of Trent, determined to introduce their treatise on the most Holy Mystery of the Eucharist with
the following summary of truths:

"At the Last Supper, on the night He was handed over, our
Lord instituted the Eucharistic Sacrifice of His Body and Blood,
to perpetuate the sacrifice on the Cross throughout the ages until
He should come, and thus entrust to the Church, His beloved Spouse,
the memorial of His death and resurrection: A sacrament of devotion, a sign of unity, a bond of charity, a paschal banquet in
which Christ is received, the soul is filled with Grace and there is
given to us the pledge of future glory" (Constit. "De Sacra Liturgia,"
ch. 2, no. 47).

In these words are highlighted both the sacrifice, which pertains
to the essence of the Mass which is celebrated daily, and the sacrament in which the faithful participate in Holy Communion by
eating the Flesh of Christ and drinking His Blood, receiving both
Grace, the beginning of eternal life, and the medicine of immortality.
According to the words of our Lord: "The man who eats my flesh
and drinks my blood enjoys eternal life, and I will raise him up
at the last day" (Jn 6, 55).

Therefore we earnestly hope that the restored sacred liturgy
will bring forth abundant fruits of Eucharistic devotion, so that the
Holy Church, under this saving sign of piety, may make daily
progress toward perfect unity (cf. Jn 17-23) and may invite all
Christians to a unity of faith and of love, drawing them gently,
thanks to the action of Divine Grace.

We seem to have a preview of these fruits and, as it were, to
gather in the early results not only in the genuine joy and eagerness
with which the members of the Catholic Church have received
both the Constitution on the Sacred Liturgy and the restoration of
the liturgy, but also in the great number of well-prepared publica-

tions which seek to investigate more profoundly and to understand more fruitfully the doctrine on the Holy Eucharist, with special reference to its relation with the mystery of the Church.

All of this is for us a cause of profound consolation and joy. It is a great pleasure for us to communicate this to you, Venerable Brothers, so that along with us you may give thanks to God, the Giver of all gifts, Who with His spirit rules the Church and enriches her with increasing virtues.

Pastoral Concern and Anxiety

However, Venerable Brothers, in this very matter which we are discussing, there are not lacking reasons for serious pastoral concern and anxiety. The awareness of our Apostolic Duty does not allow us to be silent in the face of these problems. Indeed, we are aware of the fact that, among those who deal with this most Holy Mystery in written or spoken word, there are some who, with reference either to Masses which are celebrated in private, or to the dogma of Transubstantiation, or to devotion to the Eucharist spread abroad opinions which disturb the faithful and fill their minds with no little confusion about matters of Faith. It is as if everyone were permitted to consign to oblivion doctrine already defined by the Church, or else to interpret it in such a way as to weaken the genuine meaning of the words or the recognized force of the con -cepts involved.

To confirm what we have said by examples, it is not allowable to emphasize what is called the "communal" Mass to the disparagement of Masses celebrated in private, or to exaggerate the element of sacramental sign as if the symbolism, which all certainly admit in the Eucharist, expresses fully and exhausts completely the mode of Christ's presence in this sacrament. Nor is it allowable to discuss the Mystery of Transubstantiation without mentioning what the Council of Trent stated about the marvelous conversion of the whole substance of the bread into the Body and of the whole substance of the wine into the Blood of Christ, speaking rather only of what is called "Transignification" and "Transfiguration," or finally to propose and act upon the opinion according to which, in the consecrated Hosts which remain after the celebration of the sacrifice of the Mass, Christ our Lord is no longer present.

Everyone can see that the spread of these and similar opinions does great harm to the Faith and devotion to the Divine Eucharist.

And therefore, so that the hope aroused by the council, that flourishing of Eucharistic piety which is now pervading the whole Church, be not frustrated by this spread of false opinions, we have with apostolic authority decided to address you, Venerable Brothers, and to express our mind on this subject.

We certainly do not wish to deny in those who are spreading these singular opinions the praiseworthy effort to investigate this lofty mystery and to set forth its inexhaustible riches, revealing its meaning to the men of today; rather we acknowledge and approve their effort. However, we cannot approve the opinions which they express, and we have the duty to warn you about the grave danger which these opinions involve for correct faith.

Mystery of Faith

First of all, we wish to recall something which is well known to you but which is altogether necessary for repelling every virus of rationalism, something to which many illustrious martyrs have witnessed with their blood, while celebrated Fathers and Doctors of the Church constantly professed and taught it; that is, that the Eucharist is a very great Mystery. In fact, properly speaking, and to use the words of the Sacred Liturgy, it is the Mystery of Faith. "Indeed, in it alone," as Leo XIII, our predecessor of happy memory very wisely remarked, "are contained, in a remarkable richness and variety of miracles, all supernatural realities" (Encyclical *Mirae Caritatis*).

We must therefore approach especially this Mystery with humble respect, not following human arguments, which ought to be silent, but adhering firmly to Divine Revelation.

St. John Chrysostom, who, as you know, treated of the Eucharistic Mystery with such nobility of language and insight born of devotion, instructing his faithful on one occasion about this Mystery, expressed these most fitting words:

"Let us submit to God in all things and not contradict Him, even if what He says seems contrary to our reason and intellect; rather let His words prevail over our reason and intellect. Let us act in this way with regard to the (Eucharistic) mysteries, looking not only at what falls under our senses but holding on to His Words. For His Word cannot lead us astray" (in Mat Homil. 82, 4, Migne p. g. 58, 743).

The scholastic Doctors often made similar affirmations: That in this Sacrament are the true Body of Christ and His true Blood is something that "cannot be apprehended by the senses," says St. Thomas, "but only by Faith which relies on Divine Authority. This is why, in a comment on Luke, 22, 19: ('This is my body which is given for you') St. Cyril says: 'Do not doubt whether this is true, but rather receive the Words of the Saviour in Faith, for since He is the Truth, He cannot lie'" (*Summ. Theol.* III Q. 75 A.L.C.).

Thus the Christian people, echoing the words of the same St. Thomas, frequently sing the words: "Sight, touch, and taste in Thee are each deceived, the ear alone most safely is believed. I believe all the Son of God has spoken—than truth's own word there is no truer token."

In fact, St. Bonaventure asserts: "There is no difficulty about Christ's presence in the Eucharist as in a sign, but that He is truly present in the Eucharist as He is in heaven, this is most difficult. Therefore to believe this is especially meritorious" (in IV Sent. Dist. X. P. I Art Un. Qu. I, Oper Omn. Tom. IV *Ad Claras Acquas* 1889, p. 217).

Moreover, the Holy Gospel alludes to this when it tells of the many disciples of Christ who, after listening to the sermon about eating His Flesh and drinking His Blood, turned away and left our Lord, saying: "This is strange talk, who can be expected to listen to it?" Peter, on the other hand, in reply to Jesus' question whether also the twelve wished to leave, expressed his faith and that of the others promptly and resolutely with the marvelous answer: "Lord, to whom should we go? Thy words are the words of eternal life" (Jn 6, 61-69).

It is logical, then, that we should follow as a guiding star in our investigations of this Mystery the magisterium of the Church, to which the Divine Redeemer entrusted for protection and for explanation the Revelation which He has communicated to us through Scripture or Tradition. For we are convinced that "what since the days of antiquity was preached and believed throughout the whole Church with true Catholic Faith is true, even if it is not submitted to rational investigation, even if it is not explained by means of words" (St. Augustine, Contr. Julian VI. 5, 11).

But this is not enough. Having safeguarded the integrity of the Faith, it is necessary to safeguard also its proper mode of expression, lest by the careless use of words, we occasion (God forbid) the rise of false opinions regarding faith in the most sublime of mysteries. St. Augustine gives a stern warning about this in his consideration of the way of speaking employed by the philosophers and of that which ought to be used by Christians.

"The philosophers," he says, "speak freely without fear of offending religious listeners on subjects quite difficult to understand. We, on the other hand, must speak according to a fixed norm, lest the lack of restraint in our speech result in some impious opinion even about the things signified by the words themselves" (*De Civit. Dei*, 23 P.L. 41, 300).

The Church, therefore, with the long labor of centuries and, not without the help of the Holy Spirit, has established a rule of language and confirmed it with the authority of the councils. This rule, which has more than once been the watchword and banner of orthodox faith, must be religiously preserved, and let no one pressure to change it at his own pleasure or under the pretext of new science. Who would ever tolerate that the dogmatic formulas used by the ecumenical councils for the Mysteries of the Holy Trinity and the Incarnation be judged as no longer appropriate for men of our times and therefore that others be rashly substituted for them? In the same way, it cannot be tolerated that any individual should on his own authority modify the formulas which were used by the Council of Trent to express belief in the Eucharistic Mystery. For these formulas, like the others which the Church uses to propose the dogmas of Faith, express concepts which are

not tied to a certain form of human culture, nor to a specific phase
of human culture, nor to one or other theological school. No, these
formulas present that part of reality which necessary and universal
experience permits the human mind to grasp and to manifest with
apt and exact terms taken either from common or polished language.
For this reason, these formulas are adapted to men of all times and
all places.

It must be admitted that these formulas can sometimes be more
clearly and accurately explained. In fact, the achievement of this
goal is highly beneficial. But it would be wrong to give to these
expressions a meaning other than the original. Thus, the understanding of the faith should be advanced without threat. It is,
in fact, the teaching of the First Vatican Council that "the same
signification (of sacred dogmas) is to be forever retained once
our Holy Mother the Church has defined it, and under no pretext
of deeper penetration may that meaning be weakened" (Constit.
Dogm. *De Fide Cathol.* ch. 4).

Mystery of the Eucharist Verified in Sacrifice of the Mass

For the inspiration and consolation of all, we wish to review
with you, Venerable Brothers, the doctrine which the Catholic
Church has always transmitted and unanimously teaches concerning
the Mystery of the Eucharist.

We desire to recall at the very outset what may be termed the
very essence of the dogma, namely, that by means of the Mystery
of the Eucharist, the Sacrifice of the Cross, which was once offered
on Calvary, is remarkably re-enacted and constantly recalled, and
its saving power exerted for the forgiveness of those sins which
we daily commit (*cf. Concil. Trid.*, "*Doctrina de SS. Missae Sacri-
ficio*," ch. 1.).

Just as Moses with the blood of calves has sanctified the Old
Testament (cf. Ex 24, 8), so also Christ our Lord, through the
institution of the Mystery of the Eucharist, with His own Blood
sanctified the New Testament, Whose mediator He is. For, as the
evangelists narrate, at the Last Supper "He took bread, and blessed
and broke it, and gave it to them, saying:

"This is my body, given for you; do this for a commemoration of me." And so with the cup, when supper was ended. This cup, He said, "is the New Testament, in my blood, which is to be shed for you" (Lk 22, 19-20; cf. Mt 26, 26-28; Mk 14, 22-24). And by bidding the apostles to do this in memory of Him, He made clear His Will that the same sacrifice be forever repeated. This intention of Christ was faithfully executed by the primitive Church through her adherence to the teaching of the apostles and through her gatherings summoned to celebrate the Eucharistic Sacrifice. As St. Luke carefully testifies, "these occupied themselves continually with the apostles' teaching, their fellowship in the breaking of bread, and the fixed times of prayer" (Ac 2, 41). From this practice, the faithful used to derive such spiritual strength that it was said of them that "there was one heart and soul in all the company of believers" (Ac 4, 32).

Moreover, the Apostle Paul, who has faithfully transmitted to us what he had received from the Lord (1 Cor 11, 23 ff.), is clearly speaking of the Eucharistic Sacrifice when he points out that Christians, precisely because they have been made partakers at the Table of the Lord, ought not to take part in pagan sacrifices. "Is not this cup we bless," he says, "a participation in Christ's Blood? Is not the bread we break a participation in Christ's Body? ... to drink the Lord's cup, and yet to drink the cup of evil spirits, to share the Lord's Feast, and to share the feast of evil spirits, is impossible for you" (1 Cor 10, 16). Foreshadowed by Malachias (1, 11), this new offering of the New Testament has always been offered by the Church, in accordance with the teaching of our Lord and the apostles, "not only to atone for the sins and punishment of the living faithful and to appeal for their other needs, but also to help those who have died in Christ but have not yet been completely purified" (*Concil. Trid. Doctr. de SS. Missae. Sacrif.* ch. 2).

Passing over other citations, we recall merely the testimony rendered by St. Cyril of Jerusalem, who wrote the following memorable instructions for his neophytes:

"After the spiritual sacrifice, the unbloody act of worship, has been completed, bending over this propitiatory offering we beg

God to grant peace to all the churches, to give harmony to the whole world, to bless our rulers, our soldiers, and our companions, to aid the sick and afflicted, and in general to assist all who stand in need; and then we offer the Victim also for our deceased holy ancestors and bishops and for all our dead. As we do this, we are filled with the conviction that this Sacrifice will be of the greatest help to those souls for whom prayers are being offered in the very presence of our Holy and Awesome Victim."

This holy Doctor closes his instruction by citing the parallel of the crown which is woven for the emperor to move him to pardon exiles: "In the same fashion, when we offer our prayers to God for the dead, even though they be sinners, we weave no crown, but instead we offer Christ slaughtered for our sins, beseeching our merciful God to take pity both on them and on ourselves" (Catecheses, 23 [Myst. 5], 8-18; PG, 33, 1115-1118). St. Augustine testifies that this manner of offering also for the deceased "the Sacrifice which ransomed us" was being faithfully observed in the Church at Rome (cf. Confess., IX 12, 32; PL, 32, 777; cf. ibid. IX, 11, 27; PL, 32, 775), and at the same time he observes that the Universal Church was following this custom in her conviction that it had been handed down by the earliest Fathers (cf. Serm. 172, 2; PL, 38, 936; cf. *de Cura Gerenda pro Mortuis*, 12; PL, 40, 593).

To shed fuller light on the Mystery of the Church, it helps to realize that it is nothing less than the whole Church which, in union with Christ in His role as Priest and Victim offers the Sacrifice of the Mass and is offered in it. The Fathers of the Church taught this wondrous doctrine (cf. St. Augustine, de Civit. Dei, X, 6; PL, 41, 284). A few years ago our predecessor of happy memory, Pius XII, explained it (cf. Encycl. *Mediator Dei*) and only recently the Second Vatican Council enunciated it in its treatise on the people of God as formulated in its Constitution on the Church (cf. *Const. Dogm. de Ecclesia*, ch. 2, no. 11).

To be sure, the distinction between universal priesthood and hierarchical priesthood is one of essence and not merely one of degree (cf. ibid. ch. 2, no. 10) and this distinction should be faithfully observed. Yet we cannot fail to be filled with the earnest desire that this teaching on the Mass be explained over and over until it takes root deep in the hearts of the faithful. Our desire is founded on our conviction that the correct understanding of the Eucharistic Mystery is the most effective means to foster devotion to this sacrament, to extol the dignity of all the faithful, and to spur their spirit toward the attainment of the summit of sanctity, which is nothing less than the total offering of oneself to service of the Divine Majesty.

We should also mention "the public and social nature of every Mass" (*Const. de Sacra Liturgia*, ch. 1, no. 27), a conclusion which clearly follows from the doctrine we have been discussing. For even though a priest should offer Mass in private, that Mass is not something private; It is an act of Christ and of the Church. In offering this Sacrifice, the Church learns to offer herself as a sacrifice for all. Moreover, for the salvation of the entire world she applies the single, boundless, redemptive power of the Sacrifice of the Cross. For every Mass is offered not for the salvation of ourselves alone, but also for that of the whole world. Hence, although the very nature of the action renders most appropriate the active participation of many of the faithful in the celebration of the Mass, nevertheless, that Mass is to be fully approved which, in conformity with the prescriptions and lawful traditions of the Church, a priest for a sufficient reason offers in private, that is, in the presence of no one except his server. From such a Mass an abundant treasure of special salutary graces enriches the celebrant, the faithful, the whole Church, and the entire world—graces which are not imparted in the same abundance by the mere reception of Holy Communion.

Therefore, from a paternal and solicitous heart, we recommend to priests, who bestow on us a special crown of happiness in the Lord, that they be mindful of their power, received through the hands of the ordaining bishop, of offering Sacrifice to God and of celebrating Masses both for the living and for the dead in the name of the Lord (cf. *Pontificabile Romanum*), and that they worthily and devoutly offer Mass each day in order that both they and the rest of the faithful may enjoy the benefits that flow so richly from the Sacrifice of the Cross. Thus also they will contribute most to the salvation of the human race.

Christ Is Made Sacramentally Present

By the few ideas which we have mentioned regarding the Sacrifice of the Mass, we are encouraged to explain a few notions concerning the Sacrament of the Eucharist, seeing that both Sacrifice and Sacrament pertain inseparably to the same Mystery. In an unbloody representation of the Sacrifice of the Cross and in application of its saving power, in the Sacrifice of the Mass the Lord is immolated when, through the words of consecration, He begins to be present in a sacramental form under the appearances of bread and wine to become the spiritual food of the faithful.

All of us realize that there is more than one way in which Christ is present in His Church. We wish to review at greater length the consoling doctrine which was briefly set forth in the constitution *De Sacra Liturgia* (cf. ch. 1, no. 7). Christ is present in His Church when she prays, since it is He who "prays for us and prays in us and to Whom we pray as to our God" (St. Augustine, "in Ps" 85, 1; PL, 37, 1081). It is He who has promised: "where two or three are gathered together in my name, I am there in the midst of them" (Mt 18, 20). He is present in the Church as she performs her works of mercy, not only because we do to Christ whatever good we do to one of His least brethren (cf. Mt 25, 40), but also because it is Christ, performing these works through the Church, who continually assists men with His Divine Love. He is present in the Church on her pilgrimage of struggle to reach the harbor of eternal life, since it is He who through Faith dwells in our hearts (cf. Ep 3, 17) and, through the Holy Spirit whom He gives us, pours His love into those hearts (cf. Rm 5, 5).

In still another genuine way He is present in the Church as she preaches, since the Gospel which she proclaims is the Word of God, which is not preached except in the name of Christ, by the authority of Christ, and with the assistance of Christ, the Incarnate Word of God. In this way there is formed "one flock which trusts its only Shepherd" (*Idem, "Contr. Litt. Petiliani"* III, 10, 11, PL, 43, 353).

He is present in His Church as she governs the people of God, since her sacred power comes from Christ, and since Christ, "the Shepherd of Shepherds" (St. Augustine, "in Ps" 86, 3; p. 1. 37, 1102), is present in the pastors who exercise that power, according to His promise to the apostles: "Behold I am with you all through the days that are coming, until the consummation of the world."

Moreover, in a manner still more sublime, Christ is present in His Church as she offers in His Name the Sacrifice of the Mass; He is present in her as she administers the Sacraments. We find deep consolation in recalling the accurate and eloquent words with which St. John Chrysostom, overcome with a sense of awe, described the presence of Christ in the offering of the Sacrifice of the Mass: "I wish to add something that is plainly awe-inspiring, but do not be astonished or upset. This Sacrifice, no matter who offers it, be it Peter or Paul, is always the same as that which Christ gave His disciples and which priests now offer: The offering of today is in no way inferior to that which Christ offered, because it is not men who sanctify the offering of today; it is the same Christ who sanctified His own. For just as the words which God spoke are the very same as those which the priest now speaks, so too the oblation is the very same" (*In Epist.* 2 *ad Timoth. Homil* 2, PG, 4; 612). No one is unaware that the Sacraments are the actions of Christ, Who administers them through men. Therefore, the Sacraments are holy in themselves, and by the power of Christ they pour Grace into the soul when they touch the body. The mind boggles at these different ways in which Christ is present and fill the mind with amazement. They confront the Church with a mystery ever to be pondered.

But there is yet another manner in which Christ is present in His Church, a manner which surpasses all the others; it is His presence in the Sacrament of the Eucharist, which is for this reason "a more consoling source of devotion, a more lovely object of contemplation, a more effective means of sanctification than all the other sacraments" (*Aegidius Romanus*, "Theoremata de Corpore Christi," Theor. 50, Venetiis 1521, p. 127). The reason is clear; it contains Christ Himself and it is "a kind of perfection of the spiritual life; in a way, it is the goal of all the sacraments" (St. Thomas, *Summ. Theol.* III, q. 73, a. 3c.).

This presence is called "real"—by which it is not intended to exclude all other types of presence as if they could not be "real" too, but because it is presence in the fullest sense: that is to say, it is a substantial presence by which Christ, the God-man, is wholly and entirely present (cf. Conc. of Trent, Decree on the Eucharist, ch. 3). It would therefore be wrong to explain this presence by having recourse to the "spiritual" nature, as it is called, of the glorified body of Christ, which is present everywhere, or by reducing it to a kind of symbolism, as if this august Sacrament consisted of nothing else than an efficacious sign "of the spiritual presence of Christ and of His intimate union with the faithful members of His Mystical Body" (Pius XII, Encycl. *Humani Generis*).

It is true that much can be found in the Fathers and in the scholastics with regard to symbolism in the Eucharist, especially with reference to the unity of the Church. The Council of Trent, restating their doctrine, taught that the Savior bequeathed the Blessed Eucharist to His Church "as a symbol . . . of that unity and charity with which He wished all Christians to be most intimately united among themselves," and hence "as a symbol of that one body of which He is the Head" (Decree "On the Eucharist," Proem, and ch. 2).

When Christian literature was still in its infancy, the unknown author of that work we know as the "Didache or Teaching of the Twelve Apostles" wrote as follows on this subject: "In regard to the Eucharist, give thanks in this manner: . . . Just as this bread was scattered and dispersed over the hills, but when harvested was made one, so may Your Church be gathered into Your Kingdom from the ends of the earth" ("Didache," 9:1 Funk, *"Patres Apostolici,"* 1, 20).

The same we read in St. Cyprian, writing in defense of the Church against schism: "Finally, the sacrifices of the Lord proclaim the unity of Christians, bound together by the bond of a firm and inviolable charity. For when the Lord, in speaking of bread which is produced by the compacting of many grains of wheat, refers to it as His Body,

He is describing our people whose unity He has sustained, and when
He refers to wine pressed from many grapes and berries, as His Blood,
He is speaking of our flock, formed by the fusing of many united
together" (*"Ep ad Magnum,"* 6; P.L. 1189).

But before all of these, St. Paul had written to the Corinthians:
the One Bread makes us One Body, though we are many in number
the same Bread is shared by all (1 Cor 10, 17).

While the Eucharistic symbolism brings us to an understanding of
the effect proper to this Sacrament, which is the unity of the Mystical
Body, it does not indicate or explain what it is that makes this Sacrament different from all others. The constant teaching which the
Catholic Church passes on to her catechumens, the understanding
of the Christian people, the doctrine defined by the Council of Trent,
the very words used by Christ when He instituted the Most Holy
Eucharist, compel us to acknowledge that "the Eucharist is that
flesh of our Savior Jesus Christ who suffered for our sins and whom
the Father in his loving-kindness raised again" (St. Ignatius,
"Ep. ad Smyrn." 7, 1; p.g. 5, 714). To these words of St. Ignatius
of Antioch, we may add those which Theodore of Mopsuesta, a
faithful witness to the faith of the Church on this point, addressed
to the faithful: "The Lord did not say: This is a symbol of My
Body, and this is a symbol of My Blood but: This is My Body and
My Blood." He teaches us not to look to the nature of those things
which lie before us and are perceived by the senses, for by the
prayer of thanksgiving and the words spoken over them, they have
been changed into flesh and blood" ("In Math. Comm.," ch. 26
PG, 66, 714).

The Council of Trent, basing itself on this faith of the Church,
"openly and sincerely professes that within the Holy Sacrament
of the Eucharist, after the Consecration of the Bread and Wine, Our
Lord Jesus Christ, true God and true Man, is really, truly and
substantially contained under those outward appearances." In this
way, the Savior in His humanity is present not only at the right
hand of the Father according to the natural manner of existence,
but also in the Sacrament of the Eucharist "by a mode of existence
which we cannot express in words, but which, with a mind illumined

by Faith, we can conceive, and must most firmly believe, to be possible to God" (Decree "On the Eucharist," ch. 1).

Christ Our Lord Is Present in the Sacrament of the Eucharist by Transubstantiation

To avoid misunderstanding this sacramental presence which surpasses the laws of nature and constitutes the greatest miracle of its kind (cf. Encycl. *'Mirae Caritatis,'* "Acta Leonis XIII," Vol. XXII, 1902-1903, p. 123), we must listen with docility to the voice of the teaching and praying Church. This voice, which constantly echoes the voice of Christ, assures us that the way Christ is made present in this Sacrament is none other than by the change of the whole substance of the bread into His Body, and of the whole substance of the wine into His Blood, and that this unique and truly wonderful change the Catholic Church rightly calls Transubstantiation (cf. Council of Trent, "Decree on the Eucharist," ch. 4, and can. 2). As a result of Transubstantiation, the species of bread and wine undoubtedly take on a new meaning and a new finality, for they no longer remain ordinary bread and ordinary wine, but become the sign of something sacred, the sign of a spiritual food. However, the reason they take on this new significance and this new finality is simply because they contain a new "reality" which we may justly term Ontological. Not that there lies under those species what was already there before, but something quite different; and that not only because of the Faith of the Church, but in objective reality, since after the change of the substance or nature of the bread and wine into the Body and Blood of Christ, nothing remains of the bread and wine but the appearances, under which Christ, whole and entire, in His physical "reality" is bodily present, although not in the same way that bodies are present in a given place.

For this reason the Fathers took special care to warn the faithful that in reflecting on this most august Sacrament, they should not trust to their senses, which reach only the properties of bread and wine, but rather to the Words of Christ which have power to transform, change and transmute the bread and wine into His Body and Blood. For, as those same Fathers often said, the power that accomplishes this is that same power by which God Almighty, at the beginning of time, created the world out of nothing.

"We have been instructed in these matters and filled with an unshakeable faith," says St. Cyril of Alexandria, at the end of a sermon on the Mysteries of the Faith; "that which seems to be bread, is not bread, though it tastes like it, but the Body of Christ, and that which seems to be wine, is not wine, though it too tastes as such, but the Blood of Christ . . . draw inner strength by receiving this bread as spiritual food and your soul will rejoice" ("Catecheses," 22, A9; "Myst." 4; PG, 33, 1103).

St. John Chrysostom emphasizes this point, saying: "It is not the power of man which makes what is put before us the Body and Blood of Christ, but the power of Christ Himself Who was crucified for us. The priest standing there in the place of Christ says these words but their power and grace are from God. 'This is my body,' he says, and these words transform what lies before him" (*"De Prodit. Iudae. Homil."* 1, 6, p. g. 49, 380 cf. "In Matth." "Homil." 82, 5: p. g. 58, 744).

Cyril, Bishop of Alexandria, is in full agreement with the bishop of Constantinople when he writes in his commentary on the Gospel of St. Matthew: "Christ said indicating (the bread and wine) : 'This is My Body,' and 'this is My Blood,' in order that you might not judge what you see to be a mere figure. The offerings, by the hidden power of God Almighty, are changed into Christ's Body and Blood, and by receiving these we come to share in the life-giving and sanctifying efficacy of Christ" ("In Matth." 26, 27; PG, 72, 451).

Ambrose, Bishop of Milan, dealing with the Eucharistic change, says: "Let us be assured that this is not what nature formed, but what the blessing consecrated, and that greater efficacy resides in the blessings than in nature, for by the blessing nature is changed." To confirm the truth of this Mystery, he recounts many of the miracles described in the Scriptures, including Christ's birth of the Virgin Mary, and then turning to the work of Creation, concludes thus: "Surely the word of Christ, which could make out of nothing that which did not exist, can change things already in existence into what they were not. For it is no less extraordinary to give things new natures than to change their natures" ("De Myster.," 9, 50-52; PL, 16, 422-424).

However, there is no need to assemble many testimonies. Rather let us recall that firmness of faith with which the Church with one accord opposed Berengarius, who, yielding to the difficulties of human reasoning, was the first who dared deny the Eucharistic change. More than once she threatened to condemn him unless he retracted. Thus it was that our predecessor, St. Gregory VII, ordered him to pronounce the following oath: "I believe in my heart and openly profess that the bread and wine which are placed upon the altar are, by the Mystery of the Sacred Prayer and the Words of the Redeemer, substantially changed into the true and life-giving Flesh and Blood of Jesus Christ Our Lord, and that after the Consecration, there is present the true Body of Christ which was born of the Virgin and, offered up for the salvation of the world, hung on the cross and now sits at the right hand of the Father and that there is present the True Blood of Christ which flowed from His side. They are present not only by means of a sign and of the efficacy of the Sacrament, but also in the very reality and truth of their nature and substance" (Mansi, "Coll. Ampliss. Concil." XX, 524 d).

These words fully accord with the doctrine of the Mystery of the Eucharistic Change as set forth by the ecumenical councils. The constant teaching of these councils—of the Lateran, of Constance, Florence and Trent—whether stating the teaching of the Church or condemning errors, affords us an admirable example of the unchangingness of the Catholic Faith.

After the Council of Trent, our predecessor, Pius VI, on the occasion of the errors of the Synod of Pistoia, warned parish priests when carrying out their office of teaching, not to neglect to speak of Transubstantiation, one of the articles of the Faith (Const. *Auctorem Fidei*, August 28, 1794). Similarly our predecessor of happy memory, Pius XII, recalled the bounds which those who undertake to discuss the Mystery of Transubstantiation might not cross (Allocutio Habita Die 22 Septembris 1956, 'A.A.S.' CLVII, 1956, p. 720). We ourselves also, in fulfillment of our Apostolic Office, have openly borne solemn witness to the Faith of the Church at the National Eucharistic Congress held recently at Pisa (A.A.S. LVII, 1965, pp. 588-592).

Moreover the Catholic Church has held on to this faith in the presence in the Eucharist of the Body and Blood of Christ, not only in her teaching but also in her practice, since she has at all times given to this great Sacrament the worship which is known as Latria and which may be given to God alone. As St. Augustine says: "It was in His Flesh that Christ walked among us and it is His Flesh that He has given us to eat for our salvation. No one, however, eats of this Flesh without having first adored it ... and not only do we not sin in thus adoring it, but we would sin if we did not do so" ("In Ps" 98, 9; PL, 37, 1264).

Latreutic Worship of Sacrament of the Eucharist

The Catholic Church has always offered and still offers the cult of Latria to the Sacrament of the Eucharist, not only during Mass, but also outside of it, reserving consecrated Hosts with the utmost care, exposing them to solemn veneration, and carrying them processionally to the joy of great crowds of the faithful.

In the ancient documents of the Church we have many testimonies of this veneration. The pastors of the Church in fact solicitously exhorted the faithful to take the greatest care in keeping the Eucharist which they took to their homes. "The body of Christ is meant to be eaten, not to be treated with irreverence," St. Hippolytus warns the faithful ("Tradit. Apost." Ed Botte, "La Tradition Apostolique de St. Hippolyte," Munster 1963, p. 84).

In fact the faithful thought themselves guilty, and rightly so, as Origen recalls, if after they received the body of the Lord in order to preserve it with all care and reverence, a small fragment of it fell off through negligence ("In Exod. Fragm." PG, 12, 391).

The same pastors severely reproved those who showed lack of reverence if it happened. This is attested to by Novitianus whose testimony in the matter is trustworthy. He judged as deserving condemnation anyone who came out of Sunday service carrying with him as usual the Eucharist, the Sacred Body of the Lord, "not going to his house but running to places of amusement" ("De Spectaculis" C.S.E.L. III, p. 8).

On the other hand St. Cyril of Alexandria rejects as folly the opinion of those who maintained that if a part of the Eucharist was left over for the following day it did not confer sanctification. "For," he says, "neither Christ is altered nor His Holy Body changed, but the force and power and vivifying grace always remain with it" ("Epist., ad Calosyrium" PG, 76, 1075).

Nor should we forget that in ancient times the faithful, harassed by the violence of persecution or living in solitude out of love for monastic life, nourished themselves even daily, receiving Holy Communion by their own hands when the priest or deacon was absent (cf. Basil. "Epist." 93, PG, 32, 483-486).

We say this not in order that there may be some change in the way of keeping the Eucharist and of receiving Holy Communion which was later on prescribed by Church laws and which now remain in force, but rather that we may rejoice over the Faith of the Church which is always one and the same.

This faith also gave rise to the Feast of Corpus Christi which was first celebrated in the Diocese of Liege specially through the efforts of the servant of God, Blessed Juliana of Mount Cornelius, and which our predecessor Urban IV extended to the Universal Church. From it have originated many practices of Eucharistic piety which under the inspiration of Divine Grace have increased from day to day and with which the Catholic Church is striving ever more to do homage to Christ, to thank Him for so great a gift and to implore His mercy.

Exhortation to Promote the Cult of the Eucharist

We therefore ask you, Venerable Brothers, among the people entrusted to your care and vigilance, to preserve this Faith in its purity and integrity—a Faith which seeks only to remain perfectly loyal to the Word of Christ and of the apostles and unambiguously rejects all erroneous and mischievous opinions. Tirelessly promote the Cult of the Eucharist, the focus where all other forms of piety must ultimately emerge.

May the faithful, thanks to your efforts, come to realize and experience ever more perfectly the truth of these words: "He who desires life finds here a place to live in and the means to live by.

Let him approach, let him believe, let him be incorporated so that he may receive life. Let him not refuse union with the members, let him not be a corrupt member, deserving to be cut off, nor a disfigured member to be ashamed of. Let him be a grateful, fitting and healthy member. Let him cleave to the body, let him live by God and for God. Let him now labor here on earth, that he may afterwards reign in heaven" (St. Augustine "In Ioann. Tract." 26, 13, PL, 35, 1613).

It is to be desired that the faithful, every day and in great numbers, actively participate in the Sacrifice of the Mass, receive Holy Communion with a pure heart, and give thanks to Christ Our Lord for so great a gift. Let them remember these words: "The desire of Jesus Christ and of the Church that all the faithful receive daily Communion means above all that through the sacramental union with God they may obtain the strength necessary for mastering their passions, for purifying themselves of their daily venial faults and for avoiding the grave sins to which human frailty is exposed" (*Decr. S. Congr. Concil.*, Dec. 20, 1905, *Approb. A. S. Pio X, A.A.S.* XXXVIII, 1905, p. 501).

In the course of the day the faithful should not omit to visit the Blessed Sacrament, which according to the liturgical laws must be kept in the churches with great reverence in a most honorable location. Such visits are a proof of gratitude, an expression of love, an acknowledgement of the Lord's Presence.

No one can fail to understand that the Divine Eucharist bestows upon the Christian people an incomparable dignity. Not only while the Sacrifice is offered and the Sacrament received, but as long as the Eucharist is kept in our churches and oratories, Christ is truly the Emmanuel, that is, "God with us." Day and night He is in our midst, He dwells with us, full of Grace and Truth (cf. Jn 1, 14). He restores morality, nourishes virtues, consoles the afflicted, and strengthens the weak. He proposes His own example to those who come to Him that all may learn to be, like Himself, meek and humble of heart and to seek not their own interests but those of God.

Anyone who approaches this august Sacrament with special devotion and endeavors to return generous love for Christ's own infinite love, will experience and fully understand—not without spiritual joy and fruit—how precious is the life hidden with Christ in God (cf. Col 3, 3) and how great is the value of converse with Christ, for there is nothing more consoling on earth, nothing more efficacious for advancing along the road of holiness.

Further, you realize, Venerable Brothers, that the Eucharist is reserved in the churches and oratories as in the spiritual center of a religious community or of a parish, yes, of the Universal Church and of all humanity, since beneath the appearance of the species, Christ is contained, the Invisible Head of the Church, the Redeemer of the world, the Center of all hearts, "by Whom all things are and by Whom we exist" (1 Cor 8, 6).

From this it follows that the worship paid to the Divine Eucharist strongly impels the soul to cultivate a "social" love (cf. St. Augustine, *De Gen. Ad Litt.* XI, 15, 20; PL, 34, 437), by which the common good is given preference over the good of the individual. Let us consider as our own interests of the community, of the parish, of the entire Church, extending our charity to the whole world, because we know that everywhere there are members of Christ.

The Eucharistic Sacrament, Venerable Brothers, is the sign and the cause of the unity of the Mystical Body, and it inspires an active "ecclesial" spirit in those who venerate it with greater fervor. Therefore, never cease to persuade those committed to your care that they should learn to make their own the cause of the Church in approaching the Eucharistic mystery, to pray to God without interruption, to offer themselves to God as a pleasing sacrifice for the peace and unity of the Church, so that all the children of the Church be united and think the same, that there be no divisions among them, but rather unity of mind and purpose, as the apostle insists (cf. 1 Cor 1, 10). May all those not yet in perfect communion with the Catholic Church, who, though separated from her, glory in the name of Christian, share with us as soon as possible with the help of Divine Grace that unity of Faith and Communion which Christ wanted to be the distinctive mark of His disciples.

This zeal in praying and consecrating one's self to God for the unity of the Church should be practiced particularly by Religious, both men and women, inasmuch as they are in a special way devoted to the adoration of the Blessed Sacrament, according it homage and honor on earth, in virtue of their vows.

Nothing has ever been or is more important to the Church or more consoling than the desire for the unity of all Christians, a desire which we wish to express once again in the very words used by the Council of Trent at the close of its Decree on the Most Blessed Eucharist: "In conclusion, the sacred synod with paternal love admonishes, exhorts, prays and implores 'through the merciful kindness of our God' (Lk 1, 78) that each and every Christian come at last to a perfect agreement regarding this sign of unity, this bond of charity, this symbol of concord, and, mindful of such great dignity and such exquisite love of Christ our Lord who gave His Beloved Son as the price of our salvation and 'His Flesh to eat' (Jn 6, 48 ss.), believe and adore those sacred mysteries of His Body and Blood with such firm and unwavering faith, with such devotion, piety and veneration, that they can receive frequently that super-substantial Bread (Mt 6, 11), which will be for them truly the life of the soul and unfailing strength of mind, so that fortified by its vigor (cf. K, 19, 8) they can depart from this wretched pilgrimage on earth to reach their heavenly home where they will then eat the same 'Bread of Angels' (Ps 77, 25) no longer hidden by the species which now they eat under the sacred appearances" (*Decree De SS. Eucharistia*, c. 8).

May the all-good Redeemer who shortly before His death prayed to the Father that all who were to believe in Him would be one even as He and the Father were One (cf. Jn 17, 20-21), deign speedily to hear our most ardent prayer and that of the entire Church, that we may all, with one voice and one Faith, celebrate the Eucharistic Mystery and, by participating in the Body of Christ, become One Body (cf. 1 Cor 10, 17), linked by those same bonds which He Himself desired for its perfection.

And we turn with paternal affection also to those who belong to the Venerable Churches of the Orient, from which came so many most illustrious Fathers whose testimony to the belief of the Eucharist we have so gladly cited in our present letter. Our soul is filled with intense joy as we consider your Faith in the Eucharist, which is also our Faith, and as we listen to the liturgical prayers by which you celebrate so great a Mystery, we rejoice to behold your Eucharistic devotion, and to read your theologians explaining or defending the doctrine of this most august Sacrament.

Unforgettable are the words of the holy martyr Ignatius, in his warning to the faithful of Philadelphia against the evils of division and schism, the remedy for which lies in the Eucharist: "Strive then," he says, "to make use of one form of thanksgiving for the Flesh of Our Lord Jesus Christ is one and one is the chalice in the union of His Blood, one altar, one bishop" (*Epist. Ad Philadelph.*, 4, PG, 5, 700).

Encouraged by the most consoling hope of the blessings which will accrue to the whole Church and the entire world from an increase in devotion to the Eucharist, with profound affection we impart to you, Venerable Brothers, to the priests, Religious and all those who collaborate with you and to all the faithful entrusted to your care, the Apostolic Benediction as a pledge of Heavenly Graces.

Given at Rome, at St. Peter's, the third day of September, the Feast of Pope St. Pius X, in the year 1965, the third year of our pontificate. Paul VI, Pope.

Cf. *Immensae Caritatis*—The Testament of Treasure—Treasured Love—Instruction on Facilitating Sacramental Communion in Particular Circumstances,—Sacred Congregation for the Discipline of the Sacraments, January 29, 1973. U.S.C.C.

Cf. *Sacramentum Paenitentiae*—Pastoral Norms Concerning the Administration of General Absolution—Sacred Congregation for the Doctrine of the Faith, June 16, 1972. U.S.C.C.

Cf. *Ordo Paenitentiae*—Order for the Sacrament of Penance, 1974. U.S.C.C.

Cf. Pope Paul VI, *Sacram Unctionem Infirmorum*, The Anointing of the Sick, November 30, 1972. U.S.C.C.

REVISION OF LAW ON SACRAMENTAL CONFESSION AND CANON 637

SCRSI DECREE

While the revision of Canon Law is in process, the Sacred Congregation for Religious and for Secular Institutes has judged it opportune, for a number of urgent reasons, to examine in Plenary Assembly certain questions concerning: I) the use and administration of the Sacrament of Penance, especially for women Religious, and II) fitness for the religious life in a special case.

After careful examination, the Fathers in the Plenary Assembly held on October 26 and 27, 1970, made the following decisions:

— I —

1. Religious, because of their special union with the Church which "incessantly pursues the path of penance and renewal" (Const. *Lumen Gentium*, no. 8), should value highly the Sacrament of Penance, by which the fundamental gift of "metanoia," that is, of conversion to the kingdom of Christ, first received in Baptism, is restored and strengthened in members of the Church who have sinned (cf. Ap. Const. *Paenitemini*, ΛΛS, 58, 1966, pp. 179-180).

Through this Sacrament pardon is obtained from the mercy of God for the offenses committed against Him, and we are reconciled with the Church which we wound by our sins (cf. Const. *Lumen Gentium*, no. 11).

2. Religious should likewise hold in high regard the frequent use of this Sacrament by which true knowledge of self is deepened, Christian humility is strengthened, spiritual direction is provided and grace is increased. These and other wonderful effects not only contribute greatly to daily growth in virtue, but they are highly beneficial also to the common good of the whole Community (cf. Encyclical *Mystici Corporis*, AAS 35, 1943, p. 235).

3. Therefore, Religious, in their desire to strengthen in them-

selves union with God, should strive to receive the Sacrament of Penance frequently, that is, twice a month. Superiors, on their part, should encourage this frequency and make it possible for the members to go to confession at least every two weeks and even oftener, if they wish to do so.

4. With specific reference to the confessions of women Religious, the following provisions are made:

a) All women Religious and Novices, in order that they may have proper liberty, may make their confession validly and licitly to any priest approved for hearing confessions in the locality. For this, no special jurisdiction or designation is henceforth required (c. 876).

b) In order, nevertheless, to provide for the greater good of the communities, an ordinary confessor shall be named for monasteries of contemplative nuns, for houses of formation and for large communities, and an extraordinary confessor shall be appointed at least for the monasteries mentioned above and for houses of formation without, however, any obligation on the part of the Religious to present themselves to them.

c) For other communities, an ordinary confessor may be named at the request of the community itself or after consultation with its members if, in the judgment of the Ordinary, special circumstances justify such appointment.

d) The local Ordinary should choose confessors carefully. They should be priests of sufficient maturity and possess the other necessary qualities. The Ordinary may determine the number, age and term of office of the confessors, and may name them or renew their appointment, after consultation with the Community concerned.

e) The prescriptions of Canons which are contrary to the foregoing dispositions, which are incompatible with them, or which because of them no longer apply, are suspended.

5. The provisions of the preceding paragraph (no. 4) hold also for lay communities of men in so far as they are applicable.

— II —

The final clause of Canon 637 is to be understood in the sense that a Religious in temporary vows who, because of physical or mental illness even if contracted after profession, is judged by the competent Superior with the consent of his Council on the basis of examinations by physicians or other specialists, to be incapable of living the Religious Life without personal harm or harm to the Institute, may be refused admission to renewal of vows or to final profession. The decision in such cases is to be taken with charity and equity.

His Holiness, Pope Paul VI, in the audience granted to the Secretary of this Sacred Congregation on November 20, approved these dispositions and directed that they be put into effect immediately, without any formula of execution, until such time as the revised Canon Law becomes effective.

All things to the contrary notwithstanding. December 8, 1970.

H. Card. Antoniutti
Prefect

PART THREE

RELIGIOUS ARE RELATED TO THE CHURCH BY SPECIAL BOND, REFLECTION AND EXPRESSION OF THAT BY WHICH, THROUGH THEIR PERPETUAL PROFESSION FORMALLY ACCEPTED AND RATIFIED BY THE CHURCH, THEY ARE INCORPORATED MORE DEEPLY INTO THE MYSTERY OF CHRIST, AND MORE INTIMATELY COMMITTED TO THE DIVINE SERVICE OF BUILDING UP HIS BODY, THE CHURCH.

ROOTED IN THE PERFECTION OF THEIR BAPTISMAL CONSECRATION, RELIGIOUS ARE ACTIVELY ECCLESIAL, LIVING FOR CHRIST AND HIS BODY, THE CHURCH, IN COMMITMENT TO ITS UNIVERSAL SALVIFIC MISSION. POSSESSING PROPER APOSTOLIC CHARISMS, RELIGIOUS "COMBINE CONTEMPLATION WITH APOSTOLIC LOVE" IN SERVICE, IN WITNESS TO AND AS SYMBOLS OF THE DIVINE TRANSCENDENCE OF THE EARTHLY PILGRIMAGE TO ETERNAL BEATITUDE.

CHAPTER 6

MYSTERY OF RELIGIOUS LIFE IN CHRIST'S BODY
RELIGIOUS LIFE IS ACTIVELY ECCLESIAL:
RELIGIOUS LIVE FOR CHRIST AND HIS BODY, THE CHURCH

LG 44. The faithful of Christ can bind themselves to the three previously mentioned counsels either by vows, or by other sacred bonds which are like vows in their purpose. Through such a bond a person is totally dedicated to God by an act of supreme love, and is committed to the honor and service of God under a new and special title.

It is true that through baptism he has died to sin and has been consecrated to God. However, in order to derive more abundant fruit from this baptismal grace, he intends, by the profession of the evangelical counsels in the Church, to free himself from those obstacles which might draw him away from the fervor of charity and the perfection of divine worship. This consecration gains in perfection since by virtue of firmer and steadier bonds it serves as a better symbol of the unbreakable link between Christ and His Spouse, the Church.

By the charity to which they lead, the evangelical counsels join their followers to the Church and her mystery in a special way. Since this is so, the spiritual life of these followers should be devoted to the welfare of the whole Church. Thence arises their duty of working to implant and strengthen the kingdom of Christ in souls and to extend that kingdom to every land. This duty is to be discharged to the extent of their capacities and in keeping with the form of their proper vocation. The chosen means may be prayer or active undertakings. It is for this reason that the Church preserves and fosters the special character of her various religious communities.

The profession of the evangelical counsels, then, appears as a sign which can and ought to attract all the members of the Church to an effective and prompt fulfillment of the duties of their Christian vocation. The People of God has no lasting city here below, but looks forward to one which is to come. This being so, the religious state by giving its members greater freedom from earthly cares more adequately manifests to all believers the presence of heavenly goods already possessed here below.

Furthermore, it not only witnesses to the fact of a new and eternal life acquired by the redemption of Christ. It foretells the resurrected state and the glory of the heavenly kingdom. Christ also proposed to His disciples that form of life which He, as the Son of God, accepted in entering this world to do the will of the Father. In the Church this same state of life is imitated with particular accuracy and perpetually exemplified. The religious state reveals in a unique way that the kingdom of God and its overmastering necessities are superior to all earthly considerations. Finally, to all men it shows wonderfully at work within the Church the surpassing greatness of the force of Christ the King and the boundless power of the Holy Spirit.

Thus, although the religious state constituted by the profession of the evangelical counsels does not belong to the hierarchical structure of the Church, nevertheless it belongs inseparably to her life and holiness.

(Cf. ET, no. 24)

LG 45. Since it is the duty of the hierarchy of the Church to nourish the People of God and lead them to the choicest pastures (cf. Ez 34:14), it devolves on the same hierarchy to govern with wise legislation the practice of the evangelical counsels. For by that practice is uniquely fostered the perfection of love for God and neighbor.

Submissively following the promptings of the Holy Spirit, the hierarchy also endorses rules formulated by eminent men and women, and authentically approves later modifications. Moreover, by its watchful and shielding authority, the hierarchy keeps close to communities established far and wide for the upbuilding of Christ's body, so that they can grow and flourish in accord with the spirit of their founders.

Any institute of perfection and its individual members can be removed from the jurisdiction of the local Ordinaries by the Supreme Pontiff and subjected to himself alone. This is possible by virtue of his primacy over the entire Church. He does so in order to provide more adequately for the necessities of the entire flock of the Lord and in consideration of the common good. In like manner, these communities can be left or committed to the charge of their proper patriarchical authorities. In fulfilling their duty toward the Church in accord with the special form of their life, the members of these communities should show toward bishops the reverence and obedience required by canonical laws. For bishops possess pastoral authority over individual churches, and apostolic labor demands unity and harmony.

By her approval the Church not only raises the religious profession to the dignity of a canonical state. By the liturgical setting of that profession she also manifests that it is a state consecrated to God. The Church herself, by the authority given to her by God, accepts the vows of those professing them. By her public prayer she begs aid and grace from God for them. She commends them to God, imparts a spiritual blessing to them, and accompanies their self-offering with the Eucharistic sacrifice.

(Cf. PC, nos. 1, 2, 6)

PC 20. Communities should faithfully maintain and fulfill their proper activities. Yet, they should make adjustments in them according to the needs of time and place and in favor of what will benefit the universal Church and individual dioceses. To this end they should resort to suitable techniques, including modern ones, and abandon whatever activities are today less in keeping with the spirit of the community and its authentic character.

The missionary spirit should be thoroughly maintained in religious communities, and, according to the character of each one, given a modern expression. In this way the preaching of the gospel among all peoples can be done more successfully.

Religious Share in Total Mission of Church

ET 50. To be sure, this participation in carrying out the Church's mission—as the Council urgently insists—is impossible unless religious embrace and support her "enterprises and plans in such fields as the scriptural, liturgical, dogmatic, pastoral, ecumenical, missionary and social."[1] Solicitous about doctrine that is joined with pastoral action, you will zealously work at this task, always of course "consistent with the character of the institute." You will also remember that exemption mainly concerns internal structure, and it does not dispense you from the jurisdiction of bishops, to which you are subject; it belongs to them "as the performance of their pastoral office and the right ordering of the care of souls require."[2] Besides ought not you more than others constantly reflect that by the action of the Church the action of Christ for the good of men is being continued, but only to the extent to which you follow the same plan of life as Christ, who leads all things back to His Father: "All things are yours. . . . But you belong to Christ and Christ belongs to God."[3] For the call of God directly and most efficaciously guides you on the path that leads to the eternal kingdom. Through the spiritual struggles which are inevitable in any life that is truly religious, "you give splendid and striking witness that the world cannot be transformed and offered to God without the spirit of the beatitudes."[4]

CD 33. All religious have the duty, each according to his proper vocation, of cooperating zealously and diligently in building up and increasing the whole Mystical Body of Christ and for the good of the particular churches. (In this section of the present document,

---

1. PC, no. 2.
2. CD, no. 35.
3. 1 Cor 3:22-23; GS, no. 37.
4. LG, no. 31.

it should be noted, the word religious includes members from other institutes who make a profession of the evangelical counsels.)

It is their duty to foster these objectives primarily by means of prayer, works of penance, and the example of their own life. This most sacred Synod strongly urges them ever to increase their esteem and zeal for these means. With due consideration for the character proper to each religious community, they should also enter more vigorously into the external works of the apostolate.*

CD 35. In order that the works of the apostolate be carried out harmoniously in individual dioceses and that the unity of diocesan discipline be preserved intact, these principles are established as fundamental:

1.) Religious should always attend upon bishops, as upon successors of the apostles, with devoted deference and reverence. Whenever they are legitimately called upon to undertake works of the apostolate, they are obliged to discharge their duties in such a way that they may be available and docile helpers to bishops. Indeed, religious should comply promptly and faithfully to the requests and desires of the bishops in order that they may thereby assume an even more extensive role in the ministry of human salvation. They should act thus with due respect for the character of their institute and in keeping with their constitutions which, if need be, should be adapted to this goal in accord with the principles of this conciliar Decree.

Especially in view of the urgent need of souls and the scarcity of diocesan clergy, religious communities which are not dedicated exclusively to the contemplative life can be called upon by the bishops to assist in various pastoral ministries. The particular

---

* (Men and women who are members of religious communities do not occupy an intermediate place between clergy and laity. Rather they are called by God from both states of life to bind themselves by vows to the three evangelical counsels: poverty, chastity, and obedience. The chapter on religious in the Constitution on the Church (III) treats of the internal elements of the religious state; in this decree on the bishops, the external works of the apostolate are considered.)

character of each community should, however, be kept in mind. Superiors should encourage this work to the utmost, even by accepting parishes on a temporary basis.

2.) Religious engaged in the active apostolate, however, should be imbued with the spirit of their religious community, and remain faithful to the observance of their rule and to submissiveness toward their own superiors. Bishops should not neglect to impress this obligation upon them.

3. The privilege of exemption, by which religious are called to the service of the Supreme Pontiff or other ecclesiastical authority and are withdrawn from the jurisdiction of bishops, applies chiefly to the internal order of their communities so that in them all things may be more aptly coordinated and the growth and depth of religious life better served. These communities are also exempt in order that the Supreme Pontiff may make use of them for the good of the universal Church or that any other competent authority may do so for the good of the churches under its own jurisdiction.*

This exemption, however, does not exclude religious in individual dioceses from the jurisdiction of the bishop in accordance with the norm of law, insofar as the performance of his pastoral office and the right ordering of the care of souls require.

4.) All religious, exempt and non-exempt, are subject to the

---

* "Exempt religious" are those communities withdrawn from the authority of the local ordinary and subject to the Pope alone. The purpose is "to more fully provide for the necessities of the entire flock of the Lord and in consideration of the common good." The decree on bishops explains that this special status "applies chiefly to the internal order of their communities, so that in them all things may be properly coordinated and the growth and perfection of religious life promoted . . . this exemption, however, does not exclude religious in individual dioceses from the jurisdiction of the bishop in accordance with the norm of law, insofar as the performance of his pastoral office and the right ordering of the care of souls require."

This conciliar formula for the fruitful harmony of the hierarchy and the religious communities has been drawn from historical precedent and canonical practice, especially expressed in the teaching of Leo XIII, Pius XII, and the present Pontiff.

authority of the local Ordinaries in those things which pertain to the public exercise of divine worship (except where differences in rites are concerned), the care of souls, sacred preaching intended for the people, the religious and moral education of the Christian faithful, especially of children, catechetical instruction, and liturgical formation. Religious are subject to the local Ordinary also in matters of proper clerical decorum as well as in the various works which concern the exercise of the sacred apostolate. Catholic schools conducted by religious are also subject to the authority of the local Ordinaries as regards general policy and supervision, but the right of religious to direct them remains intact. Religious also are bound to observe all those things which episcopal councils or conferences legitimately prescribe for universal observance.

5.) A well-ordered cooperation is to be encouraged between various religious communities, and between them and the diocesan clergy. There should also be a very close coordination of all apostolic works and activities. This depends especially on a supernatural attitude of hearts and minds, an attitude rooted in and founded upon charity. The Apostolic See is competent to supervise this coordination for the universal Church; bishops are competent in their own respective dioceses, and patriarchal synods and episcopal conferences in their own territory.

With respect to those works of the apostolate which religious are to undertake, bishops or episcopal conferences, religious superiors or conferences of major religious superiors should take action only after mutual consultations.

6.) In order to foster harmonious and fruitful relations between bishops and religious, at stated times and as often as it is deemed opportune, bishops and religious superiors should be willing to meet for discussion of those affairs which pertain generally to the apostolate in their territory.

CD 34. Religious priests are consecrated for the office of the presbyterate so that they may be the prudent cooperators of the episcopal order. Today they can be of even greater help to bishops in view of the mounting needs of souls. Therefore, in a certain genuine sense they must be said to belong to the clergy of the diocese inasmuch as they share in the care of souls and in carrying out works of the apostolate under the authority of the sacred prelates.

Other members of religious communities, both men and women, also belong in a special way to the diocesan family and offer great assistance to the sacred hierarchy. With the increasing demands of the apostolate, they can and should offer that assistance more every day.

APOSTOLIC LETTER, *ECCLESIAE SANCTAE*, POPE PAUL VI ISSUED AUGUST 6, 1966 IMPLEMENTING THE DECREE, *CHRISTUS DOMINUS* OF VATICAN COUNCIL II

RELIGIOUS

(Cf. nos. 33-35, Decree, *Christus Dominus*)

ES I, nos. 22-40:

22. The norms here established apply to all Religious, men and women, of whatever rite but the rights of Patriarchs for the Orientals remain intact.

23. (1) All Religious, including the exempt, who work in places where a rite different from their own is the only rite, or where the number of faithful of the other rite is so large that in common opinion it is considered the only rite, depend on the local Ordinary or hierarch of this rite in those things which pertain to the external activity of the ministry and are subject to him in accord with the norm of law.

(2) Where there are several local Ordinaries or hierarchs, however, these Religious, when engaged in work among the faithful of different rites, are bound by the norms which are given by the Ordinaries and hierarchs by mutual agreement.

24. Even though in mission areas the exemption of Religious is in effect within their own lawful sphere, nevertheless, on account of the special circumstances of exercising the sacred ministry in these areas, according to the intention of the Decree *Ad Gentes*

Divinitus, the special statutes issued or approved by the Apostolic See to regulate the relationships between local Ordinaries and Religious superiors, especially in a mission entrusted to an institute, must be observed.

25. (1) All Religious, even the exempt, are bound by the laws, decrees and ordinances enacted by the local Ordinary for various activities, in those matters which touch upon the exercise of the sacred apostolate, as well as for pastoral and social action prescribed or recommended by the local Ordinary.

(2) Likewise, they are bound by the laws, decrees, and ordinances enacted by the local Ordinary or the episcopal conference which concern the following, among other things:

(a) The public use of all media of social communication, according to the norm of nos. 20 and 21 of the Decree *Inter Mirifica;*

(b) Attendance at public entertainment;

(c) Enrollment in or cooperation with societies or associations which the local Ordinary or the episcopal conference has decreed should be avoided;

(d) Ecclesiastical attire, but without prejudice to Canon 596 of the Code of Canon Law and Canon 139 of the Oriental Code of Canon Law concerning Religious, and according to the following stipulation: the local Ordinary or the episcopal conference, to avoid things that would astonish the faithful, can forbid clerics, whether secular or Religious, even the exempt, to wear lay dress in public.

26. Moreover, Religious are also bound by the laws and decrees issued by the local Ordinary according to the norm of the law regarding the public exercise of worship in their own churches and in public and semi-public oratories if the faithful ordinarily attend them. The proper rite of the Religious remains intact which they lawfully use for their own community alone, taking into consideration the order of the Divine Office in choir and the sacred functions which pertain to the special purpose of the institute.

27. (1) The episcopal conference of any country can, after consultation with the interested Religious superiors, establish norms for seeking alms which must be observed by all Religious, including

those who by institution are called and are mendicants, though their right to beg remains intact.

(2) Likewise, Religious may not proceed in the collection of funds by public subscription without the consent of the Ordinaries of those places where the funds are collected.

28. Religious should zealously promote those works proper or special to their own institute, that is, those which with the approval of the Apostolic See were undertaken either from the institute's very foundation or by reason of venerable traditions and then were defined and ordered by the institute's constitution and other particular laws, special consideration being given to the spiritual needs of the dioceses and maintaining fraternal concord with the diocesan clergy and with other institutes which perform similar works.

29. (1) Works proper or special to the institute which are carried out in its own houses, even if these are rented, depend on the superiors of the institute who according to the constitutions rule and direct them. However, these works are also subject to the jurisdiction of the local Ordinary according to the norm of law.

(2) Works which have been entrusted to the institute by the local Ordinary, however, even though they may be proper or special to it, are under the authority and direction of the same Ordinary, without prejudice, however, to the right of Religious superiors to exercise vigilance over the life of the members of the institute, and, in combination with the local Ordinary, over the fulfillment of duties committed to them.

30. (1) When a local Ordinary entrusts an apostolic work to an institute, observing what must be observed according to law, a written agreement should be entered into between the Ordinary and the competent superior of the institute by which, among other things, the matters pertaining to the carrying out of the works, the assignment of personnel for the work and finances are clearly defined.

(2) For such works, members of the Religious institute who are truly qualified are to be selected by their own Religious superior, after mutual consultation with the local Ordinary, and if it is a case of conferring an ecclesiastical office on one of the members,

the Religious must be named by the local Ordinary on presentation by, or at least with the consent of, the Religious superior, for a definite period of time set by mutual consent.

31. Also when an office is to be entrusted to a Religious by the local Ordinary or by an episcopal conference, it should be done with the consent of his superior and with a written agreement.

32. For a grave reason any member of a Religious institute can be removed from the position assigned to him either at the will of the authority who made the appointment, after he has advised the Religious superior, or at the will of the superior after he has advised the one who made the appointment. In this matter the superior and the authority are legally equal and the action of the one does not require the consent of the other, nor is the one bound to make known to the other the reason for his judgment, much less prove it, though recourse to the Apostolic See, without suspensive effect (*in devolutivo*), remains open.

33. (1) A local Ordinary can on his own authority, with the consent of the competent Religious superior, entrust a parish to a Religious institute even by establishing a parish in the Religious church of an institute. This assignment of a parish can be in perpetuity or for a certain specified time; in either case it must be done through a written agreement between the Ordinary and the competent superior of the institute. Among other things, this agreement is to define expressly and accurately those matters which pertain to carrying out the work, the assignment of personnel for the work and financial matters.

(2) The local Ordinary can also appoint a Religious, with the permission of his superior, as pastor of a parish which is not entrusted to Religious, entering into a special and suitable agreement with the competent Religious superior.

34. (1) A Religious house belonging to exempt Religious, whether "formal" or "non-formal" cannot be suppressed without apostolic approval and consultation with the local Ordinary.

(2) Religious superiors who, for whatever reason, ask for the

suppression of any house or work, should not do so hastily. Let them remember that all Religious have the duty to work assiduously and diligently not only for building up and increasing the whole Mystical Body of Christ but also for the good of the particular churches.

(3) When, however, the suppression of a house or work is requested by superiors, especially because of insufficient personnel, the local Ordinary is to consider the request kindly.

35. Associations of the faithful which are under the leadership and direction of a Religious institute, even if they have been established by the Apostolic See, are subject to the jurisdiction and vigilance of the local Ordinary who, according to the norms of the sacred canons, has the right and the duty of holding a visitation of them.

If these associations are engaged in external works of the apostolate or in the promotion of divine worship, they must observe the prescriptions given by the local Ordinary or the episcopal conference in these matters.

36. (1) The apostolic activity of members of Institutes of perfection who lead a life which is not totally contemplative is not so circumscribed by the projects either proper to their institute or by others occasionally assumed that, in keeping with urgent spiritual needs and the lack of clergy, both priests and also all men and women members cannot be called upon by the local Ordinary, taking into account the special nature of each institute and with the consent of the competent Religious superior, to render assistance in the various ministries of dioceses or regions.

(2) If, in the judgment of the local Ordinary, the help of Religious is considered necessary or very useful to carry on the various works of the apostolate and to foster charitable projects and those of the pastoral ministry in secular parishes or diocesan associations, the requested help should be given as far as possible by Religious superiors upon request of the Ordinary.

37. In all churches and in all public and semipublic oratories belonging to Religious which de facto are habitually open to the

faithful, the local Ordinary can prescribe that episcopal documents be read publicly, that catechetical instruction be given and finally that special collections be taken up for specified parish, diocesan, national or universal undertakings; such collections are carefully to be sent to the episcopal curia.

38. The local Ordinary has the right, with respect to the observance of general laws and episcopal decrees concerning divine worship, to conduct a visitation of the churches of Religious, even exempt, and also their semipublic oratories, provided the faithful ordinarily frequent them. If he should discover abuses in this regard, and the Religious superior has been admonished in vain, he can himself by his own authority make provisions.

39. (1) According to the norm of no. 35, 4 of the Decree *Christus Dominus*, the right of Religious in regard to the direction of the schools remaining in effect, and observing the norms established there concerning the prior agreement to be mutually entered into between bishops and Religious institutes, involves the general distribution of all Catholic schools in a diocese, their common cooperation and supervision so that these schools no less than others may be adapted to pursue cultural and social aims.

(2) The local Ordinary can conduct a visitation, either personally or through a delegate, according to the norms of the sacred canons, of all schools, colleges, recreation centers, protectorates, hospitals, orphanages and other similar institutions of Religious institutes devoted to works of religion or to the temporal or spiritual works of charity, except those schools of an institute which are open exclusively to the institute's own students.

40. Norms concerning the assignment of members of Religious institutes to diocesan undertakings and ministries to be carried out under the direction of the bishops are also to be applied to other projects and ministries which go beyond the area of a diocese, with appropriate principles adapted to similar cases.

DYNAMIC FIDELITY OF RELIGIOUS TO PARTICULAR CHARISM OF FOUNDER OF THE INSTITUTE

(Cf. LG, no. 45; PC, no. 2)

Fidelity to the Charisms of Each Founder

ET 11. Only in this way will you be able to arouse the hearts of men to embrace divine truth and love according to the charisms of your founders, whom God raised up in His Church. In no other way does the Council rightly insist that religious of both sexes have the duty of faithfully preserving the spirit of their originators, the way these persons presented the Gospels, and their example of holiness. Religious must recognize here one of the fundamentals for achieving present-day renewal, and one of the most certain norms for deciding what kind of activity each institute should undertake. Certainly the charism of the religious life is not some sort of impulse born "out of human stock or will of the flesh" or of a cast of mind that "is modeled on the behavior of the world around you." It is a fruit of the Holy Spirit who is always at work in the Church.

Loyalty to the Charisms of Each Institute

ET 32. Along this path, the outstanding guide you have is the forms of life which experience, loyal to the charisms of each institute, has produced. The same experience has shown these forms of life variously combined and suggests they are the seed bed of developments still to come. But no matter how much these varieties may differ among themselves, their supportive function always looks to forming the inner man. Concern for strengthening this interior man will help you discern, among such a wide variety of inducements, which are the more appropriate forms of life. Thus an excessive desire for a kind of flexible mobility and freedom of activity can produce a situation where even the minimum of regular order in preserving customs is accused of rigidity—a minimum which the life of the community and the perfection of its members commonly demand. Minds unduly excited, which appeal to fraternal charity, or to insights which are said to have come from an inspiration of the Holy Spirit, can lead institutes to their destruction.

CHAPTER 7

UNIVERSAL APOSTOLIC MISSION OF THE CHURCH

The Works of the Apostolate by Themselves do not
Sanctify, but only as They are an Expression
of the Interior Spiritual Life

(Cf. LG, nos. 46, 48, 31, 44; PC, nos. 2, 6, 8)

PC 20. Communities should faithfully maintain and fulfill their proper activities. Yet, they should make adjustments in them according to the needs of time and place and in favor of what will benefit the universal Church and individual dioceses. To this end they should resort to suitable techniques, including modern ones, and abandon whatever activities are today less in keeping with the spirit of the community and its authentic character.

The missionary spirit should be thoroughly maintained in religious communities, and, according to the character of each one, given a modern expression. In this way the preaching of the gospel among all peoples can be done more successfully.

Proclaiming the Divine Word

ET 9. Others again are committed to the apostolate and, indeed, to its principal responsibility, which belongs to it in such a way that they proclaim the divine word to those whom God places along their path and lead them towards the faith. Such a grace presupposes a familiar intimacy with God. Supported in this way, you will be able to transmit the message of the Word Incarnate using a language which the people can understand. It is indispensably necessary, therefore, that your whole life makes you sharers in His passion, death and glory!

Renewal of Religious Life Needed for Renewal of the Church

ET 52. A very pointed question troubles us today, namely, how can the Gospel message penetrate the secular culture that character-izes the masses; how should we act in those levels of society and in territories where a culture of the spirit is developing in which a new type of man is emerging who no longer thinks that he needs redemption? Since all have been called to contemplate the mystery of salvation, you well understand how grave the lifelong obligation for each of you and what an incentive to exercise your apostolic zeal flow from these questions! Behold religious men and women, according to whatever ways the divine call demands of your spiritual families, you must reflect with intense mind on the needs of people, their problems and searchings, while witnessing in their midst, by prayer and action, to the efficacy of the Good News of love, justice and peace. The eagerness with which the whole family of mankind seeks to lead a life more suffused with brotherly love, among individuals as among nations, demands before everything else that conduct, habits of mind and conscience be transformed. While this duty is common to the whole People of God, it rests with special gravity upon you. But how can it ever be duly fulfilled if there is lacking that delight in heavenly things which arises from a kind of experience of God? This makes it perfectly clear that genuine renewal of the religious life is of capital importance for effecting the renewal of the Church herself and of the world.

Contemplation Joined with Apostolic Love

ET 10. Suppose your vocation directs you to other tasks in the service of mankind—such, for example, as the pastoral life, sacred missions, teaching in schools, works of charity, and the like. Is it not true that the intensity of spirit by which you are joined to God will be the main source of efficacy to make these tasks fruitful and, indeed, by reason of that union with God which is practiced "in secret"? If we wish to observe the doctrine of the Council faithfully, must not "the members of every institute, seeking God solely and before everything else, join contemplation with apostolic love? By the former they fix their mind and heart on Him; by the latter, they strive to be associated with the work of redemption and to extend the kingdom of God."

The People of God Need the Witness of Religious

ET 31. It is on this condition, however, that you will give the witness which the People of God are looking for. This is the witness of men and women who are strong enough to sustain the unpredictable hazards of poverty, who can be captivated by simplicity and humility, who are lovers of peace and strangers to compromise, vowing themselves to complete abnegation of self and their possessions, obedient and yet free, alert and steadfast, gentle and strong in the firmness of their faith. Certainly this grace will be given you by Christ in the measure of totality of your own gift of self which is never reclaimed. A splendid proof of this witness is offered by the recent misfortunes of so many religious men and women who in various countries have suffered for Christ with noble and ready courage. Even as We proclaim our admiration for them, We set them before all for emulation.

Modern World Needs Witness of Holiness

ET 53. Today more than ever before the world needs men and women who are outstanding for their faith in the Word of the Lord, His Resurrection and eternal life, to such an extent that they spend their entire earthly life testifying to the truth of this love which is offered to all mankind. In the course of her history, the Church has never failed to be animated and invigorated by the holiness of so many religious men and women who, following their respective form of Gospel perfection, have witnessed by their life to infinite love and to Christ the Lord. Should we not consider this a grace for the people of our age, as a divine and life-giving inspiration and a liberation from self which portends eternal and untrammeled joy? As you look forward to such divine happiness, transform with generous heart the demands of your vocation into living practice— reaffirming the truths of faith and interpreting by their norm the needs of this world in a Christian way. The time has come to apply yourselves, if need be, to a most diligent reformation of your inner mind and a re-examination of your whole life in order to achieve a more perfect loyalty.

(Cf. LG, no. 48)

AG 1. The Church has been divinely sent to all nations that she might be "the universal sacrament of salvation." Acting out of the innermost requirements of her own catholicity and in obedience to her Founder's mandate (cf. Mk 16:16), she strives to proclaim the gospel to all men. For the Church was founded upon the apostles, who, following in the footsteps of Christ, "preached the message of truth and begot Churches." Upon their successors devolves the duty of perpetuating this work through the years. Thus "the word of God may run and be glorified" (2 Th 3:1) and God's kingdom can be everywhere proclaimed and established.

The present historical situation is leading humanity into a new stage. As the salt of the earth and light of the world (cf. Mt 5:13-14), the Church is summoned with special urgency to save and renew every creature. In this way all things can be restored in Christ, and in Him mankind can compose one family and one people.

Hence this holy Synod gives thanks to God for the splendid accomplishments already achieved through the noble energy of the whole Church. At the same time she wishes to sketch the principles of missionary activity and to marshal the forces of all the faithful. Her intention is that God's people, undertaking the narrow way of the cross, may spread everywhere the kingdom of Christ, the Lord and Overseer of the ages (cf. Sir. 36:19), and may prepare the way for His coming.

(Cf. LG, nos. 31, 44)

AG 18. Right from the planting stage of the Church, the religious life should be carefully fostered. This not only confers precious and absolutely necessary assistance on missionary activity. By a more inward consecration made to God in the Church, it also luminously manifests and signifies the inner nature of the Christian calling.

Working to plant the Church, and thoroughly enriched with the treasures of mysticism adorning the Church's religious tradition, religious communities should strive to give expression to these treasures and to hand them on in a manner harmonious with the nature and the genius of each nation. Let them reflect attentively on how Christian religious life may be able to assimilate the ascetic and contemplative traditions whose seeds were sometimes already planted by God in ancient cultures prior to the preaching of the gospel.

Various forms of religious life should be cultivated in a young Church, so that they can display different aspects of Christ's mission and the Church's life, can devote themselves to various pastoral works, and can prepare their members to exercise them rightly. Still, bishops in their Conference should take care that congregations pursuing the same apostolic aims are not multiplied to the detriment of the religious life and the apostolate.

Worthy of special mention are the various projects aimed at helping the contemplative life take root. There are those who while retaining the essential elements of monastic life are bent on implanting the very rich traditions of their own order. Others are returning to simpler forms of ancient monasticism. But all are striving to work out a genuine adaptation to local conditions. For the contemplative life belongs to the fullness of the Church's presence, and should therefore be everywhere established.

AG 33. Communities engaged in missionary activity in the same territory should find ways and means of coordinating their work. Therefore, extreme usefulness recommends conferences of religious men and unions of religious women, in which all communities working in the same country or region can take part. These conferences should try to discover what things can be done by combined efforts, and should be in close touch with the Episcopal Conferences.

With equal reason, all these recommendations can be appropriately extended to include the cooperation of missionary communities in the home lands. Thus common problems and projects can be handled more easily and with less expense: for instance, the doctrinal formation of future missionaries, courses for present missionaries, relations with public authorities and with international or supranational organizations.

(Cf. CD, no. 35)

AG 34. The proper and orderly exercise of missionary activity requires that those who labor for the gospel be scientifically prepared for their task, especially for dialogue with non-Christian religions and cultures. It requires that they be effectively assisted in the carrying out of this task. Hence this Council desires that, for the sake of the missions, fraternal and generous collaboration exist on the part of scientific institutes specializing in missiology and in other sciences and arts useful for the missions. Such would be ethnology and linguistics, the history and science of religions, sociology, pastoral skills, and the like.

(Cf. CD, nos. 33-35)

AG 40. Religious communities of the contemplative and of the active life have so far played, and still do play, a very great role in the evangelization of the world. This sacred Synod gladly acknowledges their merits and thanks God for all that they have done for the glory of God and the service of souls. It exhorts them to go on untiringly in the work which they have begun, since they know that the virtue of charity impels and obliges them to a spirit and an effort which is truly Catholic. By their vocation they are bound to practice this charity with a special degree of perfection.

By their prayers, works of penance, and sufferings, contemplative communities have a very great importance in the conversion of souls. For it is God who sends workers into His harvest when He is asked to do so (cf. Mt 9:38), who opens the minds of non-Christians to hear the gospel (cf. Ac 16:14), and who makes the word of salvation fruitful in their hearts (cf. 1 Cor 3:7). In fact, these communities are urged to found houses in mission areas, as not a few of them have already done. Thus living out their lives in a manner accommodated to the truly religious traditions of the people, they can bear splendid witness there among non-Christians to the majesty and love of God, as well as to man's brotherhood in Christ.

Whether they pursue a strictly mission goal or not, communities dedicated to the active life should sincerely ask themselves in the presence of God, whether they cannot broaden their activity in favor of expanding God's kingdom among the nations; whether they might not leave certain ministries to others so that they themselves can spend their energies on the missions; whether they can undertake work among the missions, adapting their conditions if necessary, but according to the spirit of their founder; whether their members are involved as much as possible in missionary activity; and whether their type of life bears to the gospel a witness which is accommodated to the character and condition of the people.

Thanks to the inspiration of the Holy Spirit, secular institutes are increasing every day in the Church. Under the authority of the bishop, their programs can be fruitful in the missions in many ways as a sign of complete dedication to the evangelization of the world.

SCRSI, April, 1968:

In the works of the apostolate, there must be close collaboration with diocesan authority. (CD 35, 1)

Proper Works of an Institute

The proper or special works of each institute are those which with the approval of the Apostolic See have been undertaken from its foundation or on account of venerable traditions and which accordingly have been defined and regulated by the constitutions and other proper laws of the institute. These works should be zealously fostered by religious, special account being made of the spiritual necessities of the dioceses and fraternal concord being maintained with the diocesan clergy and with other institutes engaged in similar works. (ES, I, 28)

The apostolic zeal of the members of the institutes of perfection who do not profess a purely contemplative life should not be limited to works proper to each institute or to others that are occasionally assumed in such a way that local ordinaries, having considered the special characteristics of each institute and with the consent of the competent religious superior, cannot call on not only priest religious, but also on all men and women members to assist in the various ministries of the dioceses or regions because of the needs of souls and lack of clergy.

If in the judgment of the local ordinary the help of religious is thought necessary or highly useful for exercising the multiple works of the apostolate and for fostering undertakings of a pastoral nature in secular parishes or in diocesan associations, religious superiors should as far as they can furnish the desired help when the same ordinary asks for it. (ES 1, 36)

Proper Works and Particular Vocation

But your activities cannot derogate from the vocation of your various institutes, nor habitually involve work such as would take the place of their specific tasks. Nor should these activities in any way lead you toward secularization, to the detriment of your religious life. (Pope Paul VI, ET, 20)

The religious, not as a private individual but as a member of her institute, engages in apostolic work which is according to the end of her institute. (Letter SCRSI, July 10, 1972)

SCRSI and Sacred Congregation for Catholic Education
AAS 1 (1958) 100; March 31, 1971; 250

Declaration: Co-Education in Schools Conducted by Religious

The Sacred Congregation for Religious and Secular Institutes published an Instruction on December 8, 1957, after a meeting of male and female religious which had been held by the order of the Sovereign Pontiff. That Instruction decreed: "religious may not be authorized to direct a mixed secondary school except rarely, and then because of extreme necessity and after having received an apostolic indult from this Sacred Congregation."

A number of ordinaries and religious superiors have asked the Holy See if that provision still held, after the declarations of the Second Council of the Vatican. The question was submitted to the plenary assembly of the Sacred Congregation for Catholic Education, with the agreement of the Sacred Congregation for Religious and Secular Institutes. The Sacred Congregation for Catholic Education held a plenary session on October 16-17, 1970 and gave the following reply to the query. The reply was later approved by the Holy Father.

(1) According to the decree, *Christus Dominus*, "all religious, exempt and non-exempt, are subject to the authority of local ordinaries, in all that concerns . . . the religious and moral education of the faithful, especially children, catechetical instruction. . . . Catholic schools belonging to religious are also subject to the local ordinaries as regards their general organization and supervision, without, however, infringing the rights of religious in the running of them."

(2) The Motu Proprio, *Ecclesiae Sanctae*, gives the following interpretation of the application of that passage of the decree: "In accordance with number 35 of the decree, *Christus Dominus*, the general regulation of Catholic schools of religious institutes, without prejudice to their rights in the government of these schools and while observing the norms laid down there (no. 35, 5) concerning previous consultation between bishops and religious superiors, involves the general distribution of all the Catholic schools of the diocese, their co-operation with one another and their supervision, so that they shall be no less adapted than other schools to cultural and social objectives." (39, 1)

(3) If therefore a secondary school directed by religious is led to open a co-educational school, for the reasons outlined in the Motu Proprio, *Ecclesiae Sanctae*, or for other good reasons, it is no longer necessary to have recourse to the Holy See. It is sufficient, as with the other Catholic schools, that it conform with the instructions given on this score by the local ordinary or the conference of bishops.

Given at Rome, February 1, 1971.

GABRIEL MARIE CARD. GARRONE
Prefect

MARY THE EXEMPLAR

ET 56. May the most loving Mother of the Lord, after whose example you consecrated your life to God, obtain for you in the daily course of life that unchangeable joy which only Jesus can confer. Would that your life, patterned after her example, might witness "to that maternal affection by which all should be inspired to cooperate in the Church's apostolic mission of regenerating mankind" (LG, no. 65). Most beloved sons and daughters, may the joy of the Lord transfigure your life consecrated to Him, and may His love make it fruitful.

Cf. Pope Paul VI, *Marialis Cultus*—Devotion to Mary, February 2, 1974. U.S.C.C.

Cf. U.S. National Conference of Catholic Bishops, *Behold Your Mother*, November 21, 1973

Relative to Directives of Holy Mother Church concerning the Apostolate of Catholic Education

Cf. *To Teach As Jesus Did*, A Pastoral Message on Catholic Education from the U.S. National Conference of Catholic Bishops, November, 1972 U.S.C.C.

Cf. *Basic Teachings For Catholic Religious Education*, January 11, 1973 U.S.C.C.

Cf. *General Catechetical Directory*, Sacred Congregation for the Clergy, 1971 U.S.C.C.

PART FOUR

BASIC PRINCIPLES FOR AUTHENTIC RENEWAL OF RELI-
GIOUS LIFE IN THE RADICAL FOLLOWING OF CHRIST,
IN TOTAL SURRENDER TO GOD THE FATHER,
IN THE LOVE OF THE HOLY SPIRIT, AND IN
ECCLESIAL COMMITMENT TO CHRIST'S
BODY, THE CHURCH

PRIMARY ORIENTATION TO PRAYER

COMMUNAL LIFE

THE RELIGIOUS HABIT

RELIGIOUS FORMATION

CLOISTERED CONTEMPLATIVE AND MONASTIC LIFE

CHAPTER 8

PRINCIPLES FOR AUTHENTIC RENEWAL

Consistent and constant return to the sources of all Christian and religious life is necessary.

PC 2. The appropriate renewal of religious life involves two simultaneous processes: (1) a continuous return to the sources of all Christian life and to the original inspiration behind a given community and (2) an adjustment of the community to the changed conditions of the times. It is according to the following principles that such renewal should go forward under the influence of the Holy Spirit and the guidance of the Church.

a) Since the fundamental norm of the religious life is a following of Christ as proposed by the gospel, such is to be regarded by all communities as their supreme law.

b) It serves the best interests of the Church for communities to have their own special character and purpose. Therefore loyal recognition and safekeeping should be accorded to the spirit of founders, as also to all the particular goals and wholesome traditions which constitute the heritage of each community.

c) All communities should participate in the life of the Church. According to its individual character, each should make its own and foster in every possible way the enterprises and objectives of the Church in such fields as these: the scriptural, liturgical, doctrinal, pastoral, ecumenical, missionary, and social.

d) Communities should promote among their members a suitable awareness of contemporary human conditions and of the needs of the Church. For if their members can combine the burning zeal of an apostle with wise judgments, made in the light of faith, concerning the circumstances of the modern world, they will be able to come to the aid of men more effectively.

e) Since the religious life is intended above all else to lead those who embrace it to an imitation of Christ and to union with God through the profession of the evangelical counsels, the fact must be honestly faced that even the most desirable changes made on behalf of contemporary needs will fail of their purpose unless a renewal of spirit gives life to them. Indeed such an interior renewal must always be accorded the leading role even in the promotion of exterior works.

PC 5. The members of each community should recall above everything else that by their profession of the evangelical counsels they have given answer to a divine call to live for God alone not only by dying to sin (cf. Rm 6:11) but also by renouncing the world. They have handed over their entire lives to God's service in an act of special consecration which is deeply rooted in their baptismal consecration and which provides an ampler manifestation of it.

Inasmuch as their self-dedication has been accepted by the Church, they should realize that they are committed to her service as well.

The fact that they are in God's service should ignite and fan within them the exercise of virtues, especially humility, obedience, courage, and chastity. Through them they share spiritually in Christ's self-surrender (cf. Ph 2:7-8) and in His life (cf. Rm 8:1-13).

Therefore, in fidelity to their profession and in renunciation of all things for the sake of Christ (cf. Mk 10:28), let religious follow Him (cf. Mt 19:21) as their one necessity (cf. Lk 10:42). Let them listen to His words (cf. Lk 10:39) and be preoccupied with His work (cf. Cor 7:32).

To this end, as they seek God before all things and only Him, the members of each community should combine contemplation with apostolic love. By the former they adhere to God in mind and heart; by the latter they strive to associate themselves with the work of redemption and to spread the Kingdom of God.

PC 6. Those who profess the evangelical counsels love and seek before all else that God who took the initiative in loving us (cf. 1 Jn

4:10) ; in every circumstance they aim to develop a life hidden with Christ in God (cf. Col 3:3). Such dedication gives rise and urgency to the love of one's neighbor for the world's salvation and the up-building of the Church. From this love the very practice of the evangelical counsels takes life and direction.

Therefore, drawing on the authentic sources of Christian spiritu-ality, let the members of communities energetically cultivate the spirit of prayer and the practice of it. In the first place they should take the sacred Scriptures in hand each day by way of attaining "the excelling knowledge of Jesus Christ" (Ph 3:8) through reading these divine writings and meditating on them. They should enact the sacred liturgy, especially the most holy mystery of the Eucharist, with hearts and voices attuned to the Church; here is a most copious source of nourishment for the spiritual life.

Fed thus at the table of the divine law and of the sacred altar, they can bring a brother's love to the members of Christ, and a son's love to their revered pastors; thus they can live and think with the Church to an ever-increasing degree, and spend themselves completely on her mission.

(Cf. ET, no. 2)

Religious living for God alone and sharing in Christ's Paschal Mystery develop a life hidden with Christ in God and collaborate in His redemptive and sancti-fying mission in His Body, the Church.

LG 46. Religious should carefully consider that through them, to believers and non-believers alike, the Church truly wishes to give an increasingly clearer revelation of Christ. Through them Christ should be shown contemplating on the mountain, announcing God's kingdom to the multitude, healing the sick and the maimed, turning sinners to wholesome fruit, blessing children, doing good to all, and always obeying the will of the Father who sent Him.

Finally, everyone should realize that the profession of the evan-gelical counsels, though entailing the renunciation of certain values which undoubtedly merit high esteem, does not detract from a genuine development of the human person. Rather by its very nature it is most beneficial to that development. For the counsels, voluntarily undertaken according to each one's personal vocation, contribute greatly to purification of heart and spiritual liberty. They continually kindle the fervor of charity. As the example of so many saintly founders shows, the counsels are especially able to pattern the Christian man after that manner of virginal and humble life which Christ the Lord elected for Himself, and which His Virgin Mother also chose.

Let no one think that by their consecration religious have become strangers to their fellow men or useless citizens of this earthly city. For even though in some instances religious do not directly mingle with their contemporaries, yet in a more profound sense these same religious are united with them in the heart of Christ and cooperate with them spiritually. In this way the work of building up the earthly city can always have its foundation in the Lord and can tend toward Him. Otherwise, those who build this city will perhaps have labored in vain.

In summary, therefore, this sacred Synod encourages and praises the men and women, brothers and sisters, who in monasteries, or in schools and hospitals, or on the missions, adorn the Bride of Christ. They do so by their unswerving and humble loyalty to their chosen consecration, while rendering to all men generous services of every variety.

(Cf. PC, no. 6)

PC 7. Members of those communities which are totally dedicated to contemplation give themselves to God alone in solitude and silence and through constant prayer and ready penance. No matter how urgent may be the needs of the active apostolate, such communities will always have a distinguished part to play in Christ's Mystical Body, where "all members have not the same function" (Rm 12:4). For they offer God a choice sacrifice of praise. They brighten God's people with the richest splendors of sanctity. By their example they motivate this people; by imparting a hidden, apostolic fruitfulness, they make this people grow. Thus they are the glory of the Church and an overflowing fountain of heavenly graces. Nevertheless, their manner of living should be revised according to the aforementioned principles and standards of appropriate renewal, though their withdrawal from the world and the practices of their contemplative life should be maintained at their holiest.

Presence in the World through Prayer and Sacrifice

ET 49. In this way the world, too, is present in the deepest center of your life, dedicated to prayer and sacrifice, as the Council strongly declared: "Let no one think by their consecration religious have become either estranged from people or useless in the earthly city. For even though at times they do not directly mingle with their contemporaries, yet they are more deeply than ever close to them in the heart of Christ and cooperate with them spiritually. In this way the building up of the earthly city is always founded on the Lord to be directed towards Him. Otherwise those who are building the city will perhaps have labored in vain."

Religious life is centered in Christ's Eucharistic sacrifice, sacrament and sacramental presence.

(Cf. LG, no. 7; PC, no. 6)

The Eucharistic Sacrifice and Communion

ET 47. Is it further necessary to remind you of the unique importance which the Church's liturgy has in the life of your communities, whose center is the Eucharistic Sacrifice where interior prayer is joined to external worship? In the religious profession itself you were offered to God by the Church, united closely with the Eucharistic Sacrifice. Day after day, this oblation of yourselves should become a truth that must be actually and constantly renewed. The principal source of such renovation is the communion of the Body and Blood of Christ, by which your will to love truly, and reaching even to the sacrifice of your life, is unceasingly sustained.

The Real Presence, Center of Religious Communities

ET 48. The Eucharist, " the sacrament of loyalty, the sign of unity, the bond of charity," is the unqualified center of your communities, gathered together in His name. Consistent with this fact, therefore, they should be visibly united around the oratory where the presence of the most holy Eucharist signifies while it also effects what should be the most efficacious gift of each religious family as, indeed, of every Christian community. The Eucharist, through which we never cease to proclaim the death and resurrection of the Lord and dispose ourselves for His return in glory, keeps constantly in your memory the sufferings of body and soul by which Christ was tormented and yet which He freely underwent even to the agony and death on the cross. May the trials which you experience offer you the opportunity of bearing together with Christ and offering to the Father so many trials and unjust tortures inflicted on our brethren and which, in the light of faith, can acquire meaning only from the sacrifice of Christ.

Cf. *Ordo Professionis Religiosae*

CHAPTER 9

PRAYER LIFE

(Cf. PC, nos. 6, 7)

First Priority to Prayer

ET 45. Is not one of the tragedies of our age the imbalance between collectivized conditions of life and the requirements for personal reflection and, even more so, for contemplation?[1] Many people—including not a few among the youth—have lost the meaning of their life and are earnestly searching for a contemplative understanding of themselves, not realizing that Christ, through His Church, can respond to their expectation! Facts of this kind should impel you to seriously rethink what people justly expect of you, who professedly and irrevocably have undertaken the duty of leading a life in the service of the Word, "the true light, which enlightens every human being."[2] You must, therefore, be conscious of the significance that prayer has in your life, learn to give yourselves to it eagerly; for daily prayer, faithfully practiced, for each man and woman among you, remains your primary necessity. Consequently, it should be given first priority in your constitutions and your life.

Silence a Demand of Divine Love

ET 46. The interior man recognizes that times of silence are like so many demands of divine love. He ordinarily needs a certain

---

1. **Gaudium et Spes**, 8, A.A.S. 58, 1966, p. 1030.
2. Jn 1, 9.

solitude to hear God "speaking to his heart."[1] Silence, it must be stressed, which is nothing more than absence of noise and conversation and during which the spirit cannot revive its strength, clearly lacks all spiritual value and can even be an obstacle to fraternal charity, if practiced at a time when we should be dealing with other people. On the other hand, the disposition for an intimate union with God implies the need for a silence affecting one's whole being, whether those concerned are to find God in the midst of noise and confusion, or those who are dedicated to contemplation.[2] For faith, hope and a love of God ready to receive the gifts of the Holy Spirit, not to mention a fraternal love open to the mystery of other persons, require as a kind of postulate the necessity of silence.

Prayer a Criterion of the Religious Life

ET 42. Beloved religious men and women, how could you fail in longing to know Him more deeply whom you love and whom you wish to manifest to mankind? It is prayer, to be sure, that unites you to Him! If you no longer have a taste for praying, you will recover the desire by humbly returning to the practice of prayer. Do not forget the testimony of history: that sustained fidelity to prayer or its neglect are like a criterion of the vitality or decadence of religious life.

Spirit of Joy Through Prayer

ET 43. Prayer means, in fact, the attainment of intimate familiarity with God, zeal for worship and the will to ask for His help. The experience of Christian sanctity proves the fruitfulness of prayer, in which God reveals Himself to the spirit and heart of His servants. Manifold, indeed, are the gifts of the Spirit, but they always produce this effect: we enjoy such a deeply authentic knowledge of God that without it we could neither appreciate the value of a Christian or

---

1. Cf. Ho 2, 14.
2. Cf. Sacred Congregation for Religious and Secular Institutes, Instruction **Venite Seorsum** A.A.S. 61, 1969, pp. 674-690; Message of Monks dedicated to contemplative life to Synod of Bishops, Oct. 10, 1967; **La Documentation Catholique**, 64, Paris 1967, coll. 1907-1910.

religious life, nor be able to advance in it, strengthened by the joy of a hope which does not deceive.

Finding God in Others Through Prayer

ET 44. Undoubtedly the Holy Spirit also gives you the grace of finding God in the hearts of people, whom He teaches you to love as brothers. He helps you to trace the signs of His love in the complexity of human events. If only we are humbly attentive in spirit to persons and their actions, the Spirit of Jesus will enlighten us and enrich us with His wisdom, provided we are thoroughly imbued with the spirit of prayer.

Need for Quiet and Recollection

ET 35. In proportion, then, to your involvement in external affairs, you have to pass over from this kind of activity to a life of quietude concerned with the sacred, where your souls can be refreshed. Surely if you are serious about doing the work of God, you must yourselves sense the need of spending some time in quiet retreat. Together with your brethren and sisters you will change it into a time that is filled with blessings. In view of the pressing preoccupations and internal conflicts of modern life, it is agreed that special attention should be paid to these longer intervals beyond the daily program of prayers. Such prolonged periods of recollection can be variously apportioned throughout the day, depending on the character and nature of your vocation. If the houses to which you belong practice fraternal hospitality to any extent, it will be your responsibility to decide its duration and manner, so that all needless disturbance is avoided and that your guests, too, are offered effective means of an intimate union with God.

SCRSI, August, 1971:

At this time when the demands of modern life keep increasing, you must intensify your work, but subordinating it to the spirit of faith sustained by prayer. While it is very true that we must adore God in spirit and in truth, in a recollected and silent prayer, the worship that we must render God must be accompanied by exterior distinguishing forms which elevate the mind, rejoice the heart,

and give joy and serenity in the true liturgical renewal: at the foot
of the altar, the center of Eucharistic life, before the picture of the
Virgin, reciting one's rosary with fervor to ensure the happiness
of highest spirituality which reveals peace of soul and gives to the
Institute that quality of grace and progress in the sanctifying love
of Jesus and Mary.

CHAPTER 10

COMMUNAL LIFE

PC 15. The primitive Church provided an example of community life when the multitude of believers were of one heart and one mind (cf. Ac 4:32), and found nourishment in the teaching of the gospel and in the sacred liturgy, especially the Eucharist. Let such a life continue in prayerfulness and a sharing of the same spirit (cf. Ac 2:42). As Christ's members living fraternally together, let them excel one another in showing respect (cf. Rm 12:10), and let each carry the other's burdens (cf. Gal 6:2). For thanks to God's love poured into hearts by the Holy Spirit (cf. Rm 5:5), a religious community is a true family gathered together in the Lord's name and rejoicing in His presence (cf. Mt 18:20). For love is the fulfillment of the law (cf. Rm 13:10) and the bond of perfection (cf. Col 3:14); where it exists we know we have been taken from death to life (cf. 1 Jn 3:14). In fact, brotherly unity shows that Christ has come (cf. Jn 13:35; 17:21); from it results great apostolic influence.

To strengthen the bond of brotherhood between members of a community, those who are called lay brothers, assistants, or some other name, should be brought into the heart of its life and activities. Unless the state of affairs suggests otherwise, care must be taken to produce in women's communities a single category of sister. Then there may be retained only such distinction between persons as is demanded by the diversity of the works for which sisters are destined by a special call from God or by particular aptitude.

According to the norms of their constitutions, monasteries and communities of men which are not exclusively lay in their character can admit both clergy and laity on the same basis and with equal rights and duties, excepting those which result from ordination.

Community Life and Union With God

ET 34. Who, then, does not recognize how much the fraternal society of a stable form of life, when combined with a freely undertaken discipline of living, helps one attain that union? Such discipline seems more and more necessary for anyone who "returns to the heart." According to the biblical meaning of this term, it expresses something deeper than our affections, thoughts and resolutions. It is, in fact, pervaded by a sense of the infinite, the absolute, and of our eternal destiny. In the present confusion, religious must show by their witness that a person whose lively intention is focused on his proper goal, which is the living God, has actually unified and widely extended the depth and firmness of his life in God. He achieves this by the integration of his faculties, purification of mind and the spiritual transformation of his senses.

Community Life Integrates the Whole Personality

ET 33. Consequently—as you well know from experience—the value and importance of community life must not be underestimated, as much for its role of guiding the whole man—so complex and fragmented—in the path of his vocation, as for giving spiritual integration to his natural tendencies. Is not the heart often carried away by fleeting and perishable things? As a matter of fact many of you must spend your life, at least part of it, in a world that tends to alienate man from himself and threaten, along with his own spiritual unity, his union with God. It is imperative, therefore, that you learn how to find Him even in those circumstances of life which are characterized by a daily growing unrest, noise and disturbance, and the allurement of things that will pass away.

Community Spirit and Fraternal Cooperation

ET 39. Although you struggle with imperfection, as does every Christian, still you intend to create conditions of life which are favorable to fostering the spiritual growth of every community member.

But how otherwise can this be achieved except by deepening the bonds in the Lord, not excluding the common and ordinary ones, by which you are joined with each of your brethren? For charity— let us not forget this—must be like the energizing hope of the blessings by which others are sustained through our fraternal support. And the sign of its authenticity is found in the joyful simplicity by which all strive to understand what is on every one's heart. If some religious appear to be persons who look as though they are burdened by their community life, whereas it ought to make them grow, does this not happen because the kindness and friendliness which nourish hope are lacking in that life? There is no doubt that a distinctive community spirit, the intimacy of friendship, fraternal cooperation in carrying out the same apostolate, and mutual assistance in communion of life, chosen precisely the better to serve Christ, help immensely on this path of daily association with people.

Environment for Spiritual Growth

ET 38. For this reason, an obligation is incumbent on communities as well as the individuals who form them of passing from a "natural" state, as it is called, to a state which is truly "spiritual." Is not "the new man" of whom St. Paul speaks like the ecclesial fulness of Christ and, referring to every single Christian, at the same time a sharing in this plenitude? This kind of purpose in organizing one's life will make your religious families like a fertile soil where the seed of divine life, implanted in each of you by baptism, can grow into maturity and, by your consecration, expressed by living it perfectly, can produce fruits in the greatest abundance.

Evaluation of Smaller Communities

ET 40. Reflection on these facts has brought to the surface certain tendencies to form smaller communities. Something in the nature of a spontaneous reaction against the nameless crowding of people in urban centers, the felt need that a "community home" should be adjusted to small dwelling residences in today's cities, and the desire to experience more intimately the actual living conditions of the people who are to be illumined by the light of the Gospel—all of these are reasons why some institutes are led to plan having their communities consist of a small number of members. No doubt such communities can foster closer relationships among religious and their mutual and more fraternal exercise of duties. Nevertheless, while some kind of unrealistic structure can assuredly give a start to living together spiritually, anyone who believes this is enough to promote such living and multiply its devotees is deceived. For small communities, as is becoming evident, make heavier demands on their members rather than render their way of life more easy.

Estimate of Larger Communities

ET 41. Moreover, it is simply true that communities with a large number of members particularly suit many religious. It may also be necessary to create such communities, whether because of the very nature of some service rendered in the demands of charity or because of the kind of specialized work being done, or even because of the institutional requirements of contemplative or monastic life. Let perfect union of hearts and minds always flourish there, clearly consistent with the spiritual and supernatural goal toward which it is tending. Besides, prescinding from the form of the communities, whether they are small or large, they cannot sustain their members unless they are constantly nourished by the Gospel spirit, supported by prayer and distinguished by a mortification of the old man joined with magnanimity and discipline needed to form the new man along with the fruitfulness of the sacrifice of the cross.

Simplicity and Living the Beatitudes

ET 54. As We look upon you with that tender love of Christ who called His disciples "a little flock" and told them it pleased the Father to give them a kingdom, We earnestly beseech you to preserve that simplicity of "the little ones" of whom the Gospel speaks. Strive to attain it in the intimate and most familiar relationship with Christ or in whatever dealings bring you into direct contact with your brethren. For you will then experience the joyousness of a soul "exulting in the Holy Spirit," known to those who have been introduced to the secrets of the kingdom. Do not try to be added to the

number of those "learned and clever ones," whom everything con-
spires to multiply but from whom these secrets are kept away. Be
actually poor, gentle, thirsting for holiness, merciful, pure of heart,
such, in fine, through whom the world can discover the peace of God.

SCRSI, April, 1968:

Community life must be observed in principle, since it pertains
to the nature of a religious Congregation, along with certain fixed
regulations which, far from offending personal dignity, rather elevate
it in the bonds of love which safeguards genuine community. It is
inconceivable that there should be any authentic religious community
life without some form of community prayer. From the Council's
Constitution on the Sacred Liturgy we know that the first and noblest
form of community prayer is participation in the celebration of
the Eucharist.

The religious life is not to be subordinated either to the apostolate
in general or to any form of the apostolate e.g. schools. In fact, the
apostolate can only be enriched by persons who have been well
formed in holiness. Number 33 of *Christus Dominus* points out that
their first contribution to apostolic works is through prayer, works
of penance and personal example.

SCRSI, August, 1971:

Community life is a wealth for the religious life. The members
of each Institute must understand that the reason for living in community is not dependent on laws, on a psychological or anthropo-
logical discipline, but finds explanation in the fact that each consecrated person tends towards God and has a need of establishing with
the neighbor a mutual exchange of faith and charity to overcome
the difficulties which surround him.

Those who say that community life with its prescriptions of
silence and prayer is contrary to the needs of the human person,
find an answer to their objection in the daily experiences which
teaches how a life of recollection integrates the human person. It is
an unfathomable need of the mind to recollect itself and spend time
in a place set aside, far from the distractions of the world.

. . . small communities cannot mean a way of life modelled on that of lay people, without reasonable superiors, where each one may leave when she wishes, where one may dispose of money freely, where all distinctive religious sign is abandoned, where there is no room reserved for prayer. "Do not forget the witness of history; faithfulness to prayer or its abandonment are the test of the vitality or decadence of the religious life" (ET, no. 42).

CHAPTER 11

THE RELIGIOUS HABIT, SIGN OF CONSECRATION

(Cf. LG, no. 44)

PC 17. Since they are signs of a consecrated life, religious habits should be simple and modest, at once poor and becoming. They should meet the requirements of health and be suited to the circumstances of time and place as well as to the services required by those who wear them. Habits of men and women which do not correspond to those norms are to be changed.

Religious Habit, Sign of Consecration

ET 22. You are aware, beloved sons and daughters, how the needs of contemporary human society, if you test them as persons united with Christ, demand that you give a greater account of your poverty and make it more perfect. Although obviously you must consider the situation of the people among whom you live, to adapt your mode of life to theirs, yet your poverty may not be purely and simply conformed to their community. For its value as a witness derives from a whole-hearted response to the Gospel precept—while you adhere with total fidelity to your vocation—not just from a certain zeal for exhibiting poverty, which can be all too fickle and unstable. At the same time such external life styles must be avoided which clearly reflect a too worldly taste and affectation. In certain exceptional circumstances—We do, indeed, recognize it—approval can be given to lay aside a type of religious dress; but We cannot pass over in silence how much it is agreed that the habit of religious men and women should be, as the Council has ordained, a sign of their consecration and to that extent distinguished from forms that are obviously secular.

SCRSI, April, 1968:

When the habit is determined by approved Constitutions, it may not be eliminated completely, but the prescriptions of no. 17 of *Perfectae Caritatis* are to be faithfully observed. This text permits changes and adaptations of the religious habit in view of contemporary needs but does not allow the outright suppression of the habit.

SCRSI, August, 1971:

In keeping with this, the Exhortation reminds us that the religious habit must be, as the Council wishes, a sign of consecration (PC, no. 17). And a sound philosophy teaches us that this distinctive sign must be something exterior. Not only the Church and the Council, but also the lay people desire the religious habit to be humble, modest, simple and poor.

... it must be emphasized that religious who have chosen to live and work for the welfare of others cannot act as worldly men and women. The lay people, themselves, conscious of spiritual values, expect that religious be well aware of the demands of the choice they have made and demonstrate it in their lives, fulfilling at the same time, the expectations of the Council which defines them as "a sign which can and should have an effective influence on the whole Church" (LG, no. 44).

... the religious must have an accurate idea of poverty. They are to assist the Lord's privileged ones and for whom Christ became incarnate; they must undertake this task with the proper mentality and attitude (cf. G et S, 63, 5) towards them; we can never lead our communities toward revolutionary activities, for the cause of the poor is not identified with that of political movements or parties. Rather ... it calls for even exterior proofs of a simple life avoiding a style of life which denotes a certain affectedness and vanity (ET, no. 22).

SCRSI, January 22, 1972:

Change to secular dress not permitted

Nevertheless, religious institutes, in their general chapters, may, and in some cases ought to modify the traditional habit in accord with practical requirements and the needs of hygiene, but they may not abolish it altogether or leave it to the judgment of individual sisters. The basic criterion to be observed is that the habit prescribed by religious institutes, even as modified and simplified, should be such that distinguishes the religious person who wears it. On the other hand, purely secular clothes, without any recognizable exterior sign, can be permitted for particular reasons, by the competent superiors to those sisters to whom the use of the religious habit would constitute an impediment or obstacle in the normal exercise of activities which should be undertaken in certain circumstances. Even in this latter case, the dress of the religious women should not depart from the forms of poverty, simplicity and modesty proper to the religious state. It should always be in some way different from the forms that are clearly secular. . . . Similar norms are applicable to male members of religious communities.

Letter SCRSI, July 10, 1972:

Chapter decisions in this matter (religious dress) should follow the statements in the documents.

Previous statements from SCRSI excluding secular dress

"For this reason the religious habit should not be changed into a secular dress." (January 9-14, 1967)

"To cite a particular instance, the chapter is not empowered to decide, for example, . . . or the suppression of the religious habit, and the use of secular dress. (January 21, 1968)

"The increasing trend toward secularization . . . has also at times introduced a completely secular style of dress . . . the religious habit must preserve this external character of consecration as has been repeatedly reaffirmed in many documents from the Holy See". (November 24, 1969)

"With regard to the question of the religious habit, the general chapter has the right to modify it . . . but there is no right to suppress it." (August 30, 1969)

Previous replies to particular congregations of sisters excluding secular dress

This exclusion has been the constant postconciliar practice of the Sacred Congregation, as can be seen from the following:

"With regard to the question of the religious habit, the general chapter has the power to modify it provided it remains a 'sign of consecration, simple and modest, as also poor and becoming' (PC no. 17), but does not possess the right to suppress it. It is only in exceptional cases that the superior general can dispense certain religious from the wearing of the religious habit for special reasons and in determined circumstances." (August 30, 1969)

"The reasons given for departure from the prescriptions of canons 596 and 557 are not valid. The habit is a sign of consecration; this consecration is not suspended in off duty hours (cf. PC no. 17). (May 8, 1970)

"The wearing of the religious habit is not left to the free choice of the individual sister. This canon does, however, if it is interpreted properly, admit most of the reasons mentioned in your request." (April 20, 1971)

"While the Special Chapter is allowed to decide modification of the habit, it may not authorize its suppression. The Decree, *Perfectae Caritatis* no. 17, and the ET no. 22, also affirm the necessity of a religious habit." (January 11, 1972)

Habit of Extern Sisters The habit of the (Extern) Sisters shall be the same as that of the Nuns, but judiciously adapted by the Chapter to the purposes of external services according to the circumstances. (BO 'C, 5, 387, no. 7)

Habit in the same federation In monasteries of the same federation, the [Extern] Sisters as far as possible shall be dressed in the same way. (ibid.)

SACRED CONGREGATION FOR RELIGIOUS AND SECULAR INSTITUTES ON RELIGIOUS HABITS

Rome, February 25, 1972

This Congregation has been receiving reports from various

countries that religious men and women, in ever greater numbers, are abandoning the religious habit and even any distinctive sign of consecration. On the other hand, many inquiries are being made as to just what is the mind of the Holy See in this regard.

It seems opportune to inform you of the type of reply this Sacred Congregation gives in such cases, trusting that Your Excellency will find ways of making this known whenever circumstances require it.

"First of all, it is opportune to state again that the religious habit has been considered by the Second Vatican Council as a sign of consecration for those who have embraced in a public way the state of perfection of the evangelical counsels (*Perfectae caritatis*, no. 17).

"Moreover, this concept has also been confirmed by the recent apostolic exhortation of His Holiness, (*Evangelica testificatio*, no. 22).

"Nevertheless, religious institutes, in their general chapters, may, and in some cases ought to, modify the traditional habit in accord with practical requirements and the needs of hygiene but they may not abolish it altogether or leave it to the judgment of individual sisters.

"The basic criterion to be observed is that the habit prescribed by religious institutes, even as modified and simplified, should be such that it distinguishes the religious person who wears it.

"On the other hand, purely secular clothes, without any recognizable exterior sign, can be permitted, for particular reasons, by the competent superiors to those sisters to whom the use of the religious habit would constitute an impediment or obstacle in the normal exercise of activities which should be undertaken in certain circumstances. Even in this latter case the dress of the religious women should not depart from the forms of poverty, simplicity and modesty proper to the religious state. It should always be 'in some way different from the forms that are clearly secular' (*Evangelica testificatio*, no. 22)."

The foregoing applies, *mutatis mutandis,* also to male religious who should always be distinguishable from seculars by the use of the roman collar or by some other visible and appropriately distinctive sign.

I welcome this occasion to send you my very best wishes, and I remain,

Yours faithfully in our Lord,
Card. ANTONIUTTI

APOSTOLIC DELEGATION
3339 MASSACHUSETTS AVENUE
WASHINGTON, D.C. 20008

January 28, 1972

His Eminence John Cardinal Krol
President, N.C.C.B.
222 North 17th Street
Philadelphia, Pa. 19103

Your Eminence:

Under date of January 22, 1972 (no. Sp. R. 164/72) the Sacred Congregation for Religious and Secular Institutes states that its information from various countries indicates that religious, men and women, in ever increasing numbers, are abandoning the religious habit and also any distinctive external sign. The Holy See has many requests for information about its thought on the subject. It therefore considers it opportune to express itself and Your Eminence may wish to make the following known to the members of the Episcopal Conference.

"First of all, it is appropriate to state again that the religious habit has been considered by the Second Vatican Council as a sign of consecration for those who have embraced in a public way the state of perfection of the evangelical counsels. (*"Perfectae caritatis,"* no. 17)

"Moreover, this concept has also been confirmed by the recent apostolic exhortation of His Holiness, (*"Evangelica Testificatio"* no. 22)

"Nevertheless, religious institutes, in their General Chapters, may, and in some cases ought to, modify the traditional habit in accord with practical requirements and the needs of hygiene but they may not abolish it altogether or leave it to the judgment of individual Sisters.

"The basic criterion to be observed is that the habit prescribed by Religious Institutes, even as modified and simplified, should be such that it distinguishes the religious person who wears it.

"On the other hand, purely secular clothes, without any recognizable exterior sign, can be permitted, for particular reasons, by the competent Superiors to those Sisters to whom the use of the religious habit would constitute an impediment or obstacle in the normal exercise of activities which should be undertaken in certain circumstances. Even in this latter case the dress of the religious women should not depart from the forms of poverty, simplicity and modesty proper to the religious state. It should always be 'in some way different from the forms that are clearly secular.' (*Evangelica Testificatio* no. 22)"

The Cardinal Prefect concludes his comment with the statement that what has been said above, *mutatis mutandis* applies also to Religious Men who ought always to be distinguished from seculars by the roman collar or some visible and appropriate sign.

With sentiments of respect and every good wish, I remain,

Devotedly yours in Christ,
✠ Luigi Raimondi; Apostolic Delegate

ARCHDIOCESE OF PHILADELPHIA
222 North 17th Street   Philadelphia, Pa. 19103

December 20, 1973

My dear Sisters,

In your letter of December 7, you take exception to and register a great disappointment with the restrictions contained in the postscript of Father John Miller's letter—a postscript that states: "His Eminence does require that Sisters who are appointed as extraordinary ministers wear a religious garb and veil." You say that it is your understanding that the restriction is not contained in the directive from Rome regarding extraordinary ministers and you note that the . . . "wear a recognizable religious symbol but not a habit or veil."

The candor of your letter calls for equal candor in my reply. In the first place, may I assure you that your understanding about my authority to determine the garb of extraordinary ministers of Holy Communion is not accurate. The Roman Ritual *Eucharistiae Sacramentum* approved and promulgated by Pope Paul VI on June 21, 1973, no. 20, directs that the ministers of Holy Communion, if he is a priest or deacon, must wear an alb, or surplice, over his cassock and also wear a stole. Other ministers must wear a liturgical vestment which may be approved in the particular region—"aut vestem quae huic ministerio non dedeceat *et ab Ordinario probatam.*" The same norm is expressed in Article 92 for those who by order or by deputation expose the Blessed Sacrament. In both cases the approval of the Ordinary is required.

Secondly, you say that the . . . wear a recognizable religious symbol, but not a habit or veil. But the Conciliar Decree *Perfectae Caritatis*, in no. 17, calls for a religious habit, not a symbol: "the *religious habit*, an outward mark of consecration to God, should be simple and modest, poor and at the same time becoming. The Apostolic Exhortation of Pope Paul VI, *Evangelica testificatio*, in no. 22, states: "In certain exceptional circumstances—We do, indeed recognize it—approval can be given to lay aside a type of *religious dress;* but We cannot pass over in silence how much it is agreed that the *habit* of religious men and women should be as the Council has ordained, a sign of their consecration and to that extent distinguished from forms that are obviously secular."

On January 22, 1972 (no. S.P.R. 164/72), the Sacred Congregation for Religious and Secular Institutes states that information from various countries indicates that religious men and women, in ever-increasing numbers, are *abandoning the religious habit* and also any distinctive external sign. The letter continues that the Holy See has had many requests for information about its thoughts on the subject and, therefore, considers it opportune to express itself to me as President of the Episcopal Conference with the idea that

I would wish to share the information with other members of the Conference. The letter calls attention to the fact of Articles no. 17 of the Conciliar Decree and no. 22 of the Apostolic Exhortation. It continues: "Nevertheless, religious institutes, in their general chapter, may, and in some cases ought to, modify the traditional habit in accordance with the practical requirements and the needs of hygiene, but they *may not abolish it altogether or leave it to the judgment of the individual Sisters.*"

The letter continues: "The basic criterion to be observed is that the habit prescribed by religious institutes even as modified and simplified should be such that it distinguishes the religious person who wears it." The letter acknowledges circumstances in which purely secular clothes can be permitted by competent Superiors to those Sisters to whom the use of the religious habit would constitute an impediment or obstacle in the normal exercise of activities which should be undertaken in certain circumstances. However, the letter continues, "Even in this latter case, the dress of the religious woman should not depart from the forms of poverty, simplicity and modesty proper to the religious state. It should also be in some way different from the forms that are purely secular." The tenor of the letter of January 22 was communicated by a letter of the Apostolic Delegation—January 28, 1972 (no. 347/72).

On the basis of these directives, Monsignor Bennington, then Vicar for Religious, in a letter of February 14, 1972, directed to the Reverend Mothers, noted that the Holy See's statement was a simple re-affirmation of pre- and post-Conciliar legislation; that these norms are universal and oblige all religious communities that are not exempt by special indult from the Holy See. He noted that the letter refers to a habit (not merely to an emblem)—to a mode of dress that would distinguish those who wear it. Such emblems are not equated with nor are they a substitute for a religious habit. Monsignor Bennington concluded his letter with the words: "I am confident that our religious communities will continue in a spirit of obedience, compliance, and loyalty to the directives of the Holy See."

My dear Sisters, I cannot in conscience reconcile the contradiction of extending the great privilege of extraordinary ministers of Holy

Communion, a privilege extended by the Holy See, when you ignore the directives of the Holy See in the matter of a religious habit and since it is within my competence to approve the vestments to be used in exercising this extraordinary privilege, I must insist that Sisters who are to be appointed extraordinary ministers of Holy Communion wear, in conformity with the directives of the Holy See, a recognizable habit and veil.

John Cardinal Krol
Archbishop of Philadelphia

SACRED CONGREGATION FOR RELIGIOUS AND SECULAR INSTITUTES

Most Reverend LEO A. PURSLEY
Bishop of FORT WAYNE-SOUTH BEND

Your Excellency,

In regard to the Religious Habit, as you are aware, various Institutes have taken liberties far beyond what was ever intended by the Council. And if they say that Rome has approved their wearing of contemporary secular dress, they should be challenged to show proof of this. First of all, there is no question of approval of Constitutions during this period of experimentation permitted by the *Motu Proprio* "Ecclesiae Sanctae." Such approval (or disapproval) will come when the period of experimentation is over. Meantime, this Sacred Congregation has requested that the Acts of Chapters be sent here, in order to keep informed on the experimentation that is being carried on, and to have the opportunity of making the observations we believe called for. *Never has any positive approval been given to laying aside the Religious Habit.* Neither has such a provision been passed over in silence, unless, in some rare case, through an oversight. *Nor does "silence give consent" as some have contended, who presume that because they have heard nothing from this Sacred Congregation, their Interim Constitutions are approved.* The only reason they have not yet heard is because of the volume of work that is coming in as a result of Special General Chapters and follow-up Chapters, which renders prompt study and replies practically impossible.

We have recently sent out to Nuncios and Delegates of the Holy See in various countries a letter giving the mind of this Sacred Congregation on the subject of the habit. You will find enclosed a copy of this letter, translated into English.

We would ask you to continue your insistence on the habit, Your Excellency. As you know, it is not only your right but your duty, in keeping with the Motu Proprio "Ecclesiae Sanctae" I, 25, § 2, d.

With sentiments of gratitude and with every good wish, I remain

Yours sincerely in Christ
I. Cardinal Antoniutti
Prefect

CHAPTER 12

FORMATION RENEWAL

PC 18. The suitable renewal of religious communities depends very largely on the training of their members. Therefore religious men other than clerics, and religious women as well, should not be assigned to apostolic works immediately after the novitiate. In suitable residences and in a fitting manner, let them continue their training in the religious life and the apostolate, in doctrine and technical matters, even to the extent of winning appropriate degrees.

Lest the adaptations of religious life to the needs of our time be merely superficial, and lest those who by constitution pursue the external apostolate prove unequal to the fulfillment of their task, religious should be properly instructed, according to the intellectual gifts and personal endowments of each, in the prevailing manners of contemporary social life, and in its characteristic ways of feeling and thinking. If such training is harmoniously coordinated it will contribute to integrity of life on the part of religious.

Throughout their lives religious should labor earnestly to perfect their spiritual, doctrinal, and professional development. As far as possible, superiors should provide them with the opportunity, the resources, and the time to do so.

It also devolves upon superiors to see that the best persons are chosen for directors, spiritual guides, and professors, and that they are carefully trained.

The Training of Religious

(Cf. nos. ES II-II, 33-38)

33. The training of Religious beginning with the novitiate should be organized in the same way in all institutes, but the special

character of each institute should be considered. In the revision and adaptation of this training an adequate and prudent place is to be given for experience.

34. Those precepts set down in the Decree *Optatam Totius* (On the Training of Priests), adapted to suit the character of each institute, are to be observed faithfully in the education of Religious clerics.

35. Further training after the novitiate is to be given in a way suitable to each institute. This training is altogether necessary for all members, even for those living a contemplative life, for Brothers in lay religious institutes and for Sisters in institutes dedicated to apostolic works, such as now exists in many institutes and are called juniorates, scholasticates and the like. This training should generally be extended over the entire period of temporary vows.

36. This training is to be given in suitable houses and, lest it be purely theoretical, should for the sake of the inexperienced be complemented by the performance of works and duties in keeping with the nature and circumstances proper to each institute in such a way that they gradually become part of the life to be lived in the future.

37. While always maintaining the formation proper to each institute, when individual institutes cannot give adequate doctrinal or technical training this can be provided by the fraternal collaboration of many. This collaboration can take various degrees and forms: common lectures or courses, loan of teachers, associations of teachers, providing of facilities in a common school to be attended by members of several institutes.

Institutes equipped with the necessary means should willingly assist others.

38. After the completion of timely experimentation it will be the duty of each institute to formulate its own adapted norms for the training of its members.

INSTRUCTION ON THE RENEWAL OF RELIGIOUS FORMATION

Introduction

In its discussion of the question of renewal to the end that the

Church might be enriched with a greater abundance of spiritual strength and be the better prepared to proclaim the message of salvation to contemporary man, the Second Vatican Ecumenical Council devoted no small measure of attention also to those who pursue the divine gift of a religious vocation, and it set forth in a clearer light the nature, structure and importance of their way of life. Concerning their place in the body of the Church the Council affirmed: "Although the religious state constituted by the profession of the evangelical counsels does not belong to the hierarchical structure of the Church, nevertheless it belongs inseparably to her life and holiness."

Besides, "since it is the function of the hierarchy of the Church to nourish the people of God and lead them to the choicest pastures (cf. Ez 34:14), it devolves on the same hierarchy to govern with wise legislation the practice of the evangelical counsels. For by that practice is uniquely fostered the perfection of love for God and neighbor. Submissively following the promptings of the Holy Spirit, the hierarchy also endorses rules formulated by eminent men and women, and authentically approves later modifications. Moreover, by its watchful and shielding authority, the hierarchy keeps close to communities established far and wide for the upbuilding of Christ's body, so that they can grow and flourish in accord with the spirit of their founders."

It is no less true that the generous vitality, and especially the renewal of the spiritual, evangelical and apostolic life which must animate the various Institutes in the untiring pursuit of an ever greater charity is the responsibility chiefly of those who have received the mission, in the name of the Church and with the grace of the Lord, to govern these Institutes, and at the same time of the generous collaboration of all their members. It is of the very nature of the religious life, just as it is of the very nature of the Church, to have that structure without which no society, not even a supernatural one, would be able to achieve its end, or be in a position to provide the best means to attain it. Wherefore, having learned also from centuries of experience, the Church was led gradually to the formulation of a body of canonical norms, which have contributed in no small degree to the solidity and vitality of religious life in the past. Everyone recognizes that the renewal and adaptation of different Institutes, as demanded by actual circumstances, cannot be implemented without a revision of the canonical prescriptions dealing with the structure and the means of the religious life.

As "the suitable renewal of religious communities depends very largely on the training of their members," several Congregations, both of men and of women anxious to work out the renewal desired by the Council, have endeavored by serious inquiries and have often taken advantage of the preparation of the special General Chapter prescibed by the motu proprio "Ecclesiae Sanctae" (II, no. 3), in order to discover the best conditions for a suitable renewal of the various phases of the formation of their members to the religious life.

Thus it was that a certain number of requests were formulated and transmitted to the Sacred Congregation for Religious and for Secular Institutes, especially through the "Union of Superiors General." These requests were intended to secure a broadening of the canonical norms actually governing religious formation, in order to permit the various Institutes, conformably to the instructions of the Decree *Perfectae caritatis*, nos. 3 ff., to make a better adaptation of the entire formation cycle to the mentality of younger generations and modern living conditions, as also to the present demands of the apostolate, while remaining faithful to the nature and the special aim of each Institute.

It is evident that no new clear and definitive legislation can be formulated except on the basis of experiments carried out on a sufficiently vast scale and over a sufficiently long period of time to make it possible to arrive at an objective judgment based on facts. This is most true since the complexity of situations, their variations according to localities and the rapidity of the changes which affect them make it impossible for those charged with the formation of the youth of today to an authentic religious life to determine a priori which solutions might be best.

This is why this Sacred Congregation for Religious and for Secular Institutes, after careful examination of the proposals submitted regarding the different phases of religious formation, has deemed it opportune to broaden the canonical rules now in force in order to permit these necessary experiments. Nevertheless, although the juridical norms are being eased, it is important that this not be to the detriment of those basic values which the prevailing legislation undertook to safeguard. For "it must be seriously borne in mind that even the most desirable changes made on behalf of contemporary needs will fail of their purpose unless a renewal of spirit give life to them."

In order to be authentic, every revision of the means and the rules of the religious life presupposes at the same time a re-defining of the values which are essential to the religious life, since the safeguarding of these values is the aim of these norms. For this reason and in order to permit a clearer understanding of the significance of the new rulings set forth in this present Instruction, the Sacred Congregation has deemed it useful to preface them with certain explanatory remarks.

I. *Some Guidelines and Principles*

RC 1. Not only the complexity of the situations alluded to previously, but also, especially, the growing diversity of Institutes and their activities makes it increasingly difficult to formulate any useful set of directives equally applicable to all Institutes everywhere. Hence the much broader norms set forth in this Instruction give to individual Institutes the possibility of prudently choosing the solutions best suited to their needs.

It is especially important, particularly with reference to formation and education, to remember that not even the best solutions can be absolutely identical both for Institutes of men and those of women. Similarly, the framework and the means of formation must vary according as an Institute is dedicated to contemplation or is committed to apostolic activities.

RC 2. Questions raised by the faculty granted in this present Instruction to those Institutes which might deem it opportune, to replace temporary vows with some other kind of commitment, emphasizes the necessity of recalling here the nature and the proper value of Religious Profession. Such profession, whereby the members "either by vows or by other sacred bonds which are like vows in their purpose," bind themselves to living the three evangelical counsels, brings about a total consecration to God, who alone is worthy of such a sweeping gift on the part of a human person. It is more in keeping with the nature of such a gift to find its culmination and its most eloquent expression in perpetual profession, whether simple or solemn. In fact, "this consecration will be all the more perfect according as through firmer and more solid bonds there will be reflected the image of Christ united with the Church His Spouse through an unbreakable bond." Thus it is that religious profession is an act of religion and a special consecration whereby a person dedicates himself to God.

Not only according to the teaching of the Church but likewise by the very nature of this consecration, the vow of obedience, whereby a religious consummates the complete renunciation of himself and, along with the vows of religious chastity and poverty, offers to God as it were a perfect sacrifice, belongs to the essence of religious profession.

Thus consecrated to Christ, the religious is at the same time bound to the service of the Church and, according to his vocation, is led to the realization of the perfection of that apostolic charity which must animate and impel him, whether in a life entirely given over to contemplation or in different apostolic activities. This notwithstanding, it is important to note that, even though in Institutes dedicated to the apostolate "the very nature of the religious life requires apostolic action and services," this apostolic activity is not the primary aim of religious profession. Besides, the same apostolic works could be carried out quite well without the consecration deriving from the religious state although, for one who has taken on its obligations, this religious consecration can and must contribute to greater dedication to the apostolate.

Hence, although it is in order to renew religious life in its means and its forms of expression, it cannot be asserted that the very nature of religious profession must be changed or that there should be a lessening of the demands proper to it. The youth of today who are called by God to the religious state are not less desirous than before, rather they ardently desire to live up to this vocation in all its requirements, provided these be certain and authentic.

RC 3. Nevertheless, in addition to the religious vocation strictly and properly so called, the Holy Spirit does not cease to stir up in the Church, especially in these latter times, numerous Institutes, whose members, whether bound or not by sacred commitments, undertake to live in common and to practice the evangelical counsels in order to devote themselves to various apostolic or charitable activities. The Church has sanctioned the authentic nature of these different modes of life and has approved them. Still, these modes do not constitute the religious state even though, up to a certain point, they have often been likened to religious life in canonical legislation. Therefore, the norms and directives contained in this present Instruction deal directly with religious Institutes in the strict sense. Other Institutes, however, if they so wish, are free to follow them in the proper organization of their formation program and in whatever is best suited to the nature of their activities.

RC 4. The faculties granted to religious Institutes by this present Instruction have been suggested by a certain number of considerations based on experience which it is here in order to explain briefly.

It would appear that in our day and age genuine religious formation should proceed more by stages and be extended over a longer period of time, since it must embrace both the time of the novitiate and the years following upon the first temporary commitment. In this formation cycle the novitiate must retain its irreplaceable and privileged role as the first initiation into religious life. This goal cannot be attained unless the future novice possesses a minimum of human and spiritual preparation which must not only be verified but, very often, also completed.

In fact, for each candidate the novitiate should come at the moment when, aware of God's call, he has reached that degree of human and spiritual maturity which will allow him to decide to respond to this call with sufficient and proper responsibility and freedom. No one should enter religious life without this choice being freely made, and without the separation from men and things which this entails being accepted. Nevertheless, this first decision does not necessarily demand that the candidate be then able to measure up immediately to all the demands of the religious and apostolic life of the Institute, but he must be judged capable of reaching this goal by stages. Most of the difficulties encountered today in the formation of novices are usually due to the fact that when they were admitted they did not have the required maturity.

Thus, preparation for entrance into the novitiate proves to be increasingly necessary as the world becomes less Christian in outlook. In most cases, in fact, a gradual spiritual and psychological adjustment appears to be indispensable in order to prepare the way for certain breaks with one's social milieu and even worldly habits. Young people today who are attracted by the religious life are not looking for an easy life; indeed, their thirst for the absolute is consuming. But their life of faith is oftentimes based on merely elementary knowledge of doctrine, in sharp contrast to the development of their knowledge of profane subjects.

Hence it follows that all Institutes, even those whose formation cycle includes no postulancy, must attach great importance to this preparation for the novitiate. In Institutes having minor seminaries, seminaries or colleges, candidates for the religious life usually go directly to the novitiate. It will be worthwhile to reconsider if this policy should be maintained, or if it is not more advisable, in order to assure better preparation for a fully responsible choice of the religious life, to prepare for the novitiate by a fitting period of probation in order to develop the human and emotional maturity of the candidate. Moreover, while it must be recognized that problems vary according to countries, it must be affirmed that the age required for admission to the novitiate should be higher than heretofore.

RC 5. As regards the formation to be imparted in the novitiate in Institutes dedicated to the works of the apostolate, it is evident that greater attention should be paid to preparing the novices, in the very beginning and more directly, for the type of life or the activities which will be theirs in the future, and to teaching them how to realize in their lives in progressive stages that cohesive unity whereby contemplation and apostolic activity are closely linked together, a unity which is one of the most fundamental and primary values of these same societies. The achievement of this unity requires a proper understanding of the realities of the supernatural life and of the paths leading to a deepening of union with God in the unity of one same supernatural love for God and for men, finding expression at times in the solitude of intimate communing with the Lord and at others in the generous giving of self to apostolic activity. Young religious must be taught that this unity so eagerly sought and toward which all life tends in order to find its full development, cannot be attained on the level of activity alone, or even be psychologically experienced, for it resides in that divine love which is the bond of perfection and which surpasses all understanding.

The attainment of this unity, which cannot be achieved without long training in self-denial or without persevering efforts toward purity of intention in action, demands in those Institutes faithful compliance with the basic law of all spiritual life, which consists in arranging a proper balance of periods set aside for solitude with God and others devoted to various activities and to the human contacts which these involve.

Consequently, in order that novices, while acquiring experience in certain activities proper to their Institute, may discover the importance of this law and make it habitual, it has seemed advisable to grant to those Institutes which might regard it as opportune, the faculty of introducing into the novitiate formative activity and experimental periods in keeping with their activities and their type of life.

It must be emphasized that this formative activity, which complements novitiate teaching, is not intended to provide the novices with the technical or professional training required for certain apostolic activities, training which will be afforded to them later on, but rather to help them, in the very midst of these activities, to better discover the exigencies of their vocation as religious and how to remain faithful to them.

In fact, confronted with the diversity of apostolic activities available to them, let religious not forget that, differently from secular institutes, whose specific activity is carried out with the means of the world or in the performance of temporal tasks, religious must, above all, according to the teaching of the Council, be in a special manner witnesses to Christ within the Church: "Religious should carefully consider that, through them, to believers and non-believers alike, the Church truly wishes to give an increasingly clearer revelation of Christ. Through them Christ should be shown contemplating on the mountain, announcing God's kingdom to the multitude, healing the sick and the maimed, turning sinners to wholesome fruit, blessing children, doing good to all, and always obeying the will of the Father who sent Him."

There is a diversity of gifts. Wherefore, each one must stand firm in the vocation to which he has been called, since the mission of those called to the religious state in the Church is one thing; the mission of secular institutes is another thing; the temporal and apostolic mission of the laity not especially consecrated to God in an Institute, is quite another.

It is in line with this perspective on his vocation that whoever is called by God to the religious state must understand the meaning of the formation which is begun in the novitiate.

Therefore, the nature and the educational value of these periods, as well as the timeliness of introducing them into the novitiate, will be evaluated differently in congregations of men or of women, in Institutes dedicated to contemplation or to apostolic activities.

Indeed, the effectiveness of this formation, while it is imparted in an atmosphere of greater freedom and flexibility, will also depend largely on the firmness and the wisdom of the guidance afforded by the novice master and by all those who share in the formation of young religious after the novitiate. It is extremely important also to recall the importance of the role played in such formation by the atmosphere of generosity provided by a fervent and united community, in the midst of which young religious will be enabled to learn by experience the value of mutual fraternal assistance as an element of readier progress and perseverance in their vocation.

RC 6. In order then to respond to this same need of gradual

formation the question has arisen concerning the extension of the period prior to perpetual profession in which a candidate is bound by temporary vows or by some other form of commitment.

It is proper that when he pronounces his perpetual vows, the religious should have reached the degree of spiritual maturity required in order that the religious state to which he is committing himself in stable and certain fashion may really be for him a means of perfection and greater love, rather than a burden too heavy to carry. Nevertheless, in certain cases the extension of temporary probation can be an aid to this maturity, while in others it can involve drawbacks which it will not be out of place to point out. The fact of remaining for too long a time in a state of uncertainty is not always a contribution to maturity, and this situation may in some cases encourage a tendency to instability. It should be added that in the case of non-admission to perpetual profession, the return to lay life will often entail problems of readjustment, which will be all the more serious and trying according as the time spent in temporary commitment has been longer. Superiors, consequently, must be aware of their grave responsibilities in this field and should not put off until the last minute a decision which could and should have been taken earlier.

RC 7. No Institute should decide to use the faculty granted by this Instruction to replace temporary vows by some other form of commitment without having clearly considered and weighed the reasons for and the nature of this commitment.

For him who has heeded the call of Jesus to leave everything to follow Him there can be no question of how important it is to respond generously and wholeheartedly to this call from the very outset of his religious life; the making of temporary vows is completely in harmony with this requirement. For, while still retaining its probationary character by the fact that it is temporary, the profession of first vows makes the young religious share in the consecration proper to the religious state.

Yet, perpetual vows can be prepared for without making temporary vows. In fact, more frequently now than in the past, a certain number of young candidates come to the end of their novitiate without having acquired the religious maturity sufficient to bind themselves immediately by religious vows, although no prudent doubt can be raised regarding their generosity or their authentic vocation to the religious state. This hesitancy in pronouncing vows is frequently accompanied by a great awareness of the exigencies and the importance of the perpetual religious profession to which they aspire and wish to prepare themselves. Thus it has seemed desirable in a certain number of Institutes that at the end of their novitiate the novices should be able to bind themselves by a temporary commitment different from vows, yet answering their twofold desire to give themselves to God and the Institute and to pledge themselves to a fuller preparation for perpetual profession.

Whatever form such a temporary commitment may take, fidelity to a genuine religious vocation demands that it should in some way be based on the requirements of the three evangelical counsels, and should thus be already entirely orientated toward the one perpetual profession, for which it must be, as it were, an apprenticeship and a preparation.

RC 8. He who commits himself to walk in the path of the Savior in the religious life, must bear in mind Our Lord's own words that "no one, having put his hand to the plow and looking back, is fit for the kingdom of God" (Lk 9, 62). Just the same, the psychological and emotional difficulties encountered by some individuals in their progressive adaptation to the religious life are not always resolved upon the termination of the novitiate, and at the same time there is no doubt that their vocation can be authentic. In many cases, the permission for absence provided for by Canon Law will allow superiors to make it possible for these religious to spend some time outside a house of the Institute in order to be the better able to resolve their problems. But in some more difficult cases, this solution will be inadequate. Superiors can then persuade such candidates to return to lay life, using, if necessary, the faculty granted in no. 38 of this Instruction.

RC 9. Lastly, a religious formation more based on stages and judiciously extended over the different periods of the life of a young religious should find its culmination in a serious preparation for perpetual vows. It is in fact desirable that this unique and essential act whereby a religious is consecrated to God forever should be preceded by a sufficiently long immediate preparation, spent in retreat and prayer, a preparation which could be like a second novitiate.

II. *Special Norms*

The Sacred Congregation for Religious and for Secular Institutes, in its desire to promote necessary and useful experiments in view of the adaptation and renewal of religious formation, having examined these questions in its plenary meetings of June 25-26, 1968, by virtue of a special mandate from the Sovereign Pontiff, Pope Paul VI, has seen fit, by this Instruction, to formulate and to publish the following norms:

RC 10 I. Religious formation comprises two essential phases: the novitiate and the probationary period which follows the novitiate and lasts for a period adapted to the nature of the Institute, during which the members are bound by vows or other commitments.

II. A preliminary period of varying duration, obligatory in certain Institutes under the name of postulancy, usually precedes admission to the novitiate.

RC 11. I. This preliminary probation has as its purpose not merely to formulate a tentative judgment on the aptitudes and vocation of the candidate, but also to verify the extent of his knowledge of religious subjects and where need be, to complete it in the degree judged necessary and, lastly, to permit a gradual transition from the lay life to the life proper to the novitiate.

II. During this probationary period it is particularly necessary to secure assurance that the candidate for religious life be endowed with such elements of human and emotional maturity as will afford grounds for hope that he is capable of undertaking properly the obligations of the religious state and that, in the religious life and especially in the novitiate, he will be able to progress toward fuller maturity.

III. If in certain more difficult cases, the superior feels, with the free agreement of the subject, that he should have recourse to the services of a prudent and qualified psychologist known for his moral principles, it is desirable, in order that this examination may be fully effective, that it should take place after an extended period of probation, so as to enable the specialist to formulate a diagnosis based on experience.

RC 12. I. In Institutes where a postulancy is obligatory, whether by common law or in virtue of the constitutions, the General Chapter may follow the norms of this present Instruction for a better adaptation of the period of postulancy to the requirements of a more fruitful preparation for the novitiate.

II. In other Institutes it belongs to the General Chapter to determine the nature and the length of this preliminary probation, which can vary according to candidates. Nevertheless, if it is to be genuinely effective, this period should neither be too brief nor, as a general rule, be extended beyond two years.

III. It is preferable that this probation should not take place in the novitiate house. It could even be helpful that, either in whole or in part, it be organized outside a house of the Institute.

IV. During this preliminary probation, even if it takes place outside a house of the Institute, the candidates will be placed under the direction of qualified religious and there should be sufficient collaboration between these latter and the novice master, with a view to assuring continuity of formation.

RC 13. I. Religious life begins with the novitiate. Whatever may be the special aim of the Institute, the principal purpose of the novitiate is to initiate the novice into the essential and primary requirements of the religious life and also, in view of a greater charity, to implement the evangelical counsels of chastity, poverty, and obedience of which he will later make profession, "either through vows or other sacred bonds which are like vows in their purpose."

II. In those Institutes where "the very nature of the religious life requires apostolic action and services," the novices are to be gradually trained to dedicate themselves to activities in keeping with the purpose of their Institute, while developing that intimate union with Christ whence all their apostolic activity must flow.

RC 14. Superiors responsible for the admission of candidates to the novitiate will take care to accept only those giving proof of the aptitudes and elements of maturity regarded as necessary for commitment to the religious life as lived in the Institute.

RC 15. I. In order to be valid, the novitiate must be made in the house legitimately designated for this purpose.

II. It should be made in the community or group of novices, fraternally united under the direction of the novice master. The program as well as the nature of the activities and work of the novitiate must be organized in such a way as to contribute to novice formation.

III. This formation, conformably to the teachings of Our Lord in the Gospel and the demands of the particular aim and spirituality of the Institute, consists mainly in initiating the novices gradually into detachment from everything not connected with the kingdom of God, the practice of obedience, poverty, prayer, habitual union with God in availability to the Holy Spirit, in order to help one another spiritually in frank and open charity.

IV. The novitiate will also include study and meditation on holy Scripture, the doctrinal and spiritual formation indispensable for the development of a supernatural life of union with God and an understanding of the religious state and, lastly, an initiation to liturgical life and the spirituality proper to the Institute.

RC 16. I. The erection of a novitiate does not require the authorization of the Holy See. It belongs to the superior general, with the consent of his council and conformably to the norms laid down in the constitutions, to erect or to authorize the erection of a novitiate, to determine the special details of the program and to decide on its location in a given house of the Institute.

II. If necessary, in order to make more effective provision for the formation of the novices, the superior general may authorize the transfer of the novitiate community during certain periods to another residence designated by himself.

RC 17. In case of necessity, the superior general, with the consent of his council and after consultation with the interested provincial, may authorize the erection of several novitiates within the same province.

RC 18. In view of the very important role of community life in the formation of the novices, and when the small number of the novices would prevent the creation of conditions favorable to genuine community life, the superior general should, if possible, organize the novitiate in another community of the Institute able to assist in the formation of this small group of novices.

RC 19. In special cases and by way of exception, the superior general, with the consent of his council, is empowered to allow a candidate to make his novitiate validly in some house of the Institute other than the novitiate, under the responsibility of an experienced religious acting as novice master.

RC 20. For a reason which he regards as just, the major superior may allow first profession to be made outside the novitiate house.

RC 21. In order to be valid, the novitiate as described above must last twelve months.

RC 22. I. Absences from the novitiate group and house which, either at intervals or continuously, exceed three months render the novitiate invalid.

II. As for absences lasting less than three months, it pertains to the major superiors, after consultation with the novice master, to decide in each individual case, taking into account the reasons for the absence, whether this absence should be made up by demanding an extension of the novitiate, and to determine the length of the eventual prolongation. The constitutions of the Institute may also provide directives on this point.

RC 23. I. The General Chapter, by at least a two-thirds majority, may decide, on an experimental basis, to integrate into novitiate formation one or several periods involving activities in line with the character of the Institute and away from the novitiate, in the degree in which, in the judgment of the novice master and with the consent of the major superior, such an experiment would seem to be a useful contribution to formation.

II. These formation stages may be used for one or several novices or for the novitiate community as a whole. Wherever possible, it would be preferable that the novices take part in these stages in groups of two or more.

III. During these stages away from the novitiate community, the novices remain under the responsibility of the novice master.

RC 24. I. The total length of the periods spent by a novice outside the novitiate will be added to the twelve months of presence required by Art. 21 for the validity of the novitiate, but in such a way that the total duration of the novitiate thus expanded does not exceed two years.

II. These formative apostolic periods may not begin until after a minimum of three months in the novitiate and will be distributed in such a way that the novice will spend at least six continuous months in the novitiate and return to the novitiate for at least one month prior to first vows or temporary commitment.

III. In cases where superiors would deem it useful for a future novice to have a period of experience before beginning the three months of presence required at the start of the novitiate, this period could be regarded as a probation period and only after its completion would the novitiate begin.

RC 25. I. The nature of experimental periods outside the novitiate can vary according to the aims of various Institutes and the nature of their activities. Still, they must always be planned and carried out in view of forming the novice or, in certain cases, testing his aptitude for the life of the Institute. Besides gradual preparation for apostolic activities, they can also have as their purpose to bring the novice into contact with certain concrete aspects of poverty or of labor, to contribute to character formation, a better knowledge of human nature, the strengthening of the will, the development of personal responsibility and, lastly, to provide occasions for effort at union with God in the context of the active life.

II. This balancing of periods of activity and periods of retreat consecrated to prayer, meditation or study, which will characterize the formation of the novices, should stimulate them to remain faithful to it throughout the whole of their religious life. It would also be well for such periods of retreat to be regularly planned during the years of formation preceding perpetual profession.

RC 26. The major superior may, for a just cause, allow first profession to be anticipated, but not beyond fifteen days.

RC 27. In Institutes having different novitiates for different categories of religious, and unless the constitutions stipulate otherwise, the novitiate made for one category is valid likewise for the other. It belongs to the constitutions to determine eventual conditions regulating this passage from one novitiate to the other.

RC 28. The special nature and aim of the novitiate, as also the close bonds which should be found among the novices, really demand a certain separation of the novice group from the other members of the Institute. Nevertheless the novices may, according to the judgment of the novice master, have contacts with other communities or religious. Hence it will be the task of the general chapter, taking into consideration the spirit of the Institute and the demands of special circumstances, to decide what kind of contacts the novices may have with the other members of the Institute.

RC 29. I. The general chapter may permit or even impose during the regular novitiate year certain studies which may be useful for the formation of the novices. Doctrinal studies may be put at the service of a loving knowledge of God and a deepening of the life of faith.

II. Excluded from the novitiate year described in no. 21 are all formal study programs, even of theology or philosophy, as also studies directed toward the obtaining of diplomas or in view of professional training.

RC 30. All tasks and work entrusted to novices will be under the responsibility and direction of the novice master, who nevertheless may seek the aid of competent persons. The chief aim of these various tasks must be the formation of the novices, not the interests of the congregation.

RC 31. I. In the direction of the novices, particularly during the periods of formative activity, the novice master will base his direction on the teaching so clearly enunciated by the Second Vatican Council: "Therefore, in order that members may above all respond to their vocation of following Christ and may serve Christ Himself in His members, their apostolic activity should result from their intimate union with Him." "To this end, let the members of all Institutes, seeking above all only God, unite contemplation, whereby they are united with Him in mind and heart, with apostolic love, whereby they strive to associate themselves with the work of redemption and to spread the kingdom of God."

II. With this in mind he should teach the novices:

1) to seek in all things, as well in apostolic activities or the service of men as in the times consecrated to silent prayer or study, purity of intention and the unity of charity toward God and toward men;

2) when the apostolic activities of their Institute lead them to become involved in human affairs, to learn how to use this world "as though not using it";

3) to understand the limitations of their own activity without being discouraged and to work at the ordering of their own life, bearing in mind that no one can give himself authentically to God and his brethren without first getting possession of himself in humility;

4) to bring about in their lives, along with a will which is firm and rich in initiative, and conformably to the demands of a vocation to an Institute dedicated to the apostolate, the indispensable balance on both the human and the supernatural level between times consecrated to the apostolate and the service of men and more or less lengthy periods, in solitude or in community, devoted to prayer and meditative reading of the Word of God;

5) in fidelity to this program which is essential to every consecrated life, to ground their hearts gradually in union with God and that peace which comes from doing the divine will, whose demands they will have learned to discover in the duties of their state and in the promptings of justice and charity.

RC 32. I. Unity of heart and mind must reign between superiors, the novice master and the novices. This union, which is the fruit of genuine charity, is necessary for religious formation.

II. Superiors and the novice master must always show toward the novices evangelical simplicity, kindness coupled with gentleness, and respect for their personality, in order to build up a climate of confidence, docility and openness in which the novice master will be able to orientate their generosity toward a complete gift of themselves to the Lord in faith, and gradually lead them by word and example to learn in the mystery of Christ Crucified the exigencies of authentic religious obedience. Thus, let the novice master teach his novices "to bring an active and responsible obedience to the offices they shoulder and the activities they undertake."

RC 33. As for the habit of the novices and other candidates to the religious life, the decision rests with the general chapter.

RC 34. I. The general chapter, by a two-thirds majority, may decide to replace temporary vows in the Institute with some other kind of commitment as, for example, a promise made to the Institute.

II. This commitment will be made at the end of the novitiate and for the duration of the probationary period extending to perpetual profession or to the sacred commitments which are its equivalent in certain Institutes. This temporary commitment may also be made for a briefer period and be renewed at stated intervals, or even be followed by the making of temporary vows.

RC 35. I. It is altogether proper that this temporary bond should have reference to the practice of the three evangelical counsels, in order to constitute a genuine preparation for perpetual profession. It is of the utmost importance to safeguard unity of religious formation. Although the practice of this life is realized definitely at perpetual profession, it must begin quite a long time before this profession.

II. Since, therefore, the one perpetual profession assumes its full significance, it is fitting that it should be preceded by a period of immediate preparation lasting for a certain length of time, and serving as a kind of second novitiate. The duration and details will be determined by the general chapter.

RC 36. Whatever may be the nature of this temporary commitment, its effect will be to bind whoever makes it to his congregation or his Institute and it will entail the obligation of observing the rule, constitutions and other regulations of the Institute. The general chapter will determine other aspects and consequences of this commitment.

RC 37. I. The general chapter, after careful consideration of all the circumstances, shall decide on the length of the period of temporary vows or commitments which is to extend from the end of the novitiate until the making of perpetual vows. This period shall last for no less than three years and no more than nine, counting the time continuously.

II. The prescription still stands that perpetual profession must be made before the reception of Holy Orders.

RC 38. I. When a member has left his Institute legitimately, either at the expiration of his temporary profession or commitment or after dispensation from these obligations, and later requests readmission, the superior general, with the consent of his council, may grant this readmission without the obligation of prescribing the repetition of the novitiate.

II. The superior general must, nonetheless, impose on him a certain period of probation, upon the completion of which the candidate may be admitted to temporary vows or commitment for a period of no less than one year, or no less than the period of temporary probation which he would have had to complete before perpetual profession at the time he left the Institute. The superior may also demand a longer period of trial.

III. *Application of the Special Norms*

In the implementation of these present decisions the following directives shall be observed:

I. The prescriptions of common law remain in force except in so far as this present Instruction may derogate therefrom.

II. The faculties granted by this Instruction may not in any way be delegated.

III. The term "superior general" also includes the abbot president of a monastic congregation.

IV. In case the superior general is incapacitated or legitimately impeded from acting, these same faculties are granted to the one who is legitimately designated by the constitutions to replace him.

V. In the case of nuns dedicated exclusively to contemplative life, special regulations shall be inserted into the constitutions and submitted for approval. Nevertheless, the norms indicated in nos. 22, 26 and 27 may be applied to them.

VI. 1. If the special general chapter prescribed by the motu proprio "Ecclesiae Sanctae" has already been held, it will belong to the superior general and his council, acting as a body, after due consideration of all the circumstances, to decide if it is advisable to convoke a general chapter to decide the questions reserved to it, or to await the next ordinary general chapter.

2. Should the superior general with his council, as above, deem it too difficult or even impossible to convoke a new general chapter and if, at the same time, the implementation of the faculties reserved to the decision of the chapter is regarded as urgent for the welfare of the Institute, the superior general and his council, as before, is hereby authorized to implement some or all of these faculties until the next general chapter, provided that he previously consult the other major superiors with their councils and obtain the consent of at least two-thirds of their number. The major superiors in turn should make it a point to consult first their perpetually professed religious. In Institutes having no provinces, the superior general must consult the perpetually professed and obtain the consent of two-thirds.

VII. These directives issued on an experimental basis, take effect as of the date of the promulgation of the present Instruction.

Rome, January 6, on the Feast of the Epiphany of Our Lord, in the year 1969.

Promulgated, February 1, 1969

I. CARD. ANTONIUTTI

Prefect—SCRSI

CHAPTER 13

CLOISTERED AND MONASTIC INSTITUTES

PC 9. In the East and in the West, the venerable institution of monastic life should be faithfully preserved, and should grow ever-increasingly radiant with its own authentic spirit. Through the long course of the centuries, this institution has proved its merits splendidly to the Church and to human society. The main task of monks is to render to the Divine Majesty a service at once simple and noble, within the monastic confines. This they do either by devoting themselves entirely to divine worship in a life that is hidden, or by lawfully taking up some apostolate or works of Christian charity. While safeguarding the proper identity of each institution, let monasteries be renewed in their ancient and beneficial traditions, and so adapt them to the modern needs of souls that monasteries will be seedbeds of growth for the Christian people.

There are religious communities which by rule or constitution closely join the apostolic life with choral prayer and monastic observances. Let these groups, too, so harmonize their manner of life with the requirements of the apostolate belonging to them that they still faithfully preserve their form of life, for it is one which serves the highest welfare of the Church.

PC 16. The papal cloister for nuns totally dedicated to contemplation is to be retained. Still, it should be modified according to the conditions of time and place, and outdated customs done away with. In such matters, consideration should be given to the wishes of the monasteries themselves.

Other nuns institutionally devoted to external works of the apostolate should be exempt from papal cloister so that they can better discharge the apostolic tasks assigned to them. They should, however, maintain the kind of cloister required by their constitutions.

Witness of the Contemplative Life

ET 8. Some of you have been called to the contemplative life, as it is termed. An attractive force, which cannot be resisted, draws you to the Lord. Seized by God, you abandon yourselves to His sovereign action, which raises you toward Him and transforms you into Himself. All the while you are being disposed for that eternal contemplation which is the common vocation of us all. How will it be possible to advance along this path and faithfully to preserve the grace which animates you unless, motivated in your whole mind and life through a dynamism whose impulse is love, you yield to this invitation which steadfastly leads you to God? Consider, therefore, every other immediate activity that you have to carry out—such as relations with your brethren, gratuitous or remunerative labor, necessary recreation and the like—as a witness of your intimate union with God. It is a witness you are offering Him that He may give you the unifying purity of intention which is so indispensable for communing with God in times of prayer. In this way, you will contribute to the extension of the kingdom of God by the very witness of your lives and "with a hidden apostolic fruitfulness."

The Cloister of Nuns

ES II-II. 30. The papal enclosure of monasteries must be considered an ascetical institution closely joined to the special vocation of nuns. The enclosure is a sign, safeguard and special expression of their withdrawal from the world.

Nuns of the Oriental rites should observe their own enclosure in the same spirit.

ES II-II. 31. This enclosure should be arranged in such a way that material separation from the outside world is always preserved. Individual Religious families, according to their own spirit, can establish and define in their constitutions particular norms for this material separation.

ES II-II. 32. Minor enclosure is abolished. Nuns, therefore, who by their rule are devoted to external works should define their own enclosure in their constitutions. However, nuns who, although contemplative by their rule, have taken up external works, after a suitable time which is granted them to deliberate, should either retain the papal enclosure and give up their external works or, continuing these works, should define their own enclosure in their constitutions, retaining their status as nuns.

PERMISSION FOR LEAVING CLOISTER

APOSTOLIC DELEGATION
3339 Massachusetts Avenue
Washington, D. C. 20008

April 21, 1967

Your Excellency:

On April 6, 1967 (N.S.R. 1461/65) the Cardinal Prefect expressed to me the grave preoccupation of the Sacred Congregation for Religious over the facility with which Nuns of contemplative life leave the cloister for motives altogether foreign to their vocation, e.g., to participate in meetings and courses designed for religious women of the active life. In the majority of cases the Nuns are encouraged to do this by priests or sometimes also by their Bishops. These Nuns then develop a desire to go out and gradually lose the sense of the cloister, of separation from the world, and eventually the idea of the contemplative life.

It is very desirable that Nuns appreciate the demands of their vocation and that they be encouraged to resist the temptation to leave the cloister for unnecessary reasons.

Cardinal Antoniutti further observes that Bishops have the faculty *to permit* Nuns to leave the cloister "iusta et gravi de causa" (cf. motu proprio "Pastorale Munus" no. 34) but they *do not oblige them* as His Holiness emphasized in an audience granted to His Eminence on December 29, 1966: "The Holy Father wishes to make known to the Bishops the exact interpretation of no. 34 of the *motu proprio* "Pastorale Munus" about their faculty: *possunt permittere, non imponere.*"

I am further informed that the restriction "iusta et gravi de causa" is to be understood in the sense that the Bishops permit Nuns to leave the cloister for the reasons that the Sacred Congregation for Religious allowed this before the motu proprio, "Pastorale Munus." For the convenience of Your Excellency I herewith list these causes:

1. sanitas extra monasterium curanda;

2. visitatio instituenda apud medicum, praesertim in re peritum, v.g. pro oculis, pro dentibus, ad applicationem radiorum, pro observatione medicali;

3. comitari vel visitare monialem foris aegrotantem;

4. supplere sorores externas vel similes personas in casu deficientes;

5. vigilantiam exercere circa agros, fundos, aedificia, vel aedes quas sorores externae inhabitant;

6. actus administrationis vel gestionis oeconomicae magni momenti, qui aliter non aut vix recte vel male fieri possent;

7. labor monasticus tam apostolicus quam etiam manualis;

8. susceptio officii in alio monasterio, hisce similia.

The Cardinal Prefect states that Nuns are not to participate in courses and meetings of religious of the active life. The most permitted to them is that the Presidents of Federations of Nuns may form a national union distinct from the Conference of Major Superiors of the active life. If such a union is formed the meetings are to be carefully supervised so that the programs will contain nothing inimical to the contemplative life and that priests or religious making reports, giving conferences etc. will be men of proved balance and qualified to interpret the pontifical documents with wisdom and understanding.

While I apprize you of this concern of the Holy See I am confident that Your Excellency will seek to do everything possible to safeguard the contemplative life of the Nuns.

With cordial regards and best wishes, I remain

> Sincerely yours in Christ,
> Apostolic Delegate to U.S.
> ✠ Luigi Raimondi

S.C.R.S.I.
INSTRUCTION ON THE CONTEMPLATIVE LIFE
AND ON THE ENCLOSURE OF NUNS

"Come away by yourselves to a lonely place" (Mk 6:31). Numerous are those who have heard this call and have followed Christ, withdrawing into solitude to worship the Father there.

It was by this inspiration of the Spirit that some were led to establish institutions dedicated to contemplation alone, among which convents of nuns occupy a position of great distinction.

With vigilant and maternal care the Church has always watched over virgins consecrated to God, considered by St. Cyprian as "a more illustrious part of Christ's flock," and it is particularly on this account that she has defended their separation from the affairs of the world by issuing a considerable number of regulations regarding papal enclosure.

Since the Second Vatican Council likewise manifested its concern about this matter, it is the purpose of this Instruction to continue its work by legislating the norms which in the future will regulate the enclosure of nuns wholly dedicated to contemplation. These norms are prefaced by certain fundamental considerations regarding enclosure itself.

I.

Withdrawal from the world for the sake of leading a more intense life of prayer in solitude is nothing other than a very particular way of living and expressing the paschal mystery of Christ, which is death ordained toward resurrection.

This mystery is portrayed in Holy Scripture in terms of a passage or exodus, which without doubt constitutes the most important event in the development of Israelite history, inasmuch as it forms the basis of Israel's faith and of her more intimate life with God, an event which the Church recognizes as a certain prefiguration of Christian salvation.

Certainly no one is unaware to what degree the sacred liturgy and the tradition of the Fathers—as the Apostles and Evangelists themselves had already done—evoked the mystery of Christ. From the dawn of the Chosen People's history, Abraham is depicted as being called to leave his country, his family and his father's house, while the Apostle repeatedly teaches that the same calling was the beginning of a long mystical journey to a homeland which is not of this world.

What in this way was merely prefigured in the Old Testament, becomes a reality in the New. Coming from the Father and entering the world (cf. Jn 16:28) to arouse a people "that walked in darkness" (Is 9:2; Mt 4:16), the Word of God delivered us from the domination of darkness (cf. Col 1:13), that is, from sin, and through His death (cf. Jn 13:1; 16:28; and Heb 9:11-12; 10:19-20) He set us on the return road to the Father, who "raised us up with Him and made us sit with Him in the heavenly places in Christ Jesus" (Ep 2:6; cf. Col 2:12-13; 3:1). Herein lies the true essence of the paschal mystery of Christ and the Church.

But the death of Christ demands a real type of solitude, as the Apostle himself understood it, and many Fathers and Doctors of the Church after him. They attributed in fact this significance to certain episodes in Christ's life: while considering Him withdrawing into solitude or into the desert to engage in battle with "the ruler of this world" (cf. Mt 4:1; Jn 12:31; 14:30), but especially when He withdrew to pray to His Father, to whose will He was totally submitted. In this way He presignified the solitude of His passion, which the Evangelists represent to us as a new exodus.

Hence to withdraw into the desert is for the Christian tantamount to associating himself more intimately with Christ's passion, and it enables him, in a very special way, to share in the paschal mystery and in the passage of Our Lord from this world to the heavenly homeland. It was precisely on this account that monasteries were founded, situated as they are in the very heart of the mystery of Christ.

Certainly the faithful are called to follow Christ in the proclamation of His gospel of salvation, and they should at the same time contribute to the construction of the earthly city, thus becoming, as it were, a leaven by which it is transformed into the household of God. It is in this sense that the follower of Christ is said to remain in the world (cf. Jn 17:15). Yet with this mission the fulness of the mystery of the Church is not expressed, since the Church, though established for the service of God and man is likewise— and even more especially—the aggregate of all who are redeemed, that is, of those who through Baptism and the other sacraments have already passed from this world to the Father. The Church is indeed "eager to act," yet at the same time she is no less "devoted to contemplation," in such a way that in her "the human is directed and subordinated to the divine, the visible likewise to the invisible, action to contemplation."

It is therefore both legitimate and necessary that some of Christ's followers, those upon whom this particular grace has been conferred by the Holy Spirit, should give expression to this contemplative character of the Church by actually withdrawing into solitude to lead this particular type of life, in order that "through constant prayer and ready penance they give themselves to God alone" (*Perfectae Caritatis*, 7).

On the other hand, it should be quite evident that a certain degree of withdrawal from the world and some measure of contemplation must necessarily be present in every form of Christian life, as the Second Vatican Council rightly declared in reference to priests and religious dedicated to the apostolate. Indeed it is true that even outside the monastic setting there are some who through the grace of the Holy Spirit are elevated to contemplation. But just as a certain invitation of this type is extended to all Christians, so too a certain degree of separation from the affairs of this world is necessary to all, even though all do not withdraw to the desert in the same way. Monks and nuns, however, retiring to a cloistered life, put into practice in a more absolute and exemplary way an element essential to every Christian life: "From now on ... let those who deal with the world (live) as if they had no dealings with it. For the form of this world is passing away" (1 Cor 7:29, 31).

II.

To the foregoing concepts, elicited from the paschal mystery of Christ in the way the Church participates in it, those must be added which bring to light the importance of recollection and silence in rendering intimacy with God in prayer safer and easier. The way of life of those who are totally dedicated to contemplation, aiming as it does at eliminating all that might divide the spirit against itself in any way, enables them to achieve that fulness of their personalities whose hallmark is unity, and permits them to devote themselves more thoroughly to the quest for God their goal, and to attend to Him more perfectly.

Such a quest for God, moreover, for which man should renounce everything he possesses (cf. Lk 14:33), is furthered to the utmost by reading and meditating on Holy Scripture (cf. *Perfectae Caritatis,* n. 6). Reading of the Bible should therefore accompany prayer, "so that God and man may talk together; for 'we speak to Him when we pray; we hear Him when we read the divine sayings' " (cf. Const. *Dei Verbum,* n. 25; St. Ambrose, *De Officiis Ministrorum,* I, 20, 88; ML 16:50).

And by studying Holy Scripture, which is "like a mirror in which the pilgrim Church on earth looks at God, from whom she has received everything" (*Dei Verbum,* n. 7), each one "inflamed with love of God burns to contemplate His beauty" (II, II, Q. 180, art. 1, in corpore).

In such a way love and contemplation aid one another reciprocally. "The love of God is understanding Him: He is not known unless He is loved, nor is He loved unless He is known; and in reality He is known only to the degree that He is loved, and loved to the degree that He is known" (William of St. Thierry, *Expositio in cant.,* c.I: ML 180:499, C).

Thus in silence and solitude "resolute men are able to recollect themselves and, so to speak, to dwell within themselves as much as they please, cultivating the buds of virtue and feeding happily on the fruits of paradise. Here one strives to acquire that eye by whose limpid glance the bridegroom is wounded with love, and in whose purity alone may God be seen. Here one is occupied in busy leisure, and rests in quiet activity. Here, for fatigue undergone in strife, God grants His athletes the reward they have longed for, namely, a peace unknown to the world and the joy of the Holy Spirit.... This is the better part that Mary chose, that shall not be taken away from her."

III.

It must not be thought, however, that monks and nuns, because they are separated from the rest of mankind, are cut off, as it were, from the world and the Church and are aloof from them. On the contrary, they are united with them "in a more profound sense in the heart of Christ," since we are all one in Christ (cf. 1 Cor 10:17; Jn 17:20-22).

Apart from the traditional contribution of monasteries in the cultural and social domain, conclusive and unshakable evidence exists bearing witness to the great love with which men and women dedicated to contemplation alone harbor in their hearts the sufferings and anguish of all men.

From Scripture, moreover, it is evident that it was in the desert or in a mountain solitude that God revealed hidden truths to man (cf. Gn 32:25-31; Ex 3; 24:1-8; 34:5-9; 1 K 19:8-13; Lk 2: 7-9; Mt 17:1-8). These in fact are places in which heaven and earth seem to merge, where the world, in virtue of Christ's presence, rises from its condition of arid earth and becomes paradise anew (cf. Mk 1:13). How then can contemplatives be considered alien to mankind, if in them mankind achieves its fulfilment?

But however much contemplatives are entrenched, so to speak, in the heart of the world, still more so are they in the heart of the Church. Their prayers, particularly their participation in the Eucharistic sacrifice of Christ and their liturgical recitation of the Divine Office, constitute the fulfilment of a function essential to the ecclesial community, namely, the glorification of God. This in fact is the prayer that renders to the Father, through the Son and in the Holy Spirit, "a choice sacrifice of praise." Those who worship in this way are admitted to the intimacy of the ineffable conversation which Our Lord has unendingly with His heavenly Father, and in whose bosom He pours out His infinite love. This, in a word, is the prayer which is like an apex toward which converges the universal activity of the Church. In this way contemplative religious, bearing witness to the intimate life of the Church, are indispensable to the fulness of its presence.

Furthermore, by vivifying the entire Mystical Body by the fervor of their love, and by bolstering the various efforts of the apostolate, which are indeed nothing without charity (cf. 1 Cor 13:1-3), contemplatives raise the level of the spiritual life of the whole Church. "In the heart of the Church, my Mother, I shall be love," exclaimed the Saint who, without ever having stepped outside of her convent, was nevertheless declared by Pope Pius XI Patroness of all the Missions. Did not God through His charity, manifested in such proportions as to entail the sacrifice of His Son on the Cross, deliver all men from sin? Therefore, when one steeps himself in this paschal mystery of the supreme love of God for man (cf. Jn 13:1; 15:13), he necessarily participates in the redemptive mission of Christ's passion, which is the beginning of every apostolate.

Finally, religious engaged in contemplation alone sustain through their prayers the missionary activity of the Church, "for it is God who sends workers into His harvest when He is asked to do so, who opens the minds of non-Christians to hear the Gospel, and who makes the word of salvation fruitful in their hearts." In solitude, where they are devoted to prayer, contemplatives are never forgetful of their brothers. If they have withdrawn from frequent contact with their fellow men, it is not because they were seeking themselves and their own comfort, or peace and quiet for their own sake, but because, on the contrary, they were intent on sharing to a more universal degree the fatigue, the misery and the hopes of all mankind.

IV.

Truly great, therefore, is the mystery of the contemplative life. And whereas its eminent role in the economy of salvation emerges along general lines from the foregoing remarks, the mystery is seen to be enacted in a very special way in the case of cloistered nuns. These women, in fact, by their very nature, portray in a more meaningful way the mystery of the Church, the "spotless spouse of the spotless Lamb," and, seated at the Lord's feet and listening to His teaching (cf. Lk 10:39) in silence and withdrawal, seek and savor the things that are above where their lives are hidden with Christ in God, until they appear in glory with their Spouse. It is woman's role to receive the word rather than to carry it to the far ends of the earth, even though she can be summoned successfully to the latter vocation. It is her place to become thoroughly and intimately acquainted with the word and to render it fruitful, in a very clear, vivid and feminine way. For in fact, once she has attained full maturity, woman intuits more keenly the needs of others and the assistance which they hope for. Hence, she expresses more clearly the fidelity of the Church toward her Spouse, and at the same time is endowed with a more acute sense of the fruitfulness of the contemplative life. On this account the Church, as is apparent from her Liturgy, has always had particular regard for the Christian virgin. Highlighting the divine jealousy surrounding her, the Church has safeguarded with special solicitude her withdrawal from the world and the enclosure of her convent.

At this point it is impossible to pass over in silence the Blessed Virgin Mary, who welcomed into her bosom the Word of God. "Full of Faith, and conceiving Christ first in her mind before in her womb," a garden enclosed, a sealed fountain, a closed gate (cf. Sg 4:12; Ez 44:1-2), "in faith and charity she is the Church's model and excellent exemplar." The Blessed Virgin exhibits herself as a splendid model of the contemplative life, and a venerable liturgical tradition, both in the Eastern Church and the Western, appropriately applies to her these words from the Gospel: "Mary has chosen the better part" (Lk 10:38-42).

V.

Still another aspect intrinsic to the mystery of the contemplative life must be illustrated, namely, the importance of the sign and witness by which contemplatives, though especially commissioned by God to pray, are not for that reason excluded from the "apostolate of the word," even though they do not engage in direct public preaching.

In present-day society, which so easily rejects God and denies His existence, the life of men and women completely dedicated to the contemplation of eternal truth constitutes an open profession of the reality of both His existence and His presence, since such a life seeks that loving intimacy with God which "bears witness with our spirit that we are children of God" (Rm 8:16). Hence, whoever leads such a life can efficaciously reassure both those who suffer

temptations against faith and those who through error are led
to be skeptical as to whatever possibility man might have of con-
versing with the transcendent God.

Through such wondrous conversation with God, men and women
dedicated exclusively to contemplation in silence and solitude, and
to the practice of charity and the other Christian virtues, proclaim
the death of the Lord until He comes. And indeed, so much the
more do they proclaim it, since their entire life, dedicated to an
unremitting quest for God, is nothing other than a journey to the
heavenly Jerusalem and an anticipation of the eschatological Church
immutable in its possession and contemplation of God. Furthermore,
contemplatives do not only preach to the world the goal to be
reached, that is, eternal life, but they likewise indicate the way
that leads to it. If the spirit of the beatitudes, which animates
the discipleship of Christ, is to vivify any and every form of Christian life, the life of the contemplative testifies that such can be
put into practice even during one's earthly existence. This witness
will exercise a more forceful influence on men of our times to the
degree that it is collective, or rather, social. It is not, in fact, the
witness of the individual that attracts the men of today, but the
witness, fruit of a life led together with others, of a given community, or better still, of a given society already firmly established,
which, in virtue of its continuity and vigor, confirms the validity
of the principles upon which it is founded. Such indeed is the witness of the contemplative community, which Paul VI appropriately
described at Monte Cassino, speaking of "a small, ideal society in
which at last reign love, obedience, innocence, freedom from
created things, and the art of turning them to good use, in which
prevail the spirit, peace, and—in a word—the Gospel."

Yet it is easy to understand that the specific and definite commitment which is assumed in the cloistered life cannot originate
from, and still less thrive in, any ephemeral type of fervor whatever. On the contrary, it must be the product of mature reflection
and unfaltering decisiveness which enable one to renounce certain
social advantages known and esteemed at their true value. Such
maturity is required in order that this type of life be chosen with
perfect liberty of spirit in which the religious consumes his entire

earthly existence clinging to Christ alone and occupied with the affairs of heaven. On this account, vocations for the cloistered life of nuns must be placed under lengthy and careful probation, in order that the motives by which they are led become clearly discerned, and those candidates be duly excluded who, perhaps unknowingly, are not inspired by sufficiently clear and supernatural considerations, which as a result may well stand in the way of their spiritual and human development. The useful precautions prescribed by the statutes of each Institute are to be observed, not only for the admission of postulants but especially before the religious pronounce their perpetual vows.

All that is set forth in this Instruction is applicable to every Institute dedicated wholly to the contemplative life. Every religious family, nevertheless, has its own particular characteristics, determined in many instances by the Founder himself, and these must be faithfully respected. Nor is the possibility denied that within the Church, through the inspiration of the Holy Spirit, new forms of the contemplative life may originate in the future.

Thus the elements that distinguish one Institute from another are indeed recognized as legitimate, since they constitute a splendid array of variety, arising principally, as is evident, from the practical importance which each Institute attributes to mental prayer or to liturgical worship, to life led in common or characterized by elements of eremetical solitude, these being factors of diversity readily compatible with the structures of monasticism. Differences without doubt further depend on the manner in which each Institute conceives and observes material separation from the world by means of enclosure.

VI.

Confirming, then, the prescriptions of the Second Vatican Council regarding the observance and adaptation of the enclosure, which is a tried and unquestionable advantage for the contemplative life, the Sacred Congregation for Religious and Secular Institutes has undertaken to legislate the following norms approved by Pope Paul VI on July 12, 1969, for cloistered nuns dedicated wholly to contemplation.

NORMS REGULATING PAPAL ENCLOSURE OF NUNS

"The papal enclosure of convents is to be regarded as an ascetical regulation particularly consistent with the special vocation of nuns, in that it is the sign, the safeguard and the characteristic form of their withdrawal from the world" (Motu Proprio *Ecclesiae Sanctae,* II, no. 30).

1) The enclosure reserved for nuns totally dedicated to contemplation (*Perfectae Caritatis,* 16) is called papal since the norms that govern it must be sanctioned by apostolic authority, even though they are established or are to be established by particular law, by which are fitly expressed the characteristics proper to each Institute.

2) The law of papal enclosure applies to all that part of the house inhabited by the nuns, together with the gardens and orchards, access to which is reserved to the nuns themselves.

3) The area of the convent subject to the law of enclosure must be circumscribed in such a way that material separation be ensured (M.P. *Ecclesiae Sanctae,* II, 31), that is, all coming in and going out must be thereby rendered impossible (e.g., by a wall or some other effective means, such as a fence of planks or heavy iron mesh, or a thick and firmly rooted hedge). Only through doors kept regularly locked may one enter or leave the enclosure.

4) The mode of ensuring this effective separation, especially as far as choir and parlor are concerned, is to be specified in the Constitutions and in supplementary legislative documents, particular consideration being given to the diversity of each Institute's traditions and to the various circumstances of time and place (e.g., grates, lattice-work, stationary partitions, etc.). In conformity with article 1, however, the means of separation mentioned above must be previously submitted for the approval of the Sacred Congregation for Religious and Secular Institutes.

5) In virtue of the law of enclosure, the nuns, novices and postulants must live within the confines of the convent circumscribed by the enclosure itself, nor may they licitly go beyond them, except in the cases provided for by law (cf. art. 7).

6) The law of enclosure likewise forbids anyone, of whatever

class, condition, sex or age, to enter the cloistered area of the convent, except in the cases provided for by law (cf. arts. 8 and 9).

7) Besides cases provided for by particular indults from the Holy See, those mentioned in article 5 may leave the enclosure:

a) in case of very grave and imminent danger;

b) with permission of the Superior, and with at least habitual consent of the local Ordinary and of the regular superior, if there is one:

1. to consult physicians or to undergo medical treatment, provided that this is done locally or in the vicinity of the convent;

2. to accompany a sick nun, if real necessity so demands;

3. to perform manual labor or to exercise necessary surveillance in places situated outside the enclosure, yet on the premises of the convent;

4. to exercise one's civil rights;

5. to conduct business transactions which cannot be handled otherwise. Except for purposes of medical treatment, if absence from the enclosure is to be prolonged for more than one week, the Superior must previously obtain the consent of the local Ordinary and of the regular superior, if there is one.

c) except in the cases referred to under (b), the Superior must seek permission from the local Ordinary, and, if there is one, from the regular superior, by whom such permission may be granted only if there is really a serious reason, and then for just as brief a period as is necessary;

d) all absences permitted in accordance with clauses (a), (b), and (c) of this article may not be prolonged beyond three months without the authorization of the Holy See.

8) Besides cases provided for by particular indults of the Holy See, the following are permitted to enter the cloister:

a) Cardinals, who may likewise introduce their retinue; nuncios and apostolic delegates, in the areas of their own jurisdiction;

b) reigning sovereigns or heads of State, together with their wives and retinue;

c) the local Ordinary and the regular superior, for a reasonable motive;

d) canonical visitors at the time of the visitation, but only for inspection, and provided that they be accompanied by a male religious;

e) a priest, together with servers, to administer the sacraments to the sick or to hold funeral services. A priest may likewise be admitted to assist those religious suffering from a chronic or grave illness;

f) a priest, together with servers, to conduct liturgical processions, if such is requested by the Superior;

g) physicians and all others whose work or skill is required to provide for the needs of the convent, with the permission of the Superior and under the surveillance of the local Ordinary and, if there is one, of the regular superior;

h) sisters employed in the external service of the convent, in accordance with the statutes of each Institute.

9) Any particular law approved by the Holy See in accordance with article 1 may, in conformity with the spirit and characteristics of each Institute, either determine stricter prescriptions regarding enclosure, or sanction other instances in which one may enter or leave the enclosure legitimately, in order to provide for the needs of the convent or to further the good of the nuns themselves.

10) The use of the radio and television, in convents of nuns dedicated totally to the contemplative life, may be permitted only in circumstances of a religious nature.

11) Newspapers, magazines and other publications must not be either too numerous or admitted indiscriminately (cf. *Inter Mirifica*, 4). By such means, in fact, even the best religious communities can be permeated with and disturbed by the spirit of worldliness.

12) Meetings and conventions of any kind which can hardly be reconciled with the cloistered life are to be prudently avoided. If, however, current circumstances seem to justify it, nuns might sometimes, after having obtained the necessary permission, be authorized to assist at those meetings which will truly benefit the cloistered life, provided such absences from the convent do not

become too frequent. The Superiors are to bear in mind that the purity and fervor of the cloistered life depend to a great extent on the strict observance of the rules of enclosure. On this account, leaving the premises of the convent must always remain an exception.

13) The law of enclosure entails a serious obligation in conscience, for both the nuns and outsiders.

14) During the canonical visitation, whereas the Visitor must inspect the material cloister, the Superior is to report to him on the observance of the cloister prescriptions, presenting for his examination the book in which must be faithfully recorded all the instances of entering and leaving the enclosure.

15) Since the Church holds the cloistered contemplative life in great esteem, she highly praises those nuns who, updating their cloistered life in ways ever more consistent with their contemplative vocation, maintain, nevertheless, full and reverent respect for their withdrawal from the world (*Perfectae Caritatis*, 7). Those, on the other hand, who have both the right and the duty to supervise observance of the cloister laws, namely, the local Ordinary and, if there is one, the regular superior, are earnestly exhorted by the Church to safeguard such observance with the greatest diligence, and to lend, in accordance with their duty, their valuable assistance to the Superior, who is directly responsible for the enforcement of the enclosure laws.

16) Until the promulgation of the new Code of Canon Law, the penalties established for those who violate the nuns' enclosure will be inoperative.

17) Regarding the mode of procedure in updating the cloistered life, let the norms specified in part II, numbers 9, 10 and 11 of the Motu Proprio *Ecclesiae Sanctae* be faithfully observed. With reference to number 6 of the same Motu Proprio, however, experiments contrary to what is established by the present norms, which are to constitute the general law, cannot be undertaken without permission previously obtained from the Holy See.

Furthermore, those convents which have already introduced certain innovations with a view to updating papal enclosure are hereby obliged to submit such modifications to the judgment of the Sacred Congregation for Religious and Secular Institutes within six months from the date of publication of the present Instruction.

H. Card. ANTONIUTTI
Prefect

Rome, August 15, 1969

Formal Reply to Dubia Concerning Instruction *Venite Seorsum*

SACRED CONGREGATION FOR RELIGIOUS
AND SECULAR INSTITUTES

Rome, January 2, 1970

Most Reverend Luigi Raimondi
Apostolic Delegate to the U.S.A.

Your Excellency,

After the Sacred Congregation had promulgated its Instruction "VENITE SEORSUM" concerning the contemplative life and the papal enclosure of cloistered nuns, some bishops, priests, and religious proposed certain questions regarding the application of this Instruction. In order to allay all anxieties and to strengthen the cloistered nuns, I think it necessary to communicate to you the following clarifications on this matter.

1. The Instruction "Venite Seorsum" was prepared by order of Pope Paul VI, and certain norms which were added to it, were approved by the Supreme Pontiff on July 12, 1969, in such a way that these norms constitute the current law concerning the papal enclosure of cloistered nuns.

2. These norms which were established after careful examination of the wishes of cloistered nuns were welcomed with great satisfaction by the vast majority of monasteries, as is evidenced by numerous letters freely and spontaneously sent from all parts of the world to the Supreme Pontiff and to this Sacred Congregation.

3. However, there are some monasteries which have petitioned certain modifications regarding definite circumstances of time and place in the application of these Norms. Account will be taken of

these petitions when their Constitutions will be submitted to the Apostolic See for approval.

4. Some monasteries—very few however—have expressed discontent with the Instruction concerning the enclosure. As a result of mature deliberation and with the approval of the Supreme Pontiff, such monasteries will be permitted to transfer to another type of religious life after their original canonical status has been abandoned.

5. The Norms added to the Instruction *Venite Seorsum* and approved by the Supreme Pontiff by no means derogate from the provisions granted in the motu proprio, *Pastorale Munus*. According to an express interpretation made by the Supreme Pontiff in an audience of March 7, 1967, the following faculties must be respected, namely:

1) For just and grave reasons advanced by cloistered nuns, Bishops can permit them to go out from the cloister, but they cannot force the nuns to do so.

2) The reasons for permission to go outside the cloister, which are stated in the Instruction "Inter cetera" no. 24. (A.A.S. 38; 1956, pp. 516-517) still obtain, except that no longer is it necessary to have recourse to the Holy See, but the Bishops can grant this permission.

The Supreme Pontiff Paul VI deigned to confirm this interpretation in an audience on November 13, 1969, and also to approve and confirm it at a later date.

While I impart to you this information to be shared with all Ordinaries and monasteries within your territory, I exhort Your Excellency with all my power to promote the advancement of the contemplative life of cloistered nuns by supporting and defending them in their holy commitment.

Assuring you on this occasion of my sincere sentiments of deep esteem, I remain,

> Devotedly yours,
> Cardinal Antoniutti
> *Prefect*

THE ARCHDIOCESE OF ST. LOUIS
4445 Lindell Boulevard
St. Louis, Missouri 63108

May 6, 1970

Dear Sister:

Recently, the Sacred Congregation for Religious and Secular Institutes addressed a letter to me as Chairman of the Pontifical Commission for renewal among our contemplative religious. It was signed by Cardinal Antoniutti as Prefect of the Congregation and Father Heston as Secretary. I think it may be well for me to quote from the letter some pertinent comments and suggestions which were made.

After thanking the Commission for the study made, Cardinal Antoniutti had the following to say:

"We are deeply grateful to Your Eminence, to the other members of the Commission and to your zealous collaborators for the generosity with which you undertook this study on behalf of religious dedicated to the contemplative life and for the serious and disinterested efforts which made this research so profitable. The replies of the Nuns, summarized with such precision and care, eloquently confirm other information previously received at this Office and emphasize the opportuneness and necessity of the Instruction *Venite Seorsum.*

"From the statements of the Nuns themselves, as found in the survey, many invaluable insights have emerged, and the Sacred Congregation for Religious and for Secular Institutes is grateful for this composite picture of the status of contemplatives in the United States. May we ask Your Eminence to communicate this to the Nuns in the name of this Sacred Congregation, and express our appreciation for their cooperation and for the numerous and beautiful letters sent after the publication of *Venite Seorsum.*

"We beg you to encourage contemplative women religious to continued fidelity to the ideals of their esteemed vocation."

As you see the Sacred Congregation is deeply appreciative of the responses of our contemplative religious. Archbishop Leo C. Byrne, Bishop Edward Herrmann and myself join in expressing to our contemplative religious the assurance of our prayerful interest and our deep concern for the contemplative life.

We are confident that the vast majority of the contemplative religious in the United States appreciate deeply the loving concern and interest of our Most Holy Father himself for the contemplative life and its continuance as outlined in the Instruction *Venite Seorsum*.

However, it does appear evident that a small number of contemplative religious, without doubt well intentioned, are of a mind which would seek a way of life different from that set forth in the document and have expressed opposition to it.

In his letter of January 2, 1970, which was sent by Cardinal Antoniutti to the Apostolic Delegate and a copy of which was sent to the Superiors of all our contemplative religious in the United States by our Commission, the Cardinal expressed this thought in the following words.

"Some monasteries—actually a few—have expressed opposition to the cloister in the sense of the Instruction. After mature consideration of all the circumstances and by determination of the Holy Father, monasteries of this type may develop another kind of religious life, leaving their traditional canonical form of papal cloister."

You will note, dear Sister, that in his letter Cardinal Antoniutti has asked our Commission to continue our interest in the welfare of the contemplative religious of our country. We wish to assure you of our disposition to assist in this regard as soon as we have further directions from the Sacred Congregation as to their wishes.

May I ask you to communicate the contents of this letter to each member of your community.

With very prayerful good wishes, and commending you to the loving care of Our Lady, as we ask God to bless you, in the name of the Commission I remain,

Sincerely yours in Christ,
John Joseph Cardinal Carberry
Chairman, Pontifical Commission
Archbishop of Saint Louis

7

SACRED CONGREGATION FOR RELIGIOUS
AND SECULAR INSTITUTES

Rome June 13, 1970

His Eminence
John Joseph Cardinal Carberry
Archbishop of Saint Louis

Your Eminence:

It is in a spirit of deep gratitude that I reply to your letter of June 5, thanking Your Eminence not only for your correspondence of that date and the information accompanying it, but particularly for the dedicated spirit with which you are so splendidly serving and supporting the interest of contemplative nuns in the United States.

The letters of request and inquiry being received by Your Eminence from contemplatives is clearly indicative of the great confidence these good sisters are placing in you.

This Sacred Congregation also appreciates your delicate position, particularly at this time, when certain difficult situations are developing in some monasteries due to the fact that a few nuns are opposed to the cloister in the sense of the Instruction "Venite Seorsum."

In order that there may be no misinterpretation of the statement of the Cardinal Prefect of this Sacred Congregation in his letter of January 2, that those in opposition to the Norms attached to the Instruction ". . . may develop another kind of religious life, leaving their traditional canonical form of papal cloister," we wish to clarify briefly for Your Eminence the three questions which you raised in your recent letter.

a) The development of some other form of contemplative life not in conformity with the ideals and norms set forth in *Venite Seorsum* may not be done within any presently existing community.

b) If a new form of the contemplative life is desired and sought, the establishment of a totally new community without any relationship whatever to any existing contemplative community is expected and required.

c) The proper procedure to be followed by nuns who wish to experiment with new forms of contemplative life not in conformity with the Instruction "Venite Seorsum" and its norms is to petition the Sacred Congregation for Religious for dispensation from their vows and subsequently, to request of the Ordinary in whose diocese they would hope to initiate their experiment, permission to establish themselves in his diocese and under his jurisdiction, launching their new foundation as a Pious Union.

It is the mind of this Sacred Congregation that authentic contemplative life, the glory of the Church for centuries, can be maintained at its holiest only with such prudent and careful precautions. At the same time we are confident that, in this same way, what might be prompted by the Spirit of God in these times will thereby not be suppressed or lost.

Availing myself of this opportunity to express to Your Eminence my deepest gratitude and prayerful good wishes, I remain

> Faithfully yours in Christ,
> E. Heston, C.S.C.
> Secretary

THE ARCHDIOCESE OF ST. LOUIS
4445 LINDELL BOULEVARD
ST. LOUIS, MO. 68108

August 3, 1970

Reverend and dear Sister Superior:

Following upon our letter of May 6, 1970 to you, several inquiries were received from contemplative religious which contained requests for further information as to the procedure to be followed should a new form of contemplative life not in conformity with the norms of *Venite Seorsum* wish to be established.

These requests were presented to the Sacred Congregation for Religious by our Commission in a letter of June 5, 1970. Under the date of June 13, an answer was received which clearly outlines the steps to be followed.

The Sacred Congregation for Religious, through the Apostolic

Delegation, has directed that our Commission advise you and your sisters of the contents of this letter of June 13, 1970. Accordingly, we are sending the enclosed copy of the letter to you and your community.

It may be well for us to point out that our Commission has no faculties either to dispense or to approve new foundations. Such requests will be handled in the usual manner, as set forth in Father Heston's letter.

We sincerely trust that these latest directives will be of assistance to our contemplative religious whose prayers we treasure and whose lives of dedication and sacrifice are obtaining from God untold graces for the Church in these trying days. The Papal Cloister indeed is a precious form of life—a form of life the Holy See wishes to protect. But at the same time the Holy See is disposed to hear and study requests for other forms of contemplative life distinct from and not under the Papal enclosure.

In the name of Archbishop Leo C. Byrne, Bishop Edward J. Herrmann, our priest consultants, and myself, I ask God to bless you, and request a remembrance in your prayers.

> Devotedly yours in Our Lady,
> John Joseph Cardinal Carberry
> Chairman, Pontifical Commission
> Archbishop of Saint Louis

> THE ARCHDIOCESE OF ST. LOUIS
> 4445 LINDELL BOULEVARD
> ST. LOUIS MO. 63108

> August 14, 1970

Your Excellency:

To keep you fully informed of the work of the Pontifical Commission for Contemplative Religious Women, I am sending you a copy of a letter received from Father Edward Heston, C.S.C., Secretary for the Sacred Congregation for Religious, together with the covering letter addressed to all Superiors of Houses of Contemplative Religious Women in the United States.

The Pontifical Commission had asked the Sacred Congregation for clarification on the proper procedure for contemplatives who might wish to adopt a new form of contemplative life not in accord with the norms of "Venite Seorsum." I am sure you will find Father Heston's reply most informative.

May I also share with you suggestions made by Cardinal Antoniutti, Prefect of the Sacred Congregation for Religious, which were communicated to our Commission by His Excellency, the Most Reverend Apostolic Delegate.

a.) "His Eminence noted the seeming need to warn the Nuns of the dangers involved in 'sensitivity training.' The techniques used suggest an incompatibility not only with the contemplative life but with every form of consecrated life.

b. "The Sacred Congregation is also concerned because of the repeated requests about the formation of the Nuns into associations or other groupings which distract them from their specific purpose and, little by little, deprive the Church of the riches of contemplation and petition which flourish in the cloistered monasteries.

c.) "A more natural and effective way to renewal would be by way of federations within the various Orders. In accord with the decree 'Perfectae Caritatis' and the motu proprio 'Ecclesiae Sanctae' the Sacred Congregation is providing for the revision of the various Constitutions and Directories. Further, it is not in confrontation or a multiplication of assemblies that the Nuns will find renewal; rather, they should seek it in a sincere and faithful application to their own sound traditions.

d.) "Finally, Cardinal Antoniutti adverts to a delicate and difficult aspect of this situation, i.e., the problem of trying to make sure that those who speak to the Nuns about renewal are themselves imbued with a proper understanding of the teaching of the Church."

I have quoted rather extensively from the letter of the Apostolic Delegate to give you the opportunity of knowing the mind of Cardinal Antoniutti and the Sacred Congregation for Religious in these matters.

I trust that this information may be of assistance to all of us as we make every sincere effort to guard and protect the vocation to the contemplative life in the Church.

With personal best wishes, I am,

> Devotedly yours in Our Lady,
> John Joseph Cardinal Carberry
> Chairman, Pontifical Commission
> for Contemplative Religious

THE ARCHDIOCESE OF ST. LOUIS
4445 Lindell Boulevard
ST. LOUIS, MO. 63108

March 17, 1972

Reverend and dear Sister:

I am pleased to be able to inform you that a "Special Commission for Contemplative Nuns in the United States" has been established by the Sacred Congregation for Religious and Secular Institutes.

The members of this Commission are: John Joseph Cardinal Carberry, Bishops James J. Byrne, Leo C. Byrne, William W. Baum, Edward J. Herrmann, Martin N. Lohmuller and John J. Ward.

May I ask that you share this information with the members of your Community.

In the course of its work, the Commission will enlist the assistance of qualified religious men who are considered to be experts in various areas. And consultation will be sought from the religious women themselves as often as will be possible.

The formation of this Special Commission results from one of the specific recommendations submitted in the *Report* prepared for the Sacred Congregation for Religious by our first Commission. May I quote from the text of that recommendation:

"It is recommended that consideration be given to the formation of a *Commission* or *Board* that would seek to work with the Contemplative religious women in the United States toward the development of programs which would assist them without intruding on their particular spirit.

"The Pontifical Commission envisages such a *Commission* or *Board* as making proposals about the recruiting of vocations, screening of applicants, basics of formation, on-going education, and about matters of practical concern, e.g., arts and crafts, mental health, etc."

The Special Commission recently held its initial meeting in Washington, D.C. As the very first matter of business, it was decided to inform the Contemplative Religious Women of the existence of this Commission. By means of this letter, we also wish to seek your cooperation and your assistance. The Commission plans to meet again during the Bishops' meeting in Atlanta in mid-April. We would be most pleased to receive from you any suggestions or recommendations you might wish to submit to this Commission. Please feel completely free to make such known to us. You may wish to address any correspondence directly to me or to any members of this Commission.

On our part, we pledge to keep you informed of our efforts in your behalf. We earnestly request a special remembrance in all your prayers and good works so that the Holy Spirit will guide us in our work and that the Contemplative vocation will profit from our efforts.

With prayerful good wishes, and asking God to bless each of you in your special vocation, I remain,

> Sincerely yours in Christ,
> John Joseph Cardinal Carberry
> Archbishop of Saint Louis

SPECIAL COMMISSION FOR CONTEMPLATIVE NUNS IN THE UNITED STATES
April 14, 1972 (Revised: July 20, 1972)

PREAMBLE

The Special Commission for Contemplative Nuns in the United States was established by the Holy See to aid, encourage and be of service to the monasteries of contemplative religious women in the United States (Letter of the Apostolic Delegate to Cardinal

Carberry, November 3, 1971, no. 2590/71).

The Commission shall always respect the rights of the nuns themselves, of the Ordinaries of the dioceses, and major religious superiors.

GOAL

The goal of this Special Commission shall be the greater honor and glory of God and the strengthening and growth of the particular churches in the United States of America through the accomplishment of the Commission's objectives with regard to the monasteries of contemplative nuns in this nation.

OBJECTIVES

1. To be of service to monasteries of contemplative women religious in the United States.

a. Providing assistance in the development of a well balanced program of religious, liturgical and cultural formation in accord with the documents issued by the Holy See.

b. By initiating research and study with respect to the recruitment of vocations, screening of applicants and matters of practical concern, e.g., diet, arts and crafts, mental health, etc.

c. By responding, within the limits of its competency, to requests from individual monasteries or federations of monasteries seeking assistance from the Commission.

2. To be of service to the Bishops of the dioceses.

a. By recommending how they can work to effect a closer unity of the nuns and their particular bishop and to help the nuns to identify with the local Church to which they belong.

b. By proposing to them ways in which they are able to encourage the nuns in their own dioceses to fidelity to their specific vocation and can foster vocations to the contemplative life.

c. By responding to requests from individual bishops seeking assistance with regard to specific monasteries in their dioceses.

3. To be of service to major superiors of first Orders in similar ways, (cf. no. 2, above).

4. To be of service to the Holy See by carrying out specific requests directed by the Holy See to the Special Commission.

5. To initiate proposals and, if necessary, programs designed to preserve and strengthen contemplative religious communities in the United States.

PART FIVE

PRINCIPLES FOR AUTHENTIC ADAPTATION
IN RELIGIOUS LIFE THROUGH DEVELOPMENT OF LATENT
DYNAMISMS, WITHOUT LOSS OF IDENTITY,
BY RENEWAL OF THE GENUINE AND COMPLETE VOCATION
TO RELIGIOUS LIFE RECOGNIZED AND
APPROVED BY CHRIST'S BODY, THE CHURCH

PRINCIPLES FOR AUTHENTIC AND EFFECTIVE
EXPERIMENTATION IN SEARCH OF RENEWAL IN THE
PURSUIT OF PERFECT CHARITY

CHAPTER 14

NORMS FOR ADAPTATION

General Principles relevant to renewal and appropriate adaptation in regard to:

    a. various forms of religious life, PC nos. 7-11

    b. basic elements, PC nos. 12-15

    c. other elements PC nos. 7-17

    d. formation, PC no. 18

    e. apostolic works, PC no. 20

Norms for renewal and appropriate adaptation affirm need for religious of mature personality wholly dedicated by a vowed life of the evangelical counsels to God and the Church through:

    a. the continual development of the baptismal grace of each to full maturity in Christ. LG, nos. 3, 44, 46; PC, nos. 2, 5, 14, 25.

    b. fidelity to the charism of one's vocation to religious life in relation to the charism of the founder of one's institute as interpreted and guided by the living teaching authority of the Church.

ALL FITTING ADAPTATION IS THE EXPRESSION AND EFFECT OF *AUTHENTIC* RENEWAL IN THE CONSECRATED VOWED LIFE OF RELIGIOUS

(Cf. LG, no. 43)

PC 3. The manner of living, praying, and working should be suitably adapted to the physical and psychological conditions of today's religious and also, to the extent required by the nature of each community, to the needs of the apostolate, the requirements of a given culture, the social and economic circumstances anywhere, but especially in missionary territories.

The way in which communities are governed should also be re-examined in the light of these same standards.

For this reason constitutions, directories, custom books, books of prayers and ceremonies, and similar compilations are to be suitably revised and brought into harmony with the documents of this sacred Synod. This task will require the suppression of outmoded regulations.

PC 4. Successful renewal and proper adaptation cannot be achieved unless every member of a community cooperates.

In the work of appropriate renewal, it is the responsibility of competent authorities alone, especially of general chapters, to issue norms, to pass laws, and to allow for a right amount of prudent experimentation, though in all such matters, according to the norm of law, the approval of the Holy See and of local Ordinaries must be given when it is required. In decisions which involve the future of an institute as a whole, superiors should in appropriate manner consult the members and give them a hearing.

For the suitable renewal of convents of nuns, their wishes and recommendations can also be ascertained from meetings of federations or from other assemblies lawfully convoked.

Let all bear in mind, however, that the hope of renewal must be lodged in a more diligent observance of rule and of constitution rather than in a multiplication of individual laws.

Accommodation Means Activating Latent Power

ET 51. Beloved sons and daughters in Christ, religious life, to be renewed, should accommodate accidental forms to certain changes which, with increasing speed and widening extent, affect the conditions of any human life. But you will not be able to achieve this, while preserving "the stable forms of living" recognized by the Church, except by renewal of the genuine and complete vocation proper to your institutes. For the accommodation of any living being to the surroundings in which it lives does not consist in losing its true identity, but in being strengthened by the vital power peculiar to itself. Keenly perceiving the current tendencies of thought and the present desires of mankind, you must see to it that from your own wellsprings will arise forces latent with a new energy. Though perfectly aware of the difficulties, such a task is enough to set one's soul on fire.

Vitalizing the External Forms of Religious Life

ET 12. It is precisely from this source that each and every religious family will draw its own distinctive dynamic power. For although a divine vocation is renewed and expressed according to changing circumstances of place and time, nevertheless it always demands a certain constancy of direction. The generosity of soul which responds to a vocation opens up in a person's life certain basic and distinctive paths he can choose to follow. Maintaining fidelity to the elements which these paths require is the acid test by which the authentic character of religious life is preserved. Let us not forget that any human institution is subject to the weakness of becoming set in its ways and liable to accumulate a certain amount of needless customs. For external care in the observance of laws is not, of itself, sufficient to protect the excellence of a particular kind of life and the constancy of its nature in operation. Consequently these external forms must be regularly vitalized by this internal exertion of spirit, without which the externals quickly become an excessive burden.

In all this variety of forms which give each institute its individual character, and which have their root in the fulness of the grace of Christ, the highest rule of the religious life and its most certain norm must remain the following of Christ according to the teaching of the Gospel. Has it not been just this concern that, over the centuries, created the demand for a chaste and poor life dedicated to obedience?

Value of Religious Customs

ET 36. Assuredly this is the force and meaning of the customs by which the order of your daily life is carried out. An alert and attentive conscience, instead of viewing them only from the one aspect of obligating rule, judges their value from the benefits they confer since they provide the means for increased spiritual growth. Yet this must be said: religious observances require more than a suitable training of reason or education of will. They call for a person's so truly entering into them that even in the deepest core of his spirit he patterns his life on the Gospel beatitudes.

Need to Modify Some Externals

ET 5. Certainly not a few external elements recommended by the founders of orders and religious congregations are seen today as obsolete. Some of these, accumulated over the centuries, which have oppressed religious life and made it inflexible, should be modified. Accommodations must be made. New forms can even be sought and instituted with the approval of the Church. For some years now the greater part of religious institutes have eagerly pursued this very goal—sometimes too boldly—of introducing by way of experiment a new approach to the constitutions and rules. We know well and are following with careful attention these efforts at renewal desired by the Council.

LETTER OF POPE PAUL VI INTRODUCING
HIS *MOTU PROPRIO, ECCLESIAE SANCTAE*

The governing of holy Church, following the conclusion of the Second Ecumenical Vatican Council, demands indeed that new norms be established and that new adjustments be made to meet relationships introduced by the Council and which will be more and more adapted to the new goals and areas of the apostolate which through the Council have been opened up to the Church in the modern world. Because of great changes this world is in need of a shining light and longs for the supernatural flame of charity.

Prompted therefore by these considerations, as soon as the Ecumenical Council ended we appointed study commissions to apply their learning and experience to determine to the best of their ability definite norms for the implementation of the decrees of the Council for which a suspension of the effects of the law (*vacatio legis*) had been decreed. As we gladly wrote in the letter issued *motu proprio* last June 10 beginning with the words *Munus Apostolicum* those commissions devoted themselves diligently to their assigned task, and at the appointed time informed us of their conclusions.

After careful consideration of these conclusions we consider that now is the time to publish these norms. However since this involves matters pertaining to discipline, an area in which experience can still offer more suggestions, and since on the other hand a special commission is engaged in revising and improving the Code of Canon Law in which all the laws of the Church will be arranged in a more consistent, and suitable, and at the same time definitive manner, we think that we will be acting wisely and prudently if we publish these norms on an experimental basis. During this interval it will be the right of episcopal conferences to make known to us their observations and comments which the implementation of the norms will perhaps suggest to be made and to present new measures to us.

Therefore after carefully examining the matter, *motu proprio* and by our apostolic authority we decree and promulgate the following norms for the implementation of the decrees of the Council which begin with these words: *Christus Dominus* (On the Bishops' Pastoral Office in the Church), *Presbyterorum Ordinis* (On the Life and Ministry of Priests), *Perfectae Caritatis* (On the Adaptation and Renewal of Religious Life) and *Ad Gentes Divinitus* (On the Missionary Activity of the Church), and we command that they be observed by way of experiment, that is, until the new Code of Canon Law is promulgated, unless in the meantime some other provision is to be made by the Apostolic See.

These norms will begin to be in force next October 11, the feast of the Maternity of the Blessed Virgin Mary, on which day the holy Council was begun four years ago by our predecessor of venerable memory, John XXIII.

We order that whatever has been prescribed by us in this letter *Ecclesiae Sanctae* issued *motu proprio* be firm and ratified, all things to the contrary, even those worthy of most special mention, not withstanding.

Given at Rome at St. Peter's, August 6, the feast of the Transfiguration of Our Lord Jesus Christ, 1966, in the fourth year of our pontificate.

POPE PAUL VI

[Fitting adaptation should be seriously considered, implemented and evaluated according to the conciliar, papal, and ecclesial documents contemporary with and following Vatican Council II. PC, nos. 2, 3.—Ed.].

ES 11-1. 15. The norms and spirit to which adaptation and renewal must correspond should be gathered not only from the Decree *Perfectae Caritatis* but also from other documents of the Second Vatican Council, especially from chapters 5 and 6 of the Dogmatic Constitution *Lumen Gentium*.

ES 11-1. 16. The institutes should take care that the principles established in no. 2 of the Decree *Perfectae Caritatis* actually pervade the renewal of their religious life; therefore:

(1) Study and meditation on the Gospels and the whole of Sacred Scripture should be more earnestly fostered by all members from the beginning of their novitiate. Likewise, care should be taken that they share in the mystery and life of the Church in more suitable ways;

(2) The various aspects (theological, historical, canonical, etc.) of the doctrine of the religious life should be investigated and explained.

(3) To achieve the good of the Church, the institutes should strive for a genuine knowledge of their original spirit, so that faithfully preserving this spirit in determining adaptations, their religious life may thus be purified of alien elements and freed from those which are obsolete.

ES 11-1. 17. Those elements are to be considered obsolete which do not constitute the nature and purpose of the institute and which, having lost their meaning and power, are no longer a real help to religious life. Nevertheless, consideration must be given to the witness which the religious state has as its role the obligation of giving.

Adaptations should be made appropriately in relation to:

A. Elements of living *"ratio vivendi"*
> ET nos. 5, 12, 51

B. Ancient traditions
> PC no. 9
> ET no. 36
> ES 11-1, no. 17

C. *"Ratio orandi"*—the order of prayer-life: time; manner of praying in common and/or individually; interior prayer vs. a multiplicity of vocal devotions; liturgical prayer:
> PC nos. 6, 7, 8
> ET nos. 8, 49

I. The Divine Office of Brothers and Sisters

Cf. no. 3 of THE DECREE PERFECTAE CARITATIS

ES 11-11. 20. Although Religious who recite a duly approved Little Office perform the public prayer of the Church (cf. Constitution *Sacrosanctum Concilium,* no. 98), it is nevertheless recommended to the institutes that in place of the Little Office they adopt the Divine Office either in part or in whole so that they may participate more intimately in the liturgical life of the Church. Religious of the Eastern rites, however, should recite the doxologies and the Divine Lauds according to their own typika and customs.

II. Mental Prayer

No. 6 of The Decree PERFECTAE CARITATIS

ES 11-11. 21. In order that Religious may more intimately and fruitfully participate in the most holy mystery of the Eucharist and the public prayer of the Church, and that their whole spiritual life may be nourished more abundantly, a larger place should be given to mental prayer instead of a multitude of prayers, retaining nevertheless the pious exercises commonly accepted in the Church

and giving due care that the members are instructed diligently
in leading a spiritual life.

D. Characteristics of the institute in the perspective of the charism
of its founder
    PC, no. 2; ET, nos. 11, 32; ES, 11;1, nos. 15, 16

E. Apostolic service according to the needs of the Church
    "ratio operandi"
    PC, nos. 8, 9, 10

PC 18. The adaptation and renewal of religious institutes depends
chiefly on the training of their members. Therefore the non-clerical
Religious and Religious women should not be assigned to the works
of the apostolate immediately after the novitiate, but their religious,
apostolic, academic, and professional training, even the earning of
appropriate degrees, should be suitably continued in appropriate
houses.

Lest the adaptation of religious life to the needs of our time
be merely external, and lest those who according to their institute
engage in external apostolates be unequal to carrying out their
assignment, Religious should be suitably instructed, according to
their individual endowment and personal ability, in the usages of
today's social life and ways of expression and thought. Instruction
through the harmonious blending of its component parts should be
imparted in such a way as to contribute to an integrated life of
the Religious.

Throughout their whole life, however, Religious should endeavor
to perfect unceasingly this spiritual, academic, and professional
training and superiors, as far as they are able, should provide
them the opportunity, help, and time for this purpose.

It is likewise the obligation of the superiors to see to it that
moderators, spiritual directors, and teachers be most carefully selected and carefully trained.

PC 20. Religious communities should faithfully retain and carry
out their own specific apostolates, and taking into consideration the
advantage of the universal Church and dioceses, adapt them to
the needs of times and places adopting timely and even new means,

relinquishing, however, those works which today are less in keeping with the spirit and authentic nature of the institute.

(Cf. CD, nos. 33-35)

ES III. 12. Each missionary institute should immediately take steps toward its own adaptation and renewal, particularly regarding its methods of preaching the Gospel and of Christian initiation and its form of community life. (No. 3 of the Decree *Perfectae Caritatis*)

(Cf. AG, nos. 5-9)

AG 5. From the very beginning, the Lord Jesus "called to him men of his own choosing.... And he appointed twelve that they might be with him, and that he might send them forth to preach" (Mk 3:13; cf. Mt 10:1-42). Thus the apostles were the first members of the New Israel, and at the same time the beginning of the sacred hierarchy.

By His death and His resurrection the Lord completed once for all in Himself the mysteries of our salvation and of the renewal of all things. He had received all power in heaven and on earth (cf. Mt 28:18). Now, before He was taken up into heaven (cf. Ac 1:11), He founded His Church as the sacrament of salvation, and sent His apostles into all the world just as He Himself had been sent by His Father (cf. Jn 20:21). He gave them this command: "Go, therefore, and make disciples of all nations, baptizing them in the name of the Father, and of the Son, and of the Holy Spirit, teaching them to observe all that I have commanded you" (Mt 28:19 f.). "Go into the whole world; preach the gospel to every creature. He who believes and is baptized shall be saved, but he who does not believe shall be condemned" (Mk 16:15 f.).

Since then the duty has weighed upon the Church to spread the faith and the saving work of Christ. This duty exists not only in virtue of the express command which was inherited from the apostles by the order of bishops, assisted by priests and united with the successor of Peter and supreme shepherd of the Church. It exists also in virtue of that life which flows from Christ into His members: "From him the whole body (being closely joined and knit together through every joint of the system according to the functioning in due measure of each single part) derives its increase to the building up of itself in love" (Ep 4:16).

The mission of the Church, therefore, is fulfilled by that activity which makes her fully present to all men and nations. She undertakes this activity in obedience to Christ's command and in response to the grace and love of the Holy Spirit. Thus, by the example of her life and by her preaching, by the sacraments and other means of grace, she can lead them to the faith, the freedom, and the peace of Christ. Thus there lies open before them a free and trustworthy road to full participation in the mystery of Christ.

This mission is a continuing one. In the course of history it unfolds the mission of Christ Himself, who was sent to preach the gospel to the poor. Hence, prompted by the Holy Spirit, the Church must walk the same road which Christ walked: a road of poverty and obedience, of service and self-sacrifice to the death, from which death He came forth a victor by His resurrection. For thus did all the apostles walk in hope. On behalf of Christ's body, which is the Church, they supplied what was wanting of the sufferings of Christ by their own many trials and sufferings (cf. Col 1:24). Often, too, the blood of Christians was like a seed.

AG 6. This duty must be fulfilled by the order of bishops, whose head is Peter's successor, and with the prayer and cooperation of the whole Church. This duty is one and the same everywhere and in every situation, even though the variety of situations keeps it from being exercised in the same way. Hence, the differences to be found in this activity of the Church do not result from the inner nature of her mission itself, but are due rather to the circumstances in which this mission is exercised.

NORMS FOR THE IMPLEMENTATION OF
(*AD GENTES DIVINITUS*)

Since the Decree *Ad Gentes Divinitus* (On the Missionary Activity of the Church) of the Holy Second Vatican Council must be in force for the universal Church and be faithfully observed by everyone so that the whole Church may become truly missionary and the entire People of God become aware of its missionary obligation, local Ordinaries should see to it that the Decree comes to the knowledge of all the faithful. Discourses on the Decree should be given to the clergy and sermons preached to the people in which everyone's responsibility in conscience with regard to missionary activity is pointed out and inculcated.

To apply the Decree more readily and faithfully, the following are set down:

ES 111. 1. Mission Theology should be so incorporated in the teaching and development of theological doctrine that the missionary nature of the Church may be fully brought to light. In addition, the Lord's plans of preparing for the Gospel and the possibility of salvation for those to whom the Gospel has not been preached are to be examined and the necessity of evangelization and incorporation in the Church is to be made clear. (Ch. 1 of the Decree *Ad Gentes Divinitus*)

F. The method and system of government—*"ratio regiminis"*

PC, nos. 3, 14; CD, no. 35

ES 11-1. 2. The cooperation of all superiors and members is necessary to renew Religious life in themselves, to prepare the spirit of the chapters, to carry out the works of the chapters, to observe faithfully the laws and norms enacted by the chapters.

ES 11-1. 6. This general chapter has the right to alter certain norms of the constitutions, or among Orientals the norms of the Typika, as an experiment, as long as the purpose, nature and character of the institute are preserved. Experiments contrary to the common law, provided they are to be undertaken prudently, will be willingly permitted by the Holy See as the occasions call for them.

These experiments can be prolonged until the next Ordinary general chapter, which will have the faculty to continue them further but not beyond the chapter immediately following.

ES 11-1. 7. The general council has the same faculty during the time that intervenes between chapters of this kind, in accordance with conditions to be determined by the chapters, and among the Orientals in independent monasteries the Hegumen with the minor Synaxis has this power.

(Cf. ES, nos. 11-1, 18)

SCRSI, February 2, 1972

"An exclusive and collegial form of ordinary government may not be admitted contrary to the prescriptions of canon 516 for a whole religious institute, for a province, or for individual houses, in such a way that the superior, if there is one, is merely an executive. According to the mind of Vatican Council II (Decr. *Perfectae Caritatis*, no. 14) and the Pontifical Exhortation *Evangelica Testificatio*, no. 25, superiors must have personal authority, without prejudice to the practice of legitimate consultation and to the limits placed by common or particular law."

SCRSI, January 17, 1970

"The replacement of the 'local superior' by a 'local coordinator' is not permissible, precisely because the superior, according to the mind of the Second Vatican Council is not merely 'first among equals,' but is one to whom obedience is vowed as a person who holds the place of God."

SCRSI, April 16, 1970

"The mind of the Sacred Congregation for Religious on experimentation with forms of government of local houses is that the office of superior cannot be dispensed with. This, among other things, is made clear in the decree, *Perfectae Caritatis*, no. 14, which, in emphasizing the duties of the superior toward the community, by the very fact reaffirms the necessity of having a superior in a religious house. Both in this decree and in other council documents (see also *Lumen Gentium*, no. 42 dealing with the religious life), the relationships between religious and superiors are such as to be unattainable except in dealing with an individual person duly vested with authority."

SCRSI, January 11, 1972

"With regard to house structure, it is necessary to have a local superior as it is through this office that spiritual leadership should be exercised . . . statutes, of course, should provide for consultation with members of the community, and in houses where the entire community acts as a council, the matters in which collegial decisions will be made should be considered." (cf. E.T. no. 25)

G. Demands of culture, and of social and economic conditions

PC 19. When there is a question of establishing new communities, serious thought must be given to the need for them, or at least to their eminent usefulness, and also to the likelihood that they will prosper. Otherwise, lack of caution will give rise to communities which serve no purpose or are deprived of sufficient vitality.

Where the Church has newly taken root, special attention should be given to the establishment and development of fresh forms of religious life. These should take into account the natural endowments and the manners of the people, and also local customs and circumstances.

AG 10. Sent by Christ to reveal and to communicate the love of God to all men and nations, the Church is aware that there still remains a gigantic missionary task for her to accomplish. For the gospel message has not yet been heard, or scarcely so, by two billion human beings. And their number is increasing daily. These are formed into large and distinct groups by permanent cultural ties, by ancient religious traditions, and by firm bonds of social necessity.

Some of these men are followers of one of the great religions, others remain strangers to the very notion of God, while still others expressly deny His existence, and sometimes even attack it. In order to be able to offer all of them the mystery of salvation and the life brought by God, the Church must become part of all these groups for the same motive which led Christ to bind Himself, in virtue of His Incarnation, to the definite social and cultural conditions of those human beings among whom He dwelt.

ARTICLE 1: CHRISTIAN WITNESS

AG 11. The Church must be present in these groups of men through those of her children who dwell among them or are sent to them. For, wherever they live, all Christians are bound to show forth, by the example of their lives and by the witness of their speech, that new man which they put on at baptism, and that power of the Holy Spirit by whom they were strengthened at confirmation. Thus other men, observing their good works, can glorify the Father (cf. Mt 5:16) and can better perceive the real meaning of human life and the bond which ties the whole community of mankind together.

That they may be able to give this witness to Christ fruitfully, let them be joined to those men by esteem and love, and acknowledge themselves to be members of the group of men among whom they live. Let them share in cultural and social life by the various exchanges and enterprises of human living. Let them be familiar with their national and religious traditions, gladly and reverently laying bare the seeds of the Word which lie hidden in them.

At the same time, however, they should look to the profound changes which are taking place among nations. They should exert themselves lest modern man, overly intent on the science and technology of today's world, become a stranger to things divine. Rather, let them awaken in him a fiercer yearning for that truth and charity which God has revealed.

Christ Himself searched the hearts of men, and led them to divine light through truly human conversation. So also His disciples, profoundly penetrated by the Spirit of Christ, should know the people among whom they live, and should establish contact with them. Thus they themselves can learn by sincere and patient dialogue what treasures a bountiful God has distributed among the nations of the earth. But at the same time, let them try to illumine these treasures with the light of the gospel, to set them free, and to bring them under the dominion of God their Savior.

AG 18. Right from the planting stage of the Church, the religious life should be carefully fostered. This not only confers precious and absolutely necessary assistance on missionary activity. By a more inward consecration made to God in the Church, it also luminously manifests and signifies the inner nature of the Christian calling.

Working to plant the Church, and thoroughly enriched with the treasures of mysticism adorning the Church's religious tradition, religious communities should strive to give expression to these treasures and to hand them on in a manner harmonious with the nature and the genius of each nation. Let them reflect attentively on how Christian religious life may be able to assimilate the ascetic and contemplative traditions whose seeds were sometimes already planted by God in ancient cultures prior to the preaching of the gospel.

Various forms of religious life should be cultivated in a young Church, so that they can display different aspects of Christ's mission and the Church's life, can devote themselves to various pastoral works, and can prepare their members to exercise them rightly. Still, bishops in their Conference should take care that congregations pursuing the same apostolic aims are not multiplied to the detriment of the religious life and the apostolate.

Worthy of special mention are the various projects aimed at helping the contemplative life take root. There are those who while retaining the essential elements of monastic life are bent on implanting the very rich traditions of their own order. Others are returning to simpler forms of ancient monasticism. But all are striving to work out a genuine adaptation to local conditions. For the contemplative life belongs to the fullness of the Church's presence, and should therefore be everywhere established.

AG 23. Every disciple of Christ has the obligation to do his part in spreading the faith. Yet Christ the Lord always calls whomever He chooses from among the number of His disciples, to be with Him and to be sent by Him to preach to the nations (cf. Mk 3:13 f.). Therefore, through the Holy Spirit, who distributes His charismatic gifts as He wills for the common good (1 Cor 12:11), Christ inspires the missionary vocation in the hearts of individuals. At the same time He raises up in the Church certain groups which take as their own special task that duty of preaching the gospel which weighs upon the whole Church.

For there are certain priests, religious, and laymen who are prepared to undertake mission work in their own countries or abroad, and who are endowed with the appropriate natural dispositions, character, and talents. These souls are marked with a special vocation. Sent by legitimate authority, they go out faithfully and obediently to those who are far from Christ. They are set apart for the work to which they have been called (cf. Ac 13:2) as ministers of the gospel, so "that the offering up of the Gentiles may become acceptable, being sanctified by the Holy Spirit" (Rm 15:16).

AG 24. Yet a man must so respond to God's call that, without consulting flesh and blood (cf. Gal 1:16), he can devote himself wholly to the work of the gospel. This response, however, can be made only when the Holy Spirit gives His inspiration and strength. For he who is sent enters upon the life and mission of Him who "emptied himself, taking the nature of a slave" (Ph 2:7). Therefore, he must be ready to stand by his vocation for a lifetime, and to renounce himself and all those whom he thus far considered as his own, and instead to become "all things to all men" (1 Cor 9:22).

Announcing the gospel among the nations, he confidently makes known the mystery of Christ, whose ambassador he is. Thus in Christ he dares to speak as he ought (cf. Ep 6:19 f.; Ac 4:31), and is not ashamed of the scandal of the Cross. Following in his Master's footsteps, meek and humble of heart, he shows that His yoke is easy and His burden light (Mt 11:29 f.). By a truly evangelical life, in much patience, in long-suffering, in kindness, in unaffected love (cf. 2 Cor 6:4f.), he bears witness to his Lord, if need be, to the shedding of his blood. He will ask of God power and strength, so that he may come to know that abounding joy can be found even while he undergoes severe trials and the depths of poverty (cf. 2 Cor 8:2). Let him be convinced that obedience is the hallmark of the servant of Christ, who redeemed the human race by His obedience.

Let the heralds of the gospel not neglect the grace which is in them; they should be renewed day by day in spirit and in mind (cf. 1 Tm 4:14; Ep 4:23; 2 Cor 4:16). Their Ordinaries and superiors should gather the missionaries together at fixed times to strengthen them in the hope of their calling and renew them in the apostolic ministry. Houses should even be built for this purpose.

AG 25. For such an exalted task, the future missionary is to be prepared by a special spiritual and moral training. For he must be ready to take initiatives, constant in the execution of projects, persevering in difficulties, patient and strong of heart in bearing with solitude, fatigue, and fruitful labor. He must bring an open mind and heart to men, and gladly shoulder the duties entrusted to him. He needs a noble spirit for adapting himself to strange customs and changing circumstances. He needs a sympathetic mind and a responsive heart for cooperating with his brethren and with all who dedicate themselves to a common task. Thus, together with the faithful, missionaries will be of one heart and mind (cf. Ac 2:42; 4:32), in imitation of the apostolic community.

Even during a missionary's training period, these attitudes should be earnestly practiced and developed. For its part, his spiritual life should ennoble and nourish them. Imbued with a living faith and a hope that never fails, the missionary should be a man of prayer. He should glow with a spirit of strength and of love and of self-discipline (cf. 2 Tm 1:7). Let him learn to be resourceful in every circumstance (cf. Ph 4:11). Let him in the spirit of sacrifice always bear about in himself the dying of Jesus, so that the life of Jesus may work in those to whom he is sent (cf. 2 Cor 4: 10 ff.). Out of zeal for souls, let him gladly spend all and be spent himself for souls (cf. 2 Cor 12:15 f.): so that "by the daily exercise of his duty he may grow in the love of God and neighbor." Thus, joined with Christ in obedience to the will of the Father, he will continue His mission under the hierarchical authority of the Church and cooperate in the mystery of salvation.

AG 26. As good ministers of Christ, those who are going to be sent to various nations should be nourished with the "words of faith and of good doctrine" (1 Tm 4:6). These they should draw principally from the sacred Scriptures as they study the mystery of Christ, whose heralds and witnesses they will be.

Therefore, all missionaries—priests, brothers, sisters, and laymen—each according to his own state, need preparation and training if they are not to be found unequal to the demands of their future work. From the very beginning, their doctrinal training should be so planned that it takes into account both the universality

of the Church and the diversity of the world's nations. This requirement holds for all the studies by which they are prepared for the
exercise of the ministry, as also for the other branches of learning
which it would be useful for them to master. They will thereby
gain a general knowledge of peoples, cultures, and religions, a knowledge that looks not only to the past, but to the present as well.
For anyone who is going to encounter another people should have
a great esteem for their patrimony and their language and their
customs.

It is above all necessary for the future missionary to devote
himself to missiological studies: that is, to know the teachings and
norms of the Church concerning missionary activity, the roads
which the heralds of the gospel have traversed in the course of the
centuries, the present condition of missions, and the methods now
considered especially effective.

But even though this entire training program is imbued with
pastoral considerations, a special and organized apostolic training
ought to be given. It should consist of both teaching and practical
exercises.

As many brothers and sisters as possible should be well instructed
and prepared in the catechetical art, so that they can collaborate
in the apostolate to an even greater extent.

Even those who are to take only a temporary part in missionary
activity need to acquire a training which is sufficient for their
purposes.

These types of formation should be completed in the lands to
which missionaries will be sent. Thus they will gain a more thorough
knowledge of the history, social structures, and customs of the
people. They will ascertain their system of moral values and their
religious precepts, and the innermost ideas which, according to their
sacred traditions, they have formed concerning God, the world,
and man. Let missionaries learn languages to the extent of being
able to use them in a fluent and polished manner. Thus they will
find more easy access to the minds and the hearts of men. Furthermore, they should be properly introduced into special pastoral
problems.

Some should receive an especially thorough preparation in

missiological institutes or in other faculties or universities. As a result they will be able to discharge special duties more effectively and to be a help, by their learning, to other missionaries in carrying on missionary work. In our time especially, this work presents very many difficulties and opportunities.

It is also highly desirable that regional Episcopal Conferences should have available an abundance of such experts, and that in meeting the needs of their office bishops should make fruitful use of the knowledge and experience of these men. There should be no lack either of persons who are perfectly skilled in the use of practical instruments and the means of social communication. The importance of these tools should be greatly appreciated by all.

AG 27. While all these requirements are thoroughly necessary for each and every person sent to the nations, they can in reality scarcely be met by individual missionaries. Since experience teaches too that mission work itself cannot be accomplished by lone individuals, a common calling has gathered individuals together into communities. In these, thanks to united effort, they can be properly trained and will be able to carry out this work in the name of the Church and at the direction of the hierarchy.

For many centuries now, these communities have borne the burden of the day and the heat, devoting themselves to missionary labor either entirely or in part. Often, vast territories were committed to them by the Holy See for evangelization, and there they gathered together a new people for God, a local Church loyal to its own shepherds. These communities have founded Churches by their own sweat, and even their blood. In the future they will serve these Churches with their zeal and experience in a spirit of brotherly cooperation. This they can do by undertaking the normal care of souls or by discharging special assignments on behalf of the common good.

Sometimes, throughout the entire extent of some region, they will take certain more pressing tasks upon themselves; for example, the evangelization of groups or peoples who perhaps for special reasons have not yet accepted the gospel message, or who have thus far resisted it.

If need be, let them be ready to use their experience to help and train those who will devote themselves temporarily to missionary activity.

For these reasons, and since there are still many nations to be led to Christ, such communities remain especially necessary.

AG 40. Religious communities of the contemplative and of the active life have so far played, and still do play, a very great role in the evangelization of the world. This sacred Synod gladly acknowledges their merits and thanks God for all that they have done for the glory of God and the service of souls. It exhorts them to go on untiringly in the work which they have begun, since they know that the virtue of charity impels and obliges them to a spirit and an effort which is truly Catholic. By their vocation they are bound to practice this charity with a special degree of perfection.

By their prayers, works of penance, and sufferings, contemplative communities have a very great importance in the conversion of souls. For it is God who sends workers into His harvest when He is asked to do so (cf. Mt 9:38), who opens the minds of non-Christians to hear the gospel (cf. Ac 16:14), and who makes the word of salvation fruitful in their hearts (cf. Cor 3:7). In fact, these communities are urged to found houses in mission areas, as not a few of them have already done. Thus living out their lives in a manner accommodated to the truly religious traditions of the people, they can bear splendid witness there among non-Christians to the majesty and love of God, as well as to man's brotherhood in Christ.

Whether they pursue a strictly mission goal or not, communities dedicated to the active life should sincerely ask themselves in the presence of God, whether they cannot broaden their activity in favor of expanding God's kingdom among the nations; whether they might not leave certain ministries to others so that they themselves can spend their energies on the missions; whether they can undertake work among the missions, adapting their constitutions if necessary, but according to the spirit of their founder; whether their members are involved as much as possible in missionary activity; and whether their type of life bears to the gospel a witness which is accommodated to the character and condition of the people.

Thanks to the inspiration of the Holy Spirit, secular institutes are increasing every day in the Church. Under the authority of the bishop, their programs can be fruitful in the missions in many ways as a sign of complete dedication to the evangelization of the world.

AG 42. The Council Fathers together with the Roman Pontiff, aware of their most solemn duty to spread everywhere the Kingdom of God, lovingly salute all heralds of the gospel. They especially salute those who suffer persecution for the name of Christ, and they make themselves companions in their sufferings.

These Fathers and the Roman Pontiff are afire with that same love with which Christ burned toward men. But knowing that it is God who makes His kingdom come on earth, they pour forth their prayers together with all the Christian faithful, that through the intercession of the Virgin Mary, Queen of the Apostles, the nations may be led to the knowledge of the truth as soon as possible (1 Tm 2:4), and that the splendor of God which brightens the face of Jesus Christ may shine upon all men through the Holy Spirit (2 Cor 4:6).—Pope Paul VI, December 7, 1965

LINKS BETWEEN THE GOSPEL AND CULTURE

GS 58. There are many links between the message of salvation and human culture. For God, revealing Himself to His people to the extent of a full manifestation of Himself in His Incarnate Son, has spoken according to the culture proper to different ages.

Living in various circumstances during the course of time, the Church, too, has used in her preaching the discoveries of different cultures to spread and explain the message of Christ to all nations, to probe it and more deeply understand it, and to give it better expression in liturgical celebrations and in the life of the diversified community of the faithful.

But at the same time, the Church, sent to all peoples of every time and place, is not bound exclusively and indissolubly to any race or nation, nor to any particular way of life or any customary pattern of living, ancient or recent. Faithful to her own tradition and at the same time conscious of her universal mission, she can enter into communion with various cultural modes, to her own enrichment and theirs too.

The good news of Christ constantly renews the life and culture of fallen man. It combats and removes the errors and evils resulting from sinful allurements which are a perpetual threat. It never ceases to purify and elevate the morality of peoples. By riches coming from above, it makes fruitful, as it were from within, the spiritual qualities and gifts of every people and of every age. It strengthens, perfects, and restores them in Christ. Thus by the very fulfillment of her own mission the Church stimulates and advances human and civic culture. By her action, even in its liturgical form, she leads men toward interior liberty.

H. Mental and physical health
　　PC, no. 12; ET, no. 33

Renewal and adaptation according to Pope Paul VI

(Cf. RR 32 [1973] 1277-1278)

"Yes, it is the witness of saints that the world needs, for, as the Council reminds us, 'in them God Himself addresses us and furnishes us with a sign of His kingdom, to which we are strongly drawn'." (December 8, 1970, TPS, 15-1971-331)

"But there is another reform, in the ascetical sense, to which we attach great value, that does not always regard precise norms of law but is the work of each one of us, of our way of thinking, of acting, and of serving with a spirit of faith and sacrifice; it is a more intimate and deeper reform, or spiritual renovation, even if less evident, that is realized in persons." (December 22, 1967, AAS, 60-1968-21)

"The renewal of religious life desired by the Council does indeed aim at a wiser discipline and a more modern way of coming into contact with society, but not at the expense of the true, authentic meaning of religious life, which consists mainly in continual progress in charity, the spirit of sacrifice, and adherence to the word and cross of Christ." (June 12, 1972, TPS, 17-1972-158)

"But if this (renewal and adaptation) certainly requires that there be removed anything that has become less relevant, less correct, or superfluous, care must yet be taken that everything, without any distinction, is not fundamentally changed. This is more destruction than renovation." (January 22, 1968, AAS, 60-1968-201)

"But the Church has also suffered (after Vatican II) and is still suffering from a whirlwind of ideas and facts that are certainly not from the good Spirit and do not promise that vital renovation that the Council promised and promoted ... for some the idea of change has taken the place of the idea of adaptation, ... but two things especially cannot be placed in discussion: the truths of faith, authoritatively sanctioned by tradition and the ecclesiastical teaching authority, and the constitutional laws of the Church, with the consequence of obedience to the ministry of pastoral government, that Christ established and the Church has developed ... renewal, *yes*; arbitrary change, *no*." (April 25, 1968, AAS, 60-1968-328)

"Besides, would not the real scandal be to perceive that, on the pretext of adaptation, you are renouncing these requirements of prayer, humility, poverty, sharing, purity, simplicity, and unselfish service that Christ has asked of His disciples?" (October 19, 1972, TPS, 17-1972-202)

"No, the Council is a renewal, not a revolution, and you will see that the first criterion that guides its intervention in your sector is that of fidelity to your origin rather than an abandonment of your genuine traditions." (October 28, 1966, AAS, 58-1966-1156)

"But if, on the other hand, the wind of dissatisfaction causes you to yield to the modern mentality, to allow ephemeral and changeable fashions and attitudes, to mimic the world's forms without discernment and without having any criteria, then you may be sure that the results will be truly deplorable.... Like the priest and the male religious—but with a different perspective from theirs—the woman religious is faced with a terrible dilemma: either to be a saint totally and without compromise, and attain the greatest measure of sanctity possible; or to be reduced to a joke, a caricature, an unsuccessful and, let us say, abortive being. The dangers of secularization are evident in every aspect, especially as regards poverty, when an attempt is made to obtain an economic autonomy that contrasts with the spirit of renunciation proper to the Gospel and to religious life." (November 22, 1969, TPS, 14-1970-365)

"First of all, you must have at heart loyalty toward the spirit of your founder. Religious institutes exist and flourish just as long as the complete mentality of their founder remains and inspires the members in their discipline and work and in their conduct and life, Any adaptation, therefore, to the changed circumstances of the times, any renewal of discipline is to be attained in such a way that the distinctive nature and character of the institute remain intact. Accordingly, no undertaking or work opposed to the primary end of the institute is to be engaged in, no change in discipline that is in any way foreign to the mind of the founder." (August 26, 1967, AAS, 59-1967-861)

"Some imagine that the only genuine renewal of the Church is one which is born from the ideas of a few, admittedly zealous, people who not infrequently consider themselves divinely inspired ... as in many of the faithful, who think that the reform of the Church should consist principally in adapting its way of thinking and acting to the customs and temper of the modern world. ... Hence, those who are not deeply rooted in the faith and in the observance of the Church's laws, readily imagine that the time is ripe to adjust themselves to worldly standards of living. ... We are also confronted with the growing tendency to prune away from the Christian life everything that requires effort or causes inconvenience. It rejects as vain and futile the practice of Christian asceticism and the contemplation of the things of God." (August 6, 1964, TPS, 10-1965-270-1)

RENEWAL AND APPROPRIATE ADAPTATION
ARE OBLIGATORY FOR RELIGIOUS

I. Imposed by the very nature of the mystery of religious life in the Mystery of Christ and His Body, the Church; by the theology of religious life; by the unique vocation assigned it in the Church and in the world.

> *PERFECTAE CARITATIS* is a normative and obligatory document; it is reaffirmed and further explicated in *EVANGELICA TESTIFICATIO* and subsequent papal decrees and documents from the SACRED CONGREGATION FOR RELIGIOUS AND SECULAR INSTITUTES.
>
> (Cf. PC, nos. 1, 2, 3)

PC 25. The communities for which these norms of appropriate renewal are decreed should react with a willing spirit to their divine calling and their contemporary mission in the Church. This sacred Synod has high regard for the character of their life—virginal, poor, and obedient—of which Christ the Lord Himself is the model. The Council places steady hope in the immense fruitfulness of their labors, both the unseen ones and the obvious.

Let all religious therefore spread throughout the whole world the good news of Christ by the integrity of their faith, their love for God and neighbor, their devotion to the Cross, and their hope of future glory. Thus will their witness be seen by all, and our Father in heaven will be glorified (cf. Mt 5:16). Thus, too, with the prayerful aid of that most loving Virgin Mary, God's Mother, "whose life is a rule of life for all," religious communities will experience a daily growth in numbers, and will yield a richer harvest of fruits that bring salvation.

Mary, the Exemplar of Religious Sanctity and Zeal

ET 56. May the most loving Mother of the Lord, after whose example you consecrated your life to God, obtain for you in the

daily course of life that unchangeable joy which only Jesus can
confer. Would that your life, patterned after her example, might
witness "to that maternal affection by which all should be inspired
to cooperate in the Church's apostolic mission of regenerating mankind." Most beloved sons and daughters, may the joy of the Lord
transfigure your life consecrated to Him and may His love make
it fruitful. In His name We bestow on you from the heart the
Apostolic Blessing.

(Cf. ET, nos. 1, 2, 3, 52)

LG 65. In the most holy Virgin the Church has already reached
that perfection whereby she exists without spot or wrinkle (cf. Ep
5:27). Yet the followers of Christ still strive to increase in holiness
by conquering sin. And so they raise their eyes to Mary who shines
forth to the whole community of the elect as a model of the virtues.
Devotedly meditating on her and contemplating her in the light of
the Word made man, the Church with reverence enters more intimately into the supreme mystery of the Incarnation and becomes
ever increasingly like her Spouse.

For Mary figured profoundly in the history of salvation and
in a certain way unites and mirrors within herself the central truths
of the faith. Hence when she is being preached and venerated, she
summons the faithful to her Son and His sacrifice, and to love for
the Father. Seeking after the glory of Christ, the Church becomes
more like her exalted model, and continually progresses in faith,
hope, and charity, searching out and doing the will of God in all
things. Hence the Church in her apostolic work also rightly looks
to her who brought forth Christ, conceived by the Holy Spirit and
born of the Virgin, so that through the Church Christ may be born
and grow in the hearts of the faithful also. The Virgin Mary in her
own life lived an example of that maternal love by which all should
be fittingly animated who cooperate in the apostolic mission of the
Church on behalf of the rebirth of men.

LG 68. In the bodily and spiritual glory which she possesses in
heaven, the Mother of Jesus continues in this present world as the

image and first flowering of the Church as she is to be perfected in the world to come. Likewise, Mary shines forth on earth, until the day of the Lord shall come (cf. 2 P 3:10), as a sign of sure hope and solace for the pilgrim People of God.

LG 69. It gives great joy and comfort to this most holy Synod that among the separated brethren, too, there are those who give due honor to the Mother of our Lord and Savior. This is especially so among the Easterners, who with ardent emotion and devout mind concur in reverencing the Mother of God, ever virgin.

Let the entire body of the faithful pour forth persevering prayer to the Mother of God and Mother of men. Let them implore that she who aided the beginnings of the Church by her prayers may now, exalted as she is in heaven above all the saints and angels, intercede with her Son in the fellowship of all the saints. May she do so until all peoples of the human family, whether they are honored with the name of Christian or whether they still do not know their Savior, are happily gathered together in peace and harmony into the one People of God, for the glory of the Most Holy and Undivided Trinity.

II. Right of the Holy See to interpret the norms of religious life for the Universal Church and the local churches.

SCRSI, April, 1968:

The Decree "Perfectae Caritatis" (no. 4) and the Motu Proprio "Ecclesiae Sanctae" (no. 6) entrust to the Religious Institutes the responsibility of carrying on the desired adaptation, but do not exempt the Holy See from the obligation of supervising so that everything is accomplished in accordance with the Conciliar prescriptions.

The Sacred Congregation which is responsible for the renewal of the religious institutes (Reg. Ecc. no. 73, 5) has not only not blocked but has encouraged in every way orderly updating of the religious life.... At the same time, however, the Sacred Congregation must insist that the norms laid down by the Second Vatican Council be duly respected.... Nowhere does the Council grant Religious unrestricted authority to experiment. Even the Special

General Chapter is limited by the provisions of "Perfectae Caritatis" and "Ecclesiae Sanctae."

SCRSI, April, 1968

The genuine renewal as it is stated in the Decree *Perfectae Caritatis* (no. 2), must always be carried out under the influence of the Spirit and the guidance of the Church.

Anyone who feels that the necessary and ardently desired renewal of the Religious Life can be built on: the use of secular and worldly dress, the elimination of community life, subordination of the Religious life to external activities, independence from the Local Ordinary in the Apostolate is falling into serious error and evidences an attitude basically contrary to that genuine renewal as it is stated in "Perfectae Caritatis," (no. 2).

SCRSI, December, 1971

It is understood that renewal and adaptation in the religious life are to be based on the documents of Vatican II, especially in "Lumen Gentium" VI, "Perfectae Caritatis" and on the recent "Evangelica Testificatio" of Our Holy Father, as well as on all other pertinent documents issued by the Holy Father since Vatican II.

"Ecclesiae Sanctae" does not allow unlimited experimentation and changes. Moreover, on-going experimentation needs effective evaluation and control; decisive judgment is the competency of the Holy See.

SCRSI, August, 1971

You have the responsibility of your life; but you have freely committed it to God in the hands of your superiors, for the welfare of your brothers, 'by a dedication of your will as a sacrifice of yourself to God' (PC no. 14).

Today, more than ever, we have need of generous souls who are willing to give themselves to God with ardor; who accept the unknown of poverty, who are able to submit to discipline, who show themselves free and obedient, spontaneous and tenacious, . . . in their apostolate.

Lay Religious in the Life of the Institute

1. Lay brothers are to be brought into the heart of the life and activities of the institute (PC no. 15, AAS, 61 [1969] 739-40).

2. The general chapters of clerical religious institutes may enact that lay religious be permitted to fill merely administrative offices such as that of treasurer, director of a bookstore, and others of such a nature that they do not have a direct relation with the strictly priestly ministry. (ibid.)

3. The general chapters of clerical religious institutes may grant active and passive voice for chapters on any level to the same religious and for elections and the treating of affairs in the same chapters, according to the measure and conditions established by the nature of the matters and by the general chapter itself. (ibid.)

4. Monasteries and institutes of men not exclusively lay in character can admit both clergy and laity on the same basis and with equal rights and duties, excepting those arising from sacred orders. (PC no. 15)

5. Institutes of brothers may admit some members to holy orders for priestly ministrations for their own houses. (PC no. 10)

6. Care is to be taken to effect one class of sister in institutes of women. (PC no. 15)

PC 10. The lay religious life, for both men and women, constitutes a state which of itself is one of total dedication to the profession of the evangelical counsels. This sacred Synod highly esteems such a life, since it serves the pastoral work of the Church so usefully by educating the young, caring for the sick, and discharging other services. The Council supports such religious in their vocation, and entreats them to adapt their life to modern needs.

This sacred Synod declares that there is no objection to religious congregations of brothers admitting some members to holy orders, to supply needed priestly ministrations for their own houses, provided that the lay character of the congregation remains unchanged and that it is the general chapter that makes the decision.

III. Manner of promoting renewal and adaptation of religious life.

a. E.S. II-Introduction

That the fruits of the Council may carefully mature, it is necessary that Religious institutes promote first of all a renewal of spirit, and then that they take care to carry out this renewal adapted to their life and discipline prudently and yet skillfully by applying themselves assiduously to the study especially of the Dogmatic Constitution *Lumen Gentium* (chapters 5 and 6) and the Decree *Perfectae Caritatis*, and by putting into effect the norms and teachings of the Council.

To speed up the implementation of the Decree *Perfectae Caritatis* the following norms which will affect all Religious, whether Latin or Oriental, with suitable adjustments, establish a procedure and give certain rules.

b. Persons bound to promote.

(Cf. ES II-I, 1-11; PC, 4)

ES II-1. 1. The most important role in the adaptation and renewal of the Religious life belongs to the institutes themselves, which will accomplish it especially through general chapters or, among the Orientals through synaxes. The task of the chapters is not completed by merely making laws, but especially by promoting spiritual and apostolic vitality.

ES II-1. 2. The cooperation of all superiors and members is necessary to renew Religious life in themselves, to prepare the spirit of the chapters, to carry out the works of the chapters, to observe faithfully the laws and norms enacted by the chapters.

ES II-1. 3. A special general chapter, ordinary or extraordinary, should be convened within two or at most three years to promote the adaptation and renewal in each institute.

This chapter can be divided into two distinct periods, separated generally by not more than a year, if the chapter itself so decides by secret vote.

ES II-1. 4. The general commission in preparing this chapter should suitably provide for full and free consultation of the members and arrange the results of this consultation in time so that the work of the chapter may be helped and directed It will be possible to accomplish this, for example, by consulting conventual and provincial chapters, by establishing commissions, by proposing series of questions, etc.

ES II-1. 5. For stauropagial monasteries it shall be the duty of the patriarch to set forth the norms for pursuing this consultation.

ES II-1. 6. This general chapter has the right to alter certain norms of the constitutions, or among Orientals the norms of the typika, as an experiment, as long as the purpose, nature and character of the institute are preserved. Experiments contrary to the common law, provided they are to be undertaken prudently, will be willingly permitted by the Holy See as the occasions call for them.

These experiments can be prolonged until the next ordinary general chapter, which will have the faculty to continue them further but not beyond the chapter immediately following.

ES II-1. 7. The general council has the same faculty during the time that intervenes between chapters of this kind, in accordance with conditions to be determined by the chapters, and among the Orientals in independent monasteries the Hegumen with the minor Synaxis has this power.

ES II-1. 8. The definitive approval of the constitutions is reserved to the competent authority.

ES II-1. 9. As far as the revision of the constitutions of nuns is concerned, each monastery by means of a chapter, or even the individual nuns, should make known their wishes which, to safeguard the unity of the Religious family in keeping with its nature, should be collected by the highest authority of the order, if she is present, otherwise by the delegate of the Holy See; among Orientals, by the patriarch or the local hierarch. The wishes and opinions can be sought from the assemblies of the federations or from other gatherings legitimately called together. The bishops' pastoral solicitude should also lend benevolent assistance to this end.

ES II-1. 10. If at times in monasteries of nuns certain experiments with respect to observances are judged opportune for an interval, these can be permitted by the superiors general or by delegates of the Holy See, and among Orientals by the patriarch or the local hierarch. Yet special consideration should be given to the special outlook and frame of mind of those who are cloistered and who have so great a need for stability and security.

ES II-1. 11. It shall be the duty of those authorities mentioned above to provide for the revision of the texts of the constitutions with the help and consultation of the monasteries themselves and for their submission for the approval of the Holy See or the competent hierarch.

IV. Revision of Constitutions:

Code of life to transmit to religious the wealth of the Gospels and of the Church, indicating the path of life to follow.

(Cf. PC, no. 3)
(Cf. ES, II-1, nos. 12-14; 15-17)

ES II-1. 12. The general laws of each institute (constitutions, Typica, rules or whatever name they bear) should ordinarily include these elements:

(a) The evangelical and theological principles of the religious life and of its union with the Church and suitable and clear words in which "the spirit of the founders and their specific aims and healthy traditions, all of which constitute the patrimony of each institute, are acknowledged and preserved." (no. 2b *Perfectae Caritatis*)

(b) The necessary juridical norms for defining clearly the character, purpose and means of the institute, which norms should not be excessively multiplied but should always be presented in an adequate manner.

ES II-1. 13. The union of both elements, spiritual and juridical, is necessary so that the principal codes of the institutes have a stable foundation and that the true spirit and life-giving norms pervade them; care must therefore be taken that a merely juridical or purely exhortatory text is not composed.

ES II-1. 14. Those matters which are now obsolete, or subject to change according to a particular era, or which correspond with merely local usages, should be excluded from the fundamental code of the institutes.

Those norms however which correspond with the needs of the present time, the physical and psychological conditions of the members and particular circumstances should be set down in supplementary codes called "directories," books of customs, or in books bearing other titles.

V. Criteria for renewal and adaptation.

ES II-1. 15. The norms and spirit to which adaptation and renewal must correspond should be gathered not only from the Decree *Perfectae Caritatis* but also from other documents of the Second Vatican Council, especially from chapters 5 and 6 of the Dogmatic Constitution *Lumen Gentium*.

ES II-1. 16. The institutes should take care that the principles established in no. 2 of the Decree *Perfectae Caritatis* actually pervade the renewal of their religious life; therefore:

(1) Study and meditation on the Gospels and the whole of Sacred Scripture should be more earnestly fostered by all members from the beginning of their novitiate. Likewise, care should be taken that they share in the mystery and life of the Church in more suitable ways;

(2) The various aspects (theological, historical, canonical, etc.) of the doctrine of the religious life should be investigated and explained.

(3) To achieve the good of the Church, the institutes should strive for a genuine knowledge of their original spirit, so that faithfully preserving this spirit in determining adaptations, their religious life may thus be purified of alien elements and freed from those which are obsolete.

ES II-1. 17. Those elements are to be considered obsolete which do not constitute the nature and purpose of the institute and which, having lost their meaning and power, are no longer a real help to religious life. Nevertheless, consideration must be given to the witness which the religious state has the obligation of giving.

ES II-1. 18. The form of government should be such that "the chapters and councils . . . each in its own way express the participation and concern of all the members for the welfare of the whole community" (no. 14 of the Decree *Perfectae Caritatis*). This will be realized especially if the members have a really effective part in selecting the members of these chapters and councils. Similarly the form of government should be such that the exercise of authority is made more effective and unhindered according to modern needs. Therefore, superiors on every level should be given sufficient powers so that useless and too frequent recourse to higher authorities is not multiplied.

ES II-1. 19. Nevertheless, suitable renewal cannot be made once and for all but should be encouraged in a continuing way, with the help of the zeal of the members and the solicitude of the chapters and superiors.

VI. Some Things to be Adapted and Renewed in the Religious Life

I. *The Divine Office of Brothers and Sisters*
(Perfectae Caritatis, no. 3)

ES II-11. 20. Although Religious who recite a duly approved Little Office perform the public prayer of the Church (cf. Constitution *Sacrosanctum Concilium*, no. 98), it is nevertheless recommended to the institutes that in place of the Little Office they adopt the Divine Office either in part or in whole so that they may participate more intimately in the liturgical life of the Church. Religious of the Eastern rites, however, should recite the doxologies and the Divine Lauds according to their own typika and customs.

2. *Mental Prayer*
(Perfectae Caritatis, no. 6)

ES II-11. 21. In order that Religious may more intimately and fruitfully participate in the most holy mystery of the Eucharist and the public prayer of the Church, and that their whole spiritual life may be nourished more abundantly, a larger place should be given to mental prayer instead of a multitude of prayers, retaining nevertheless the pious exercises commonly accepted in the Church and giving due care that the members are instructed diligently in leading a spiritual life.

3. *Mortification*
(*Perfectae Caritatis, nos 5, 12*)

ES II-11. 22. Religious should devote themselves to works of penance and mortification more than the rest of the faithful. However, the special penitential practices of institutes should be revised insofar as it is necessary so that, taking into account traditions, whether of the East or of the West, and modern circumstances, the members may in practice be able to observe them, adopting new forms also drawn from modern conditions of life.

4. *On Poverty*
(*Perfectae Caritatis, no. 13*)

ES II-11. 23. Institutes especially through their general chapters should diligently and in concrete manner promote the spirit and practice of poverty according to the intention of no. 13 of the Decree *Perfectae Caritatis* while also seeking and urging new ways in keeping with the nature of their institute to make the practice and witness of poverty more effective in modern times.

ES II-11. 24. It is the right of institutes with simple vows to decree in general chapter whether the renunciation of inheritances which have been acquired or will be acquired should be incorporated in the constitutions and, if this is done, whether such renunciation should be obligatory or optional. They should also decide when this is to be done, that is, whether before perpetual profession or after some years.

5. *Living The Common Life*
(*Perfectae Caritatis, no. 15*)

ES II-11. 25. In institutes devoted to works of the apostolate the common life, which is so important for Religious as a family united in Christ to renew fraternal cooperation, should be promoted by every means possible in a manner suitable to the vocation of the institute.

ES II-11. 26. In institutes of this kind the order of the day cannot always be the same in all their houses, nor at times in the same house for all the members. The order, however, is always to be so arranged that the Religious, aside from the time given to spiritual things and works, should also have some periods to themselves and be able to enjoy suitable recreation.

ES II-11. 27. General chapters and synaxes should explore ways in which members who are called "conversi," "cooperators," or by any other such name, may gradually obtain an active vote in specified community actions and elections and also a passive vote in the case of certain offices. Thus indeed it will come about that they are closely joined with the life and works of the community and the priests will be able to devote themselves more freely to their own ministry.

ES II-11. 28. In monasteries where the stage of having one class of nun has been achieved, choir obligations should be defined in the constitutions, taking into consideration the diversity of persons which the distinction of activities and special vocations requires.

ES II-11. 29. Sisters devoted to the external service of the monasteries, whether called oblates or some other name, should be governed by special statutes in which consideration should be given to the needs of their vocation which is not contemplative only and also to the needs of the vocation of the nuns with whom their lives are joined, even though they themselves are not nuns.

The superioress of the monastery has a grave obligation to have solicitous care for these Sisters, to provide them with a fitting religious training, to treat them with a true sense of charity and to promote a bond of sisterliness between them and the community of nuns.

CHAPTER 15

NORMS FOR EXPERIMENTATION

Purpose to strengthen renewal of religious life;
not to put it in danger.

NATURE: Temporary suspension or substitution of norms of an
institute in view of determining definitive norms; it is not left
to individuals, but is to be decided on, and approved by competent
authority.

SCRSI, August, 1971

We must ... discard in communities the experiments which put
aside the directives and the teaching of superiors, and establish
a style of life which is in opposition to the letter and spirit of
the Council.

1. Authority
    Cf. PC, nos. 4, 3
    Cf. ES, II-1, nos. 1, 3, 4, 6
    Cf. CD, no. 35
    Cf. ET, nos. 7, 25, 50

2. Scope and limit
    a. Experiments may not interfere with the purpose, nature, and
       character of the institute.
       Cf. PC, nos. 2, 20, 17
    b. Limited by the general law specified for religious in the
       Code of Canon Law unless revised.
    c. Limited by prudence: experiments which cannot be sanctioned
       by the Church when time comes for definitive approval of
       the Constitutions should be avoided.

3. Excluded from experimentation (without prior permission of the Holy See)

   a. Code of Canon Law relative to
      1) admission, cs. 538-552
      2) novitiate, cs. 553-571
      3) obligations of religious, cs. 592-612
      4) elections, cs. 162-168
      5) dismissal and separation, cs. 637-672

   b. Common law for religious institutes

   c. Norms of *Sedes Sapientiae,* and the Statutes which apply it

   d. Articles containing doctrinal, spiritual or apostolic principles

4. Approval
   Cf. c. 492

ES II-I. 8. The definitive approval of the constitutions is reserved to the competent authority.

SCRSI, July 10, 1972

Things to be included in the constitutions

   1. *Union of spirituality and law.* In view of writing future constitutions, it is well to remark here that there should be a union of spirituality and law. Above all, *the spirit of the Gospel* should be the basis of constitutions, emphasizing that the essence of the consecrated life is in the total gift of self to God. The *spirit of the founder,* that special charism given to an institute . . . should permeate the constitutions which embody the spiritual heritage of the members.

   2. *Things not determined in Canon Law.* The general legislation of the Church permits each institute to decide what will be done in some judicial matters, e.g., who will have active and passive voice, the practice of poverty within the institute, the manner of admittance to profession; therefore these should be expressed in the constitutions.

Experimental authority of religious institutes

   1. Provided . . . the purpose, nature and character of the institute are preserved. (Cf. ES, II-1, no. 6)

2. Every derogation from common law must have a dispensation explicitly granted. In some cases, it might easily have happened that the Sacred Congregation omitted to call attention to some change contrary to the law in force. This would have been due to an oversight and may not be interpreted as an explicit concession. (SCRSI, July 10, 1972)

Canon law in general not abrogated nor suspended

1. The laws which our most provident Mother the Church has established in the Code of Canon Law and in other documents issued afterward, and which she has not revoked, We (Paul VI) declare unchanged and sacred, unless the Second Ecumenical Council of the Vatican has clearly abrogated or modified or derogated from them in some respects.

2. These norms which apply to religious of the entire Church leave intact the general laws of the Church, whether of the Latin Church or of the Eastern Churches, as well as the proper laws of religious institutes unless these norms change them explicitly or implicitly.
(SCRSI, July 10, 1972)

SACRED CONGREGATION FOR RELIGIOUS AND SECULAR INSTITUTES

Rome, July 10, 1972

Dear Reverend Mother,

In a letter dated December 4, 1967 the Sacred Congregation for Religious and Secular Institutes requested Institutes to send the Acts of their Special General Chapters which were to be held according to the *Motu Proprio, Ecclesiae Sanctae* part II., no. 3.

In making this request the Sacred Congregation wished to be aware of the experiments in progress and also to know if the chapters remained within the limits set by the *Motu Proprio*. This permitted modifications of the constitutions "ad experimentum" as long as the nature, end and purpose of the Institute would be preserved.

Following this letter, many Institutes sent their capitular acts and this sacred Congregation has responded to many, making the necessary observations and also permitting experiments contrary to common law.

The examination of capitular decrees up to this time shows that Institutes have had to face many similar problems and, consequently, observations sent by the Sacred Congregation have also been similar. However, since six years have passed following the publication of the Motu Proprio and it is not possible to make as complete a study as we would like of the remaining acts of Chapters from English-speaking communities, the Sacred Congregation believes it opportune to send a list of principal observations and suggestions. In this way each Institute will be able to see those things which should be modified or improved.

Several comments are in order at this point. In this period of experimentation the Sacred Congregation does not approve new constitutions. This does not prevent the Acts of the General Chapters from becoming immediately effective provided, as mentioned above, the purpose, nature and character of the institute are preserved. (*Ecclesiae Sanctae*, part II., no. 6)

However, every derogation from common law must have a dispensation explicitly granted. In some cases, it might easily have happened that the Sacred Congregation omitted to call attention to some change contrary to the law in force. This would have been due to an oversight and may not be interpreted as an explicit concession.

We wish here to recall some observations which the Sacred Congregation has made most frequently about Acts of Chapters and which we hope will be guiding norms for you in the serious work of writing Constitutions.

Vows in general: A clear definition of each vow is necessary.

1. Chastity or Consecrated Celibacy

"Chastity is decisively positive, it witnesses to preferential love for the Lord and symbolizes in the most eminent and absolute way the mystery of the union of the Mystical Body with its Head, the union of the Bride with her eternal Bridegroom." (*Evangelica testificatio*, n. 13)

The term, *virginity*, has a specific meaning and should not be substituted for the word, *chastity*.

2. Poverty

The matter of the vow of poverty and its practice should be accurately specified by the Chapter. Several factors should be included in this explanation.

Religious must recognize the importance and dignity of work in earning their livelihood. Their life style, characterized as it should be by simplicity, will result in genuine fraternal sharing, an intrinsic part of both poverty and common life. A correct sense of dependence must be included not only in legislation but also in actual living. Chapter decisions which tend to dispense with any kind of dependence or accountability are not acceptable.

"The forms of poverty of each person and of each community will depend on the type of institute and on the form of obedience practised in it. Thus will be brought to realization, in accordance with particular vocations, the character of dependence which is inherent in every form of poverty." (*Evangelica testificatio*, no. 21, also nos. 16-22)

3. Obedience

The necessity for consultation and collaboration should be included but the obligation and the right of the Superior to exercise prudently the role of personal authority should be respected.

"Thus, far from being in opposition to one another, authority and individual liberty go together in the fulfillment of God's Will, which is sought fraternally through a trustful dialogue between the superior and his brother in the case of a personal situation, or through a general agreement regarding what concerns the whole community."

"This labour of seeking together must end, when it is the moment, with the decision of the superiors whose presence and acceptance are indispensable in every community." (*Evangelica testificatio*, no. 25)

4. "The formula for religious profession for each congregation should be based on the ritual *Ordo Professionis,* and should be

approved by the Sacred Congregation for Religious. This formula, pronounced by each Sister, has to be the same since each member professes vows especially recognized by the Church and since obligations and privileges deriving from it are the same for all. This, however, does not prevent a Sister from adding something personal before or after the formula itself. (*Ordo Professionis: Ritual*, February 2, 1970—Sacred Congregation for Divine Worship)

GOVERNMENT

1. Method of election of the Superior General

Although direct election has been permitted at the request of some small communities, this has been by way of exception.

2. General Chapter

Provision should be made for the collaboration of the members of the institute and for adequate representation. Although some institutes give active voice to those members in temporary commitment, whether by vows or by promises, it is not considered feasible to give them passive voice since they have not yet made a permanent commitment of themselves in the particular institute. Those in temporary commitment may not hold positions of authority in the institute.

3. Enlarged Councils

Powers given to enlarged councils (e.g., Council members, Provincials and/or Local Superiors) should be clearly determined. Enlarged Councils are of considerable help in the task of evaluation of experiments but they should not interfere in legislative functions of General Councils.

4. Local Councils

There is nothing to prevent the entire community from being members of the local council, especially in small communities. But, in larger communities the usual type of council would be necessary particularly when rather delicate matters must be discussed; however, in other items of general interest the consultation of the entire local community is to be favored.

5. Smaller communities

There is no objection to these provided the "life style" be that of a religious community with a person in authority, no matter what the title. Experience of many Institutes indicates that small communities should not be composed of only peer groups nor according to personal choice.

COMMON LIFE

1. Prayer

Since the Eucharistic mystery is truly the center of the liturgy and even of the entire Christian life, it is normal that it hold first place in the life of religious communities and of each consecrated person. (Instruction: *Eucharisticum Mysterium*, S.C. Rites, May 25. 1967)

In the light of *Perfectae caritatis* and of *Evangelica testificatio*, as well as from the experience of common life itself, Chapters should not hesitate to prescribe a minimum of time for daily prayer, providing for both communal and personal prayer.

2. Apostolate

The religious, not as a private individual but as a member of her Institute, engages in apostolic work which is according to the end of her Institute. "But your activities cannot derogate from the vocation of your various institutes. . . ." (*Evangelica testificatio*, no. 20).

3. Religious dress

Chapter decisions in this matter should follow the statements in the documents.

"The religious habit, an outward mark of consecration to God, should be simple and modest, poor and at the same time becoming." (*Perfectae caritatis*, no. 17 ff.)

"While we recognize that certain situations can justify the abandonment of a religious type of dress, we cannot pass over in silence the fittingness that the dress of religious men and women should be, as the Council wishes, a sign of their consecration and that it should be in some way different from the forms that are clearly secular." (*Evangelica testificatio*, no. 22)

The letter sent from this Sacred Congregation on February 25, 1972 re-affirms the above directives.

4. Other matters

Some Chapters leave to the individual the responsibility for decisions on recreation, vacations, going out, visits, correspondence. In these matters Superiors cannot totally abdicate their authority, since "Superiors are responsible for the souls confided to their care. . . ." (*Perfectae caritatis,* no. 14)

In view of writing future constitutions, it is well to remark here that there should be a union of spirituality and law. Above all, the Spirit of the Gospel should be the basis of constitutions, emphasizing that the essence of the consecrated life is in the total gift of self to God. The Spirit of the Foundress should permeate the constitutions which embody the spiritual heritage of her daughters.

The general legislation of the Church permits each institute to decide what will be done in some juridical matters, e.g., who will have active and passive voice, the practice of poverty within the institute, the manner of admittance to profession; therefore, these should be expressed in the constitutions.

The above observations are intended to be of assistance in answering the questions and in resolving in some degree the problems facing religious institutes today. Not all these observations will affect the present legislation of all institutes but the members of the institutes and the participants in General Chapters will see those things which refer to their respective institutes.

It is hoped that these observations will serve as guidelines for the writing of constitutions which eventually must be submitted to the competent authority for approval.

It is the fervent prayer of all those privileged to assist religious institutes that the foregoing information will enable you and your Sisters by means of generous efforts to bring to living reality not only the necessary external changes but also to render fruitful that spiritual renewal which the Church asks of all of us.

Devotedly in Our Lord
✠ Aug. Mayer—Secretary

PART VI

MISCELLANEOUS DIRECTIVES

FEDERATION OF RELIGIOUS INSTITUTES
CONFERENCES OF MAJOR SUPERIORS
DISSOLUTION OF DECLINING INSTITUTES
ESTABLISHMENT OF NEW COMMUNITIES

PROMOTION OF VOCATIONS
SECULAR INSTITUTES

CHAPTER 16

SPECIFIC DIRECTIVES

1. Union or Federation of Institutes

PC 22. Where opportunity and the Holy See permit, independent communities and monasteries should work towards making a federation of themselves if they belong in some sense to the same religious family; or, if their constitutions and customs are practically the same and a kindred spirit animates them, they should try to form a union, especially when of themselves they are excessively small; or let them enter into an association if they engage in external activities of an identical or similar nature.

ES II-11. 39. Promoting any kind of union between institutes presupposes a suitable spiritual, psychological and juridical preparation, according to the intention of the Decree *Perfectae Caritatis*. For this purpose it will often be profitable that the institutes be helped by some assistant approved by the competent authority.

ES II-11. 40. In the aforementioned cases and circumstances the good of the Church is to be kept in view, but with due consideration for the specific character of each institute as well as to the freedom of individual members.

2. Suppression of Institutes

PC 21. If after consulting the appropriate Ordinaries, the Holy See decides that certain communities or monasteries no longer offer any reasonable hope of flourishing, these should be forbidden thereafter to accept novices. If it can be done, they should be absorbed by a more vigorous community or monastery which approximates their own purpose and spirit.

ES II-11. 41. Among the criteria that can contribute to forming a judgment on the suppression of an institute or monastery, taking all the circumstances into account, the following especially are to be considered together: the small number of Religious in proportion to the age of the institute or the monastery, the lack of candidates over a period of several years, the advanced age of the majority of its members. If a decision for suppression is reached, provision should be made that the institute be joined "if it is possible, with another more vigorous institute or monastery not much different in purpose and spirit." (no. 21 of the Decree *Perfectae Caritatis*) The individual Religious, however, should be consulted beforehand and all should be done with charity.

3. Conferences or Unions of Major Superiors of Men and Women

PC 23. Favor is to be shown to conferences or councils of major superiors which have been established by the Holy See. These can make splendid contributions to several goals: helping individual communities fulfill their purpose more adequately; fostering more successful cooperation on behalf of the Church; distributing workers in a given territory more advantageously; and working on affairs of common concern to religious communities.

Where the exercise of the apostolate is involved, appropriate coordination and collaboration with episcopal conferences should be established. Similar conferences can also be set up for secular institutes.

ES II-11. 42. Care is to be taken that the union of superiors general of men and women can be heard and consulted by means of a council established at the Sacred Congregation for Religious.

ES II-11. 43. It is of greatest importance that national conferences or unions of major superiors of men and women cooperate with episcopal conferences with confidence and reverence (cf. no. 35 of the Decree *Christus Dominus*; no. 33 of the Decree *Ad Gentes Divinitus*).

Therefore it is hoped that questions involving both sides be discussed in mixed commissions composed of both bishops and major superiors of men or women.

4. Establishment of New Communities

PC 19. When there is a question of establishing new communities, serious thought must be given to the need for them, or at least to their eminent usefulness, and also to the likelihood that they will prosper. Otherwise, lack of caution will give rise to communities which serve no purpose or are deprived of sufficient vitality.

Where the Church has newly taken root, special attention should be given to the establishment and development of fresh forms of religious life. These should take into account the natural endowments and the manners of the people, and also local customs and circumstances.

5. Promotion of Vocations

PC 24. Priests and Catholic teachers should make serious efforts* on behalf of religious vocations, so that a new supply may be at hand for meeting the Church's needs adequately.** Candidates should be appropriately and carefully selected. Ordinary sermons should treat more often of the evangelical counsels and the choice of the religious state. Parents should develop and protect religious vocations in the hearts of their children by training them to behave like Christians.

Communities have the right to spread knowledge of themselves by way of attracting vocations, and to seek out candidates as well. Only, they should do so with proper prudence, adhering to the norms set down by the Holy See and the local bishop.

---

*Orders of priests, brothers, and sisters have rightly established the office of vocation director, vocation recruiter, etc.

The first task of the vocation director is to **discover the invitation of the Holy Spirit. The director will often meet candidates who are directed by the Holy Spirit to serve in the diocesan clergy or in some congregation other than his own. In such a case it will be his function to encourage such a candidate to follow this invitation—an attitude that will promote the ultimate well-being of his own institute and the entire Church.

Religious should not forget that the good example of their own lives affords the highest recommendation for their community, and the most appealing invitation to embrace the religious life.

(Cf. ET, nos. 3, 12, 45, 55)

Young girls desirous of becoming religious ... wrote:

"... We want something more challenging which will facilitate for us the practice of sacrifice and mortification, something which will free us from earthly vanity and give us a visible sign of our consecration to God, so that we might be an obvious witness to the Church in the service of the people of God." These words demonstrate how youth do not fear sacrifice, mortification and privations —inescapable conditions of religious life. (SCRSI, August, 1971)

CHAPTER 17

SECULAR INSTITUTES

Secular institutes* differ from religious institutes in this: their profession of poverty, chastity, and obedience is by some act other than *public* vows, and community of life is not required. This form of the life of evangelical perfection in the world was first given official recognition by the Holy See in the constitution *Provida Mater* (Feb. 2, 1947). The secular institute form of life should not be confused with either the religious life or lay apostolates such as Catholic Action.**

PC 11. Secular institutes*** are not religious communities but they carry with them in the world a profession of the evangelical counsels which is genuine and complete, and recognized as such by the Church. This profession confers a consecration on men and women, laity and clergy, who reside in the world. For this reason they should chiefly strive for total self-dedication to God, one

---

*Secular institutes are associations of priests or laity or both. Their members live the life of the vows or promises of poverty, chastity and obedience without the protections of religious habit, cloistered room, or spiritual exercises in common. Secular institutes differ from Third Order groups, Sodalities, and Catholic Action organizations because the institutes involve profession of poverty, chastity, and obedience and have been given a special place in the canonical structure of the Church.

**As indicated by Pope John in originally summoning the Council, this renewal was primarily a "New Pentecost." The "fresh air" he longed to see within the Church was chiefly the breath of the Holy Spirit in renewal.

***"Institutes" is a more literal translation of the word used in the Latin text here. "Community" is widely used by religious congregations to mean what the technical word "institute" stands for, i.e., a whole order, society, or congregation (as is clear from Art. 13, speaking of "provinces and houses of a religious community."—Ed.

inspired by perfect charity. These institutes should preserve their proper and particular character, a secular one, so that they may everywhere measure up successfully to that apostolate which they were designed to exercise, and which is both in the world and, in a sense, of the world.

Yet they should surely realize that they cannot acquit themselves of so immense a task unless their members are skillfully trained in matters both human and divine, and can thus be a genuine leaven in the world for strengthening and enlarging Christ's body. Therefore directors should give especially serious care to the spiritual training of members and to the promotion of more advanced formation as well.

APOSTOLIC CONSTITUTION

PROVIDA MATER ECCLESIA

CONCERNING CANONICAL STATES AND SECULAR INSTITUTES FOR THE ATTAINMENT OF CHRISTIAN PERFECTION

Our far-seeing Mother, the Church, has ever striven with great diligence and motherly affection to make her favored sons, who consecrate their whole lives to Christ the Lord and follow him freely and perseveringly in the way of the counsels, worthy of their heavenly purpose and angelic vocation; in her wisdom she regulates their manner of life. To this many documents and acts of Popes, Councils and Fathers bear witness and the whole course of the history of the Church and the general trend of canonical discipline clearly show it even down to our own times.

Indeed, from the very beginnings of Christianity the Magisterium of the Church has been concerned to elucidate the teaching and example of Christ and the apostles summoning men to perfection, and has taught with assurance how a life dedicated to perfection should be led and regulated. In her work and ministry she has favored and encouraged this complete gift and dedication to Christ to such a degree that from the very beginning Christian communities spontaneously offered for the evangelical counsels a good soil ready to receive the seed and giving sure promise of an abundant harvest.

Shortly afterwards—as the writings of the apostolic Fathers and ancient ecclesiastical writers clearly prove—the perfect state of life was so flourishing in the various Churches that those who embraced it began to form within the Christian community a special order and social category clearly designated by various names such as ascetics, celibates, virgins and so on, winning approval and veneration from many.

The Church, faithful to Christ her Bridegroom and to her principles, in the course of centuries, gradually, and under the guidance of the Holy Spirit, drew up with sure and unfaltering steps the regulations concerning the life of perfection down to the promulgation of the present Code of Canon Law. With motherly solicitude for all those who wholeheartedly and in different forms profess the life of perfection she has never ceased to encourage them in their holy resolution. She has done this in a two-fold way: firstly, she has not only accepted and recognized the individual profession of perfection, provided it was made in the face of the Church and in public, like the ancient and venerable consecration of virgins which was formerly a liturgical ceremony, but she has wisely confirmed it and strenuously defended it, bestowing on it many canonical prerogatives: secondly, the Church's principal care and favor have been very rightly directed, from the fourth century onwards, to that complete and more strictly public profession of perfection which, after the "peace of the Church" under Constantine, was made in associations and communities established with her permission or approbation or by her command.

It is well known how essentially bound up together have been the history of the Church's holiness and her universal apostolate with the history and glorious achievements of canonical religious life. This latter, ever quickened by the grace of the Holy Spirit, has developed in wondrous diversity and has been strengthened in marvellous, ever deeper and more closely-knit unity. It is not surprising, then, that the Church should have faithfully followed, in the field of law, this movement that a wise Providence so clearly intimated, and that she should have regulated the canonical state of perfection to the extent of raising upon it the structure of ecclesiastical legislation, as one of its chief corner stones. Hence, from the first, the public state of perfection was included among the three principal ecclesiastical states and from it alone the Church has derived the second order and canonical degree of persons (c. 107). This is worth serious and attentive consideration: the two other canonical orders of persons, namely of clerics and layfolk, by divine law (and ecclesiastical institution, cs. 107 and 108 § 3) form part of the Church as a hierarchically constituted and appointed society; the category of religious, intermediate between clerics and layfolk and comprising both (c. 107), is derived entirely from its close and special relationship with the purpose of the Church, that is, sanctification effectively pursued by adequate means.

Nor was this enough. In order that public and solemn profession of a holy way of life should not be doomed to frustration and failure the Church, with ever increasing vigor, has only recognized this canonical state of perfection in those societies established and regulated by herself, that is, in those religious orders (c. 488, § 1) whose general form and constitution, after long and serious examination she has approved by her Magisterium, in every instance subsequently exercising control, scrutinizing their organization and constitutions not only from the doctrinal and abstract point of view but in fact and in practical experience. All this has been so rigorously and absolutely laid down by Canon Law that in no case, without any exception whatsoever, can the canonical state of perfection be recognized unless profession of it be made in a religious order approved by the Church. Lastly, the canonical legislation applying to the state of perfection, in so far as it is a public state, thus regulated by a wise disposition of the Church, requires that in clerical religious orders, in all matters concerning the clerical life of the religious, the religious order takes the place of the diocese and admission to this religious order is equivalent to incardination in a diocese (c. 111 § 1; 115; 585).

The Code of Pius X and Benedict XV (in the second part of Book II, devoted to religious) by its legislation concerning religious —accurately compiled and carefully collated and examined—had in many ways confirmed the canonical state of perfection, viewed always as a public state. Wisely concluding the work begun by Leo XIII of happy memory, in his Constitution *Conditae a Christo*, it admitted congregations taking simple vows among religious orders properly so called. There seemed then nothing remaining to be added to the discipline regarding the canonical state of perfection. But the Church, in her magnanimity, decided in her maternal solicitude to add to the legislation concerning religious a concise section to complete it in a manner suited to the times (tit. XVII, Bk. II).

In it the Church decided to give a full measure of equality with the canonical state of perfection to those societies which had deserved well of her and frequently of civil society also. These associations, though lacking certain juridical forms, public vows, for example, required for full constitution in the canonical state of perfection (cs. 488 § 1 and 7; 487) are nevertheless closely allied to religious orders properly so called by close resemblance and by a certain necessity, because they possess the other features that are regarded as belonging to the substance of the life of perfection.

All this wise, prudent and benevolent legislation had amply provided for the needs of numberless souls who, having left the world, desired to embrace the new canonical state of perfection properly so called, solely and entirely devoted to the winning of perfection. But our loving Lord who, no respecter of persons, has ever and again invited all the faithful to pursue and practise perfection everywhere, has desired by an admirable design of his divine Providence that even in the world, made corrupt by so many vices, there should flourish, especially in our times, several bands of chosen souls. He has desired that these, remaining in the world not indeed from lack of zeal for their personal perfection, but in virtue of a special call from God, should find new and excellent forms of association, especially suited to the needs of our time in which they can lead a life entirely conducive to the attainment of Christian perfection.

While commending with all our hearts to the prudence and zeal of spiritual directors the generous efforts of souls striving after perfection in the spiritual sphere, we turn our attention at present to those associations which endeavor publicly in the Church to lead their members, as it were by the hand, to a life of solid perfection. There is, however, no question here of all those associations which sincerely pursue Christian perfection in the world, but only of those which by their internal constitution, by the hierarchical nature of their government, by the complete self-dedication, free from every other bond, which they require of their members properly so called, in the profession of the evangelical counsels, and lastly by the way in which they exercise their ministry and apostolate, more nearly approach the canonical state of perfection, so far as its substance is concerned, and especially the association without public vows (tit. XVII) although they may take other external forms than those of religious life in common.

These associations, which will be called hereafter Secular Institutes, began to be established, by a special inspiration of divine Provindence, in the first half of the last century. Their purpose was to practise faithfully "in the world the evangelical counsels and to undertake with greater freedom the duties of charity which owing to the evils of the times were made difficult or were entirely forbidden to the religious orders." The oldest of these Institutes proved their worth; increasingly they have sufficiently shown by their works and deeds that, by reason of the stringent and prudent selection of their members and of the careful and lengthy training they received in a flexible and stable rule of life well-adapted for its purpose, it is certainly possible to obtain, even in the world, by a special vocation from God and with the help of grace, not only an external but also an inward consecration to the Lord, almost comparable to the religious life. They have thus provided a timely instrument of apostolic endeavor and penetration. For these manifold reasons not infrequently "has the Holy See commended these associations of the faithful as real religious congregations."

The fortunate increase of these institutes has shown with increasing clarity what varied aid and effective support they can furnish to the Church and souls. In all times and places their members can lead the life of perfection; they can embrace it in certain cases when the canonical religious life is impossible or ill-adapted to the circumstances; they can act as the leaven of rechristianization for families, professions and civil society by reason of their close and daily contact with a life of complete and perfect dedication to holiness; they can exercise the apostolate in many ways and carry out manifold ministerial tasks that place, time or circumstances forbid or render very difficult for priests and religious. Such are the tasks entrusted to these Institutes. On the other hand, experience has shown the difficulties and dangers sometimes occasioned, and even quite easily, by this life of perfection, voluntarily led without the external support of the religious habit and community life, beyond the supervision of the diocesan bishop, to whom it may easily be unknown or of religious superiors who are often at a distance.

Discussion has also arisen concerning the juridical nature of these institutes and the mind of the Holy See in approving them. Here we have considered it timely to mention the decree *Ecclesia catholica*, published by the Congregation of Bishops and Regulars, and approved on August 11, 1889 by Leo XIII, our predecessor of immortal memory. Without withholding praise and approval for these institutes, the decree however laid down that when the Congregation bestowed praise and approbation on them it was certainly not as religious orders of solemn vows, or as true religious congregations of simple vows, but merely as devout associations in which, apart from the absence of other conditions required by the present discipline of the Church, no religious profession in the proper sense of the word is made and the vows, if they are taken, are deemed to be private vows and not public ones like those received by a legitimate superior in the name of the Church.

In addition, as the same Congregation went on to say, these associations are praised and approved only under the essential condition that they are fully and perfectly known to their respective diocesan bishops and wholly subject to their jurisdiction. These prescriptions and declarations of the Congregation of Bishops and Regulars were a timely contribution in that they defined the nature of these institutes and regulated, but without impeding it, their evolution and progress.

In this century the Secular Institutes have unobtrusively increased, assuming many and varied forms. Some are autonomous, others are united more or less closely with religious orders or congregations. The Constitution *Conditae a Christo*, which was concerned only with religious Congregations, did not legislate for Secular Institutes. The Code of Canon Law purposely omitted mention of them, leaving for future legislation the task of framing their organization since it seemed premature to do so at that time.

These matters we considered on several occasions, impelled by the consciousness of our office and of our paternal love for souls seeking so generously holiness in the world. For we were persuaded also that it must be made possible to make a wise and severe discrimination between these associations, only recognizing as real institutes those which make authentic profession of the life of perfection in all its fullness. We desired to avoid the danger of the continual foundation of fresh institutes—for they are often imprudently and insecurely established—and also to give to the institutes deserving of approbation the special juridical status aptly fitted to their nature, aims and requirements. We have resolved and decided to do for the Secular Institutes what our predecessor of immortal memory, Leo XIII, so wisely and prudently achieved by the Apostolic Constitution *Conditae a Christo* for the Congregations of simple vows. Therefore, by this present letter we approve the general statute of Secular Institutes which the Supreme Congregation of the Holy Office has carefully examined concerning all that falls within its competence and which Congregation of Religious has drawn up and revised, at our command and under our direction. In virtue of our Apostolic Authority we declare, decree and enact as follows; further, we appoint the Congregation of Religious for the execution of this law as set forth in the decree above, and we grant it all the faculties necessary and expedient for the purpose.

THE SPECIAL LAW
GOVERNING SECULAR INSTITUTES

Article I

Clerical or lay Associations whose members, in order to attain to Christian perfection, and the full exercise of the apostolate, make profession of practising the evangelical counsels in the world, receive the special name of Institutes or Secular Institutes in order to be clearly distinguished from other general associations of the faithful (Code of Canon Law, IIIrd pt; Bk. II).

These Institutes are subject to the laws of this Apostolic Constitution.

Article II

1. Since Secular Institutes neither take the three public vows of religion (cs. 1308 § 1, and 488, 1) nor impose community life or domicile in common on all their members, according to Canon Law (cs. 487 ff.; 673):

1. By law, ordinarily, they cannot strictly speaking be called religious orders or societies of common life.

2. They are not bound by the special law proper to religious or societies of common life. Nor may they take advantage of such law, unless some prescription thereof, and especially of that proper to Societies without public vows, is, exceptionally, applied or adapted to them.

2. Secular Institutes, without prejudice to the general rules of Canon Law applying to them, are governed by the following as by law special to them and more precisely adapted to their special character and condition:

1. By the general rules of this Apostolic Constitution which form the special statute of all Secular Institutes.

2. By the regulations that the Congregation of Religious, as necessity requires or experience counsels, shall lay down for all or some Secular Institutes whether by interpretation, elaboration or application of this Apostolic Constitution.

3. By special Constitutions approved according to the following articles (5-8) which prudently adapt the general rules of the law and the special rules laid down above (1. and 2.) to the very different aims, needs and circumstances of each Institute.

Article III

1. For any devout association of the faithful to be established as a Secular Institute, in accordance with the following articles, in addition to the ordinary requirements it must fulfil the following conditions:

2. As regards dedication of life and profession of Christian perfection:

Associates who desire to belong to the Institute as members in the strict sense, in addition to the exercises of piety and mortification undertaken by all those who aspire to perfection of Christian life, must effectively tend to this same perfection by the special means here enumerated:

1. By profession, made before God, of celibacy and perfect chastity, secured, in accordance with their Constitutions, by a vow, oath and consecration obliging in conscience.

2. By the vow or promise of obedience, so that bound by a firm bond they dedicate themselves wholly to God and to works of charity or apostolate, and that in all things they remain morally under the authority and guidance of superiors, according to the Constitutions.

3. By the vow or promise of poverty in virtue of which they enjoy not the free use of their temporal goods but a defined and restricted use according to the Constitutions.

3. As regards the incorporation of members in their Institute and the bond resulting therefrom:

The bond joining the Secular Institute and its members properly so called must be:

1. Lasting (*stabile*) according to the Constitutions, either for life or for a determined period, and in the latter case it must be renewed on expiry.

2. Mutual and complete so that in accordance with the Constitutions the member gives himself wholly to the Institute and the Institute takes care of the member and is responsible for him.

4. As regards the residences and common houses of Secular Institutes:

Secular Institutes, even if they do not oblige their members (art II, § 1) in accordance with Canon Law to life in common or to living under the same roof, for reasons of necessity or convenience must nevertheless possess one or several common houses in which:

1. The superiors of the Institute, especially general or regional superiors, can live.

2. The members of the Institute can live or gather to receive or perfect their training, to make their retreats or for purposes of this nature.

3. Members can be accommodated who, by reason of ill-health or some other circumstance, are incapable of providing

for themselves, or for whom it is considered inexpedient that they should live in a private house either alone or with others.

Article IV

1. Secular Institutes (art. I) are under the jurisdiction of the Congregation of Religious, saving for the rights of the Congregation for the Propagation of the Faith, in accordance with c. 252 § 3, in the case of societies and seminaries intended for the foreign missions.

2. Societies outside the definition of, or whose aims are not completely in accordance with, the requirements of art. I, those also lacking in one of the elements enumerated in arts. I and III of the associations of the faithful (cs. 684 following) and are under the present Apostolic Constitution, are governed by the law concerning jurisdiction of the Congregation of the Council except for the prescriptions of c. 252 § 3, concerning missionary territories.

Article V

1. Bishops, but not vicars capitular or vicars general, can establish Secular Institutes and give them the status of moral persons, in accordance with c. 100 § 1 and 2.

2. However, bishops cannot found these Institutes nor allow them to be founded without previous consultation of the Congregation of Religious in accordance with c. 492 § 1, and the following article.

Article VI

1. For the Congregation of Religious to grant permission to found Secular Institutes to bishops who, in accordance with art. V § 2, have previously consulted it regarding their establishment of Institutes, it must be informed on the points specified in the Rules that it has laid down (nos. 3-5) for the establishment of diocesan congregations or societies of common life, making those adaptations that it considers necessary; it must be informed also on those points which have been or will subsequently be introduced in the practice and customs of the same Congregation.

2. Once the authorization of the Congregation of Religious has been obtained nothing prevents bishops making use in all freedom of their own rights and establishing the foundation. They must not

omit officially to notify the same Congregation of the foundation that has been made.

Article VII

1. Secular Institutes which have obtained from the Holy See the decree of approbation or commendation become Institutes of pontifical jurisdiction.

2. For diocesan Secular Institutes to obtain the decree of approbation and commendation there are required in general, in addition to the adaptations judged necessary by the Congregation of Religious, all the formalities laid down or to be laid down, in the future, by the Rules (6 ff) and customs and practice of this same Congregation for congregations and societies of common life.

3. For the first approbation of an Institute and its Constitutions, for its renewal, if necessary, and for the definitive approbation, the following procedure will be adopted:

1. The case having been prepared in the normal manner and elucidated by the recommendation and report of at least one consultor, it will be discussed in the first instance at the commission of consultors under the presidency of the secretary of the Congregation of Religious or his delegate.

2. The whole matter will be subjected to examination and decision by the full assembly of the Congregation, presided over by His Eminence the Cardinal Prefect; competent consultors, or others even more expert, will be invited to study the case more thoroughly should it be necessary or expedient.

3. The decision of the assembly will be communicated to the Holy Father at a pontifical audience by the Cardinal Prefect or by the Secretary of the Congregation and submitted to his supreme judgment.

Article VIII

In addition to their own laws, at present in force or subsequently to be enacted, Secular Institutes are subject to their local diocesan bishops according to the prescriptions of Canon Law for non-exempt congregations leading a common life.

Article IX

The internal government of Secular Institutes can be hierarchic, according to the nature, aims and character of each one, on the pattern of the government of religious orders and societies of common life, after adaptations have been made as judged necessary by the Congregation of Religious.

Article X

Nothing is changed by the present Apostolic Constitution in the laws and obligations of the Institutes already founded and approved by the bishops after consultation of the Holy See or by the Holy See itself.

We proclaim, declare and sanction these things aforementioned, decreeing likewise that this Apostolic Constitution shall always be and remain permanent, effective and valid, and that it must obtain its full effects, notwithstanding all things to the contrary, even those deemed worthy of special mention. Let it be lawful for no one to transgress or otherwise with impunity oppose this Constitution promulgated by us.

Given at St. Peter's in Rome on the second day of February, the feast of the Purification of the Blessed Virgin Mary in the year 1947, the eighth of our pontificate.

PIUS PP. XII

MOTU PROPRIO PRIMO FELICITER

IN PRAISE AND APPROBATION OF SECULAR INSTITUTES

A year has happily passed since the promulgation of our Apostolic Constitution *Provida Mater*. At the sight of this great number of souls hidden "with Christ in God" who aspire to perfection in the world and gladly with generous heart and willing mind consecrate their whole life to God in the new Secular Institutes, we cannot refrain from giving thanks to the Divine Goodness for this new militia come to augment the army of those who practise the evangelical counsels and also for the powerful help which in these troubled and sorrowful times providentially strengthens the Catholic apostolate.

The Holy Spirit who unceasingly re-creates and renews the

face of the earth, daily made desolate and stained by many and great evils, has called to himself, by a great and especial grace, many beloved sons and daughters whom with great affection we bless in the Lord, so that gathered together and organized in Secular Institutes they may be for this dark world which has lost its savor, a world to which they do not belong and in which by divine dispensation they must nevertheless remain, the salt, the light and the leaven: the incorruptible salt which, renewed by the effect of vocation, does not grow savorless; the light which shines amid the darkness of the world and is not put out; the leaven, small in quantity yet ever active, which always and everywhere at work, mingled with all grades of society, from the highest to the lowest, strives by word, example and in every way to reach and permeate them each and all until the whole mass is transformed and wholly leavened in Christ.

In order that so many Institutes, which have arisen in all nations as a result of this consoling outpouring of the Spirit of Jesus Christ, may be effectively guided by the provisions of the Apostolic Constitution *Provida Mater Ecclesia* and that they may bear in great abundance the excellent fruits of sanctity which are looked for from them; and also in order that solidly and wisely organized into an army they may courageously fight God's battles in common or individual works of the apostolate, we confirm this Apostolic Constitution with great joy and, after mature deliberation, in this *Motu Proprio*, with certain knowledge and in the fullness of our Apostolic power, we declare, decree and establish as follows:

I. Societies of clerics or layfolk who profess Christian perfection in the world, and who seem certainly and completely to possess the characteristics and requirements laid down by the Apostolic Constitution *Provida Mater Ecclesia*, neither ought to, nor may, under any pretext whatsoever, be left arbitrarily among the ordinary associations of the faithful (cs. 684-725) but must of necessity be brought and raised to the proper state and form of Secular Institutes which perfectly correspond to their character and needs.

II. In effecting this raising up of societies of the faithful to the higher status of Secular Institutes (cf. I) and in the organization, both general and special, of all Institutes, it must be kept in mind that the proper and special character of these Institutes, that is, their *secular* character, which constitutes their whole reason for existence, must always stand out clearly in everything. Therefore, nothing must be withdrawn from the complete profession of Christian perfection, solidly founded on the evangelical counsels and authentically religious in its substance, but this perfection must be pursued and professed in the *world;* it must therefore be adapted to secular life in all that is lawful and in accordance with the obligations and works of this same perfection.

In its entirety the life of the members of Secular Institutes ought to be directed towards the apostolate. The exercise of this apostolate in constancy and holiness must derive from such purity of intention, close union with God, generous forgetfulness of self and mortification, from so great a love for souls, that it should reveal the interior spirit which informs it and must continually nourish and renew it. This apostolate, which embraces the whole of their life, is usually so deeply and sincerely regarded in these Institutes that, with the help and under the inspiration of divine Providence, the burning thirst for souls seems not to be confined to the provision of a suitable opportunity for a dedicated life, but to a great extent to have stamped it with its own form and nature and, even more wonderfully, to have required and brought into being its specific and even its generic purpose.

This apostolate of the Secular Institutes is to be faithfully exercised not only *in the world* but, as a consequence, its profession, activities, forms, places and other circumstances are to correspond to this secular condition.

III. The laws concerning canonical discipline of the religious state do not apply to Secular Institutes and legislation for religious in general should not be applied to them nor regarded as valid for them in accordance with the rules laid down by the Apostolic Constitution *Provida Mater Ecclesia* (art. II, § 1). On the other hand those things which in the Institutes are in accordance with their character as secular, provided that they in no wise impair the complete consecration of the whole life and are in conformity with the Constitution *Provida Mater Ecclesia,* may be preserved.

IV. An hierarchical, interdiocesan and universal constitution after the manner of an organized body can be applied to Secular Institutes (*ibid.* art. IX) and this application must certainly obtain for them internal strength, a wider and more effective influence and also stability. Nevertheless, in this organization, which must be adapted to each Institute, account must be taken of the nature of the end pursued by the Institute, of its purpose of greater or less expansion, of its stage of development and its degree of maturity, of the circumstances in which it is situated and other matters of this kind. Those forms of Institutes which are established as a confederation and which desire to retain and encourage with due moderation their local character in each nation, region or diocese, must not be rejected or despised provided that this character is good and permeated with the sense of the catholicity of the Church.

V. The Secular Institutes, because their members, although living in the world, consecrate themselves wholly to God and souls with the approval of the Church, and because they possess, in differing degrees, an internal hierarchic, interdiocesan and universal organization, are very rightly, and in accordance with the conditions of the Apostolic Constitution *Provida Mater Ecclesia,* included among the states of perfection ordained and recognized by the Church herself. Deliberately, therefore, these Institutes have been entrusted and assigned to the competence and care of that Congregation which is concerned with the government and protection of the *public states of perfection.* Consequently, though without prejudice to the rights of the Congregation of the Council over pious associations and sodalities of the faithful (c. 252, § 2) and those of the Congregation for the Propagation of the Faith over ecclesiastical societies and seminaries in missionary territories (c. 252, § 3) we have decreed that all societies everywhere—even though they enjoy episcopal or pontifical approbation—shall obligatorily and immediately be converted to the new form of Secular Institutes according to the rule laid down above (I) whenever they are found to possess the characteristics and fulfill the requisite conditions. In order to preserve unity of direction they must depend upon and be assigned to the Congregation of Religious alone, within which a special section has been established for Secular Institutes.

VI. We address ourselves to directors and assistants of Catholic Action movements and other associations of the faithful within which are trained to a fully Christian life, and initiated into the exercise of the apostolate, a numerous *élite* of young men and women called by God to a higher vocation either in religious orders and societies of common life or even in Secular Institutes; paternally we commend to them the generous encouragement of these holy vocations calling on them to lend assistance not only to the religious orders and societies but also to these truly providential Secular Institutes, and willingly make use of their help while preserving their own internal discipline.

In virtue of our authority we entrust the faithful execution of all these things here laid down by *Motu Proprio* to the Congregation of Religious mentioned above, to local diocesan bishops and to the directors of the societies in question, to the extent to which they pertain to each.

What we have determined by these letters, given by *Motu Proprio*, we decree to be valid and binding always, all things to the contrary notwithstanding.

Given at Rome at St. Peter's on the twelfth day of March, 1948, at the beginning of the tenth year of our pontificate.

PIUS PP. XII

CUM SANCTISSIMUS

INSTRUCTION ON SECULAR INSTITUTES FROM THE SACRED CONGREGATION OF RELIGIOUS

When His Holiness promulgated the Apostolic Constitution *Provida Mater Ecclesia*, he saw fit to assign all those things which were wisely set forth in the Constitution for their ready fulfilment to the Sacred Congregation of Religious to whose competence Secular Institutes belong (Lex peculiaris, art. IV, § 1 and 2), and he bestowed on it all the faculties necessary and proper to this end.

Among the duties and offices laid on the Sacred Congregation by this pontifical delegation of power, according to the express definition of the Constitution, we recall this in particular: that "as necessity arises or experience dictates, whether by interpretation or elaboration and application of the Apostolic Constitution" this Congregation may lay down norms that are deemed necessary or useful to Secular Institutes in general or to any one of them (art. II, § 2 b).

Moreover, although the complete and definitive norms respecting Secular Institutes are better deferred to a more opportune time lest the present evolution of these Institutes be restricted, yet it is necessary that certain things, which were not clearly perceived or correctly interpreted by everyone in the Apostolic Constitution *Provida Mater Ecclesia*, should be at once more plainly and securely stated. This, however, is to be carried out according to the prescriptions enunciated in His Holiness's *Motu proprio* Letter *Primo feliciter*, of March 12. Therefore, the Sacred Congregation has decided, by way of an Instruction, to collect the main norms and clearly to publish the substance of those that are deservedly regarded as basic to the initial and secure foundation and organization of Secular Institutes:

1. In order that any Association, however much it may be dedicated to the profession of Christian perfection and apostolate in the world, may justly and rightly assume the name and title of *Secular Institute*, it is not only necessary that it should have each and all of those elements that are laid down by the Apostolic Constitution *Provida Mater Ecclesia* as being held and defined necessary for, and integral to, Secular Institutes (arts. I and III); it is also necessary that it should be approved and erected by a Bishop after consultation with this Sacred Congregation (art. V, § 2; art. VI).

2. Associations of the faithful having the nature and characteristics described in the Apostolic Constitution all depend by law, according to the same Constitution (art. IV, § 1 and 2), on the this Sacred Congregation of Religious everywhere, both in countries under the common law and in Missionary countries, and subject to the *Lex peculiaris* of the Constitution. Nor for whatsoever reason or

title, according to the Letter *Primo feliciter* (no. V), may they remain as ordinary Associations of the faithful (C.J.C., Bk. II, pt. III), having respect to no. 5 of this Instruction.

3. To obtain permission for the erection of a new Secular Institute, a diocesan Bishop, and no other, should approach this Sacred Congregation, and he must inform it in detail regarding all those things laid down in the Norms issued by the Sacred Congregation of Religious for the erection and approval of Congregations (March 6, 1921, nn. 3-8), but with necessary modifications (art. VII). At the same time, at least six copies of the proposed Constitutions must be submitted in Latin or in some other tongue acceptable to the Curia, and with these must go Directories and such other documents that may serve to reveal the nature and spirit of the Association. The Constitutions must contain everything that concerns the nature of the Institute, the types of membership, the internal government, the form of consecration (art. III, § 2), the bond which arises from the incorporation of the members in the Institute (art. III, § 3), the common houses (art. III, § 4), the means of formation of the members and their spiritual exercises.

4. Associations which previous to the Constitution *Provida Mater Ecclesia* were legitimately erected or approved by Bishops according to the norms of older laws, or which had obtained some pontifical approval as lay Associations, must submit the following to this Sacred Congregation in order to be recognized by it as Secular Institutes— of either diocesan or pontifical right: documents of erection or approval, the Constitutions by which they have hitherto been governed, a brief history of the Association, of its discipline and apostolate, and also, particularly if it be only of diocesan right, evidence from the Ordinaries in whose diocese they reside. Once all these have been thoroughly and carefully examined under the regulations of articles VI and VII of *Provida Mater Ecclesia*, a permission for erection or a Decree of praise may be granted according to the nature of the case.

5. It would be better that Associations which have not been thus previously established, or have not yet been sufficiently devel-

oped, or are now being founded, even though they may have every hope that, if things continue as they are, well established and genuine Secular Institutes may arise out of them, should not be immediately proposed to the Sacred Congregation for permission to be erected. As a general rule, admitting exceptions only for serious and clearly proven reasons, these new Associations should be kept and directed under the immediate and watchful care of the diocesan Authority until they manifest sufficient signs of vitality. At first they should be treated as mere Associations which exist in fact rather than by right; and then step by step, and by degrees without any by-passing, they should evolve under some special form of Association of the faithful, as Pious Unions, Sodalities, Confraternities, as the case may be.

6. Regarding these said developments (cf. no. 5)—from which it is to be shown that a true Association is in question, having before its eyes a complete dedication to the life of perfection and apostolate and having all the other characteristics requisite for a Secular Institute—it should be noted that, as they evolve, great care is to be exercised lest anything internal or external be allowed within the Association that exceeds their present status and seems to belong specifically to the essence and nature of Secular Institutes. In particular those things are to be avoided that would militate against the future permission of erection as a Secular Institute, and could not easily be removed or abolished and so would appear to bring pressure to bear on the authorities to approve them or too readily to agree to them.

7. In order to safeguard a sure and practical judgment regarding any association having the true nature of a Secular Institute, in other words to ascertain whether it effectively draws its members, in a secular state and condition, to that full consecration and dedication which, even in the exterior (*in foro externo*), bears the mark of the complete state of perfection, in substance true religious, the following points must be accurately weighed:

(a) Whether the members, insofar as they are inscribed in the Association as members in the strict sense, seriously profess "in addition to those exercises of devotion and self-denial," without which the life of perfection would be a vain illusion, the three evangelical counsels according to one of the forms recognized by the Apostolic Constitution (art. III, § 2). However, members in a broad sense may be admitted, who are incorporated in the Association to a greater or less degree, provided they aspire to evangelical perfection and try to live it in their own state, even though they do not or cannot embrace each evangelical counsel in the highest degree.

(b) Whether the bond by which the members strictly so called and the Association are held together is *stable, mutual and comprehensive* (*stabile, mutuum ac plenum*), in such fashion that according to the regulations of the Constitution the individual member dedicates himself entirely to the Association and the Association is, or seriously anticipates being, in such a position that it will and can take care of the member and be legally responsible for him (art. III, § 3, b).

(c) Whether and under what description and title the common centres prescribed by the Apostolic Constitution (art. III, § 4) are actually in existence or are being set up so as to achieve the purpose for which they are required.

(d) Whether such things as are not consonant with the nature and essence of a Secular Institute are excluded, e.g., clothes or habits unlike the ordinary dress of the world, a common life that is externally organized (art. II, § 1; art. III, § 4) in the same way as religious community life or is equivalent to it (tit. XVII, L. II, C.J.C.).

8. According to art. II, § 1, b, of the Apostolic Constitution *Provida Mater Ecclesia* and having respect to arts. X and II, § 1, a, of the same Constitution, Secular Institutes are not subject to the proper and particular law regarding Religious Institutes or Societies of common life, nor may they use that law. Nevertheless the Sacred Congregation, by way of exception, according to the meaning of the Constitution (art. II, § 1, b) may prudently demand that certain particular prescriptions of the law of Religious, which are suited to Secular Institutes, be accommodated and applied to them; and

that, similarly, certain more or less general standards, which have been proved by experience and correspond closely to the nature of things, be so accommodated and applied.

9. In particular:

(a) Though the prescriptions of c. 500, § 3, do not strictly apply to Secular Institutes, nor is there any need to apply them as they stand, nevertheless from them it is possible to obtain a clear standard and directive for approving and organizing Secular Institutes.

(b) Though according to c. 492, § 1, there is nothing to prevent Secular Institutes, by special concession, from being attached to Religious Orders or other Religious Institutes, and being helped by them in various ways and even in some way being morally directed by them, nevertheless other forms of more strict dependence which may possibly detract from the autonomy of the Secular Institute's government and put it under a more or less stringent control, can only with difficulty be granted even when such dependence is desired and sought—especially by female Institutes; and permission can be granted only with due restrictions and after the good of the Institute has been carefully considered and the nature and essence of its spirit and apostolate have been weighed up.

10. (a) Secular Institutes, according to the state of complete perfection which they profess and to the total consecration to the apostolate which they undertake, are clearly called to greater things in this order of perfection and apostolate than those which may seem to suffice for the faithful, even among the best, working in merely lay Associations or in Catholic Action or in other devout activities.

(b) Nevertheless they should undertake the works and service of the apostolate proper to the special aims of the Institutes in such a way that their members, carefully shunning possible confusions, may with energy stand forth as evident examples to the rest of the faithful who will observe them, examples of self-sacrificing, humble and sustained cooperation with the Hierarchy, while, of course, always preserving the internal discipline of the Institutes (cf. Motu Proprio *Primo feliciter*, no. VI).

11. (a) The Ordinary, having obtained the permission of the Holy See for the erection of a Secular Institute—which has previously been in existence as an Association *de facto*, or as a Pious Union or Sodality—may, while he proceeds to the erection, define whether it is expedient to take cognizance of what has been hitherto accomplished—e.g., probation, consecration, etc.—in order to establish the condition of the persons and to assess the requirements of the Institute's Constitutions.

(b) In the first ten years of a Secular Institute, from the date of its erection, the diocesan Bishop may dispense from the requisites regarding age, time of probation, years of consecration and such like prescriptions, general to all Institutes or proper to any particular one, when it is a question of offices, duties, degrees and other legal matters.

(c) The houses or centers established before the canonical erection of the Institute that were set up by permission of the two Bishops prescribed by c. 495, § 1, by the very deed of erection become part of the Institute.

Given at Rome from the Offices of the Sacred Congregation of Religious, on the 19th of March, feast of St. Joseph, Spouse of the Blessed Virgin Mary, in the year 1948.

ALOYSIUS CARDINAL LAVITRANO
Prefect

ALLOCUTION ON SECULAR INSTITUTES

Pope Paul VI

On September 20, 1972, members of the International Congress of Leaders of Secular Institutes were granted an audience with His Holiness, Pope Paul VI. During the audience the Holy Father delivered the following allocution, presented in the *Osservatore romano*, English language weekly edition, October 5, 1972, pages 3-4.

Beloved Sons and Daughters in the Lord, once more we have the opportunity of meeting you, Leaders of the Secular Institutes, who are and represent a vigorous and flourishing section of the Church at this moment of history. The circumstance that has brought you before us is, this time, the International Congress which you have carried out and are about to conclude here in Nemi, near our summer residence at Castel Gandolfo, and at which you examined the statutes of the "World Conference of Secular Institutes" (C.M.I.S.), about to be erected.

We do not wish to discuss your work, which was certainly carried out with thoroughness and enthusiasm, under the watchful care and with the participation of the competent Sacred Congregation. We hope that it will reap rich fruits in relation to the increase of your institutions.

Your Presence a Testimony

We rather desire to dwell on some reflections about what the function of the secular institutes could be in the mystery of Christ and in the mystery of the Church.

When we look at you and think of the thousands and thousands of men and women of whom you are part, we cannot but feel consoled, while a deep sense of joy and gratitude to the Lord comes over us. How strong and flourishing the Church of Christ appears in you! This venerable Mother of ours, whom some people today, even among her sons, take as the butt of harsh, pitiless criticism; about whom some delight in describing fanciful symptoms of decrepitude and in predicting ruin; here we see her, on the contrary, bursting continuously into bud and blossoming beyond all expectation with initiatives of holiness. We know that it must be so and could not be otherwise, because Christ is the divine inexhaustible source of the vitality of the Church; and your presence offers us a further testimony of this, and is for all of us an opportunity for renewed consciousness.

But we wish to scan your face more closely, in the family of the People of God. You, too, reflect a "specific way" in which the mystery of Christ can be lived in the world, and a "specific way" in which the mystery of the Church can be manifested.

Christ the Redeemer is such a fullness, which we will never be able to understand or express completely. He is everything for His Church. In her, what we are we are just because of Him, with Him, and in Him. Also for the secular institutes, therefore, He remains the ultimate example, the inspirer, the source on which to draw.

Based on Christ the Savior and following His example you are carrying out, in your own characteristic way, an important mission of the Church. But the Church, too, in her way, like Christ, is such a fullness, such riches, that no one by himself, no institution by itself, will ever be able to understand her and express her adequately. Nor would it be possible for us to discover her dimensions, because her life is Christ, who is God. So also the reality of the Church, and the mission of the Church, can be expressed completely only in the plurality of members. It is the doctrine of the Mystical Body of Christ, the doctrine of the gifts and charisms of the Holy Spirit.

A Consecrated Secularity

This is the point, as you have understood, to ask ourselves about your particular way of carrying out the mission of the Church. What is your specific gift, your characteristic role, the "quid novum" brought by you to the Church of today? Or: in what way are you the Church today? You know the answer; you have by now clarified it to yourselves and to the Christian community.

You are at a mysterious confluence between the two powerful streams of Christian life, welcoming riches from both. You are laymen, consecrated as such by the sacraments of baptism and confirmation but you have chosen to emphasize your consecration to God with the profession of the evangelical counsels assumed as obligations with a stable and recognized bond. You remain laymen, engaged in the secular values characteristic of, and peculiar to, the laity (*Lumen gentium*, 31), but yours is a "consecrated secularity" (Paul VI, *Discorso ai Dirigenti e Membri degli Istituti Secolari nel XXV della "Provida Mater,"* L'Osservatore Romano, February 3, 1972), you are "secular consecrated" (Paul VI, *Discorso ai partecipanti al Congresso Internazionale degli Istituti Secolari,* September 26, 1970, *Insegnamenti* VIII, p. 939).

Though "secular," your position differs in a certain way from that of mere laymen, since you are engaged in the same worldly values, but as consecrated beings: that is, not so much to affirm the intrinsic validity of human things in themselves, but to direct them explicitly according to the evangelical beatitudes. On the other hand you are not religious, but in a certain way your choice is concordant with the religious, because the consecration you have made sets you in the world as witnesses to the supremacy of spiritual and eschatological values, that is, to the absolute character of your Christian charity. The greater the latter is, the more relative it makes the values of the world seem, while at the same time it helps their correct implementation by yourselves and by your other brothers.

Both Aspects Essential

Neither of the aspects of your spiritual nature can be overrated at the expense of the other. They are both equally essential.

"Secularity" indicates your involvement in the world. But it does not mean only a position, a function, which coincides with living in the world by practicing a trade, a "secular" profession. It must mean in the first place awareness of being in the world as "your specific place of Christian responsibility." To be in the world, that is, to be engaged in secular values, is your way of being the Church and of making her present, of saving yourselves and of announcing salvation. Your existential and sociological condition becomes your theological reality; it is your way to realize and testify to salvation. Thus you are an advanced wing of the Church "in the world"; you express the will of the Church to be in the world in order to mold it and sanctify it "from within, in the manner of leaven" (*Lumen gentium*, 31), a task, too, which is mainly entrusted to the laity. You are a particularly concrete and efficacious manifestation of what the Church wishes to do to construct the world described and desired by *Gaudium et Spes*.

"Consecration," on the other hand, indicates the intimate and secret carrying structure of your being and your acting. Here is your deep and hidden wealth, which the men in the midst of whom you live cannot explain and often cannot even suspect. Baptismal consecration has been further radicalized as a result of an increased aspiration for love aroused in you by the Holy Spirit; not in the same form as the consecration of religious, but nevertheless such as to induce you to make a fundamental option for life according to the evangelical beatitudes. So that you are really consecrated and really in the world. "You are in the world and not of the world, but for the world," as we ourself described you on another occasion (Paul VI, *Discorso ai partecipanti al Congresso Internazionale degli Istituti Secolari,* September 26, 1970, *Insegnamenti,* VII, p. 939). You live a real consecration according to the evangelical counsels, but without the fullness of "visibility" characteristic of religious consecration; a visibility that is constituted, in addition to the public vows, by a closer community life and by the "sign" of the religious habit. Yours is a new and original form of consecration, prompted by the Holy Spirit to be lived in the midst of temporal realities, and to bring the strength of the evangelical counsels—that is, of divine and eternal values—into the midst of human and temporal values.

The Cross of Christ

Your choices of poverty, chastity and obedience are ways of participating in the cross of Christ, because they associate you with Him in the renunciation of goods which are elsewhere permissible and legitimate; but they are also ways of participating in the victory of the risen Christ, since they free you from the hold that these values might have on the full availability of your spirit. Your poverty tells the world that it is possible to live among temporal goods and use the means of civilization and progress, without being enslaved by any of them. Your chastity tells the world that it is possible to love with disinterestedness and the inexhaustibility that draws on God's heart, and to dedicate oneself joyfully to everyone without tying oneself to anyone, taking care particularly of the most abandoned. Your obedience tells the world that it is possible to be happy without stopping at a comfortable personal choice, but remaining fully at the disposal of God's will, as it appears from daily life, from the signs of the times, and from the aspirations to salvation of the world of today.

Thus, also your activity in the world—both personal and collective, in the professional sectors in which you are engaged individually or as a community—receives from your consecrated life a more marked orientation towards God, it, too, being somehow involved and swept along in your consecration. And in this singular and providential configuration, you enrich the Church of today with a particular exemplarity in her "consecrated" life, living it as secular persons.

Priests in Secular Institutes

At this point we would like to dwell on a particularly fruitful aspect of your institutions. We are referring to the numerous groups of those who, consecrated to Christ in the ministerial priesthood and wishing to be united to him with a further bond of donation, embrace the profession of the evangelical counsels, joining the secular institutes in their turn. We are thinking of these brothers of ours in Christ's priesthood, and we wish to encourage them, while we admire in them, once more, the action of the Spirit, indefatigable in arousing desire for ever greater perfection. What has been said so far certainly applies to them, too, but it would require further study and clarifications. In fact, they arrive at consecration in the evangelical counsels and commitment to "secular" values not as laymen, but as ecclesiastics, that is, bearers of a sacred mediation in the People of God. In addition to baptism and confirmation, which constitute the basic consecration of the laity in the Church, they have received a subsequent sacramental specification in holy orders, which have constituted them holders of certain ministerial functions with regard to the Eucharist and the Mystical Body of Christ. This has left the "secular" nature of Christian vocation intact, and they can therefore enrich it by living it as "consecrated" persons in the secular institutes. The requirements of their spirituality are very different, however, as well as certain external implications in their practice of the evangelical counsels and in their secular commitment.

Ecclesial Communion

In conclusion we wish to address a pressing and fatherly invitation to everyone: to cultivate and increase ecclesial communion, to have it at heart always and particularly. You are vital articulations of this communion, because you, too, are the Church; never make an attack on their efficiency. It is impossible to conceive or understand an ecclesial phenomenon outside the Church. Never let yourselves be overcome by, or even give thought to, the temptation, too easy today, that authentic communion with Christ is possible without real harmony with the ecclesial community governed by the legitimate pastors. It would be misleading and illusory. Of what value would an individual or a group be, however lofty and perfect their intentions might be subjectively, without communion? Christ asked us for it as a guarantee to admit us to communion with Him, just as He asked us to love our neighbor as documentation of our love for Him.

You are, therefore, of Christ and for Christ, in His Church; this Church is your local community, your institute, your parish, but always in the communion of faith, of Eucharist, of discipline, and of faithful and loyal collaboration with your bishop and with the hierarchy. Your structures and your activities should never lead you—be you priests or laymen—to a "bipolarity" of positions, or to an "alibi" of interior and exterior attitude, far less to positions in opposition to your pastors.

This is our invitation; this is our wish, in order that you may be in the midst of the world authentic operators of the one saving mission of the Church, in your own characteristic way, to which you have been called and invited. May the Lord thus help you to prosper and fructify further, with our Apostolic Blessing.

APPENDIX

June 29, 1974

His Eminence Timothy Manning
Archbishop of Los Angeles
1531 West 9th Street
Los Angeles, California

Your Eminence:

I learned with great pleasure that, from August 29 through September 2, your Eminence will sponsor an Assembly for the promotion of consecrated life in the light of Vatican II and the subsequent documents issued by the Apostolic See. The zeal of your Eminence, a member of the Sacred Congregation for Religious and Secular Institutes, for the advancement of consecrated life in the Church is well known to us. I find it gratifying to be able to send a message to the participants at this Assembly who look to the Apostolic See for encouragement and guidance.

Religious life must be set on its own theology, built on the sound basis of the Gospel, Tradition and the Magisterium of the Church. It would be incorrect to say that Religious Life has no theology, that it is just a historical fact. Its roots sink deep into the Word of God, Tradition and the Magisterium, today more solemn than ever, with the rich patrimony of doctrine and pastoral orientation offered by Vatican II and the Apostolic See in the post-Council period. As the Church, Religious Life, an expression of her mystery, recognizes in the Holy Father the Supreme Authority that he generally exercises towards consecrated life through the Sacred Congregation for Religious and Secular Institutes. This authority "keeps its indispensable constitutional and mystical value, as a vehicle of the mysteries of God." (Paul VI, October 9, 1968).

The Church is a communion; union is her trade-mark. No wonder that the Holy Father has repeatedly expressed his concern about anything that divides. "We must have," he said June 16, 1974, "a special sensibility and dynamic care of unity, not *of* the Church, but also *in* the Church." There should always be an organic and fraternal union within and among the Institutes of Perfection as well as in their relations with the Hierarchy.

Religious Life is essentially a consecration; a consecration, not to something, to a program or project, but to *Someone*. Indeed, consecrated people are also dedicated by their commitment to the service of the world, of the brethren, as a practical application of the demands of the Gospel. It is a necessary consequence of their consecration to the Person of Christ. As Christ, they pray, they help the helpless, they use faithfully and generously their charisms, they embrace sacrifice and spend themselves for the human family.

This is a most fruitful idea, with precious consequences. It blends dynamically theology and sociology, the vertical and the horizontal. True religious, being consecrated people, seek unity and avoid polarization. Dialogue and cooperation are no problem when there is good will and humility. We can all teach each other something; we must all help each other. It is Christ, the living Gospel, that counts. He is the living epitome of consecrated chastity, poverty and obedience. His life is His most convincing gift to us.

May the blessings of the Lord, the fire of the Holy Spirit and the intercession of the Virgin Mary, Mother of the Church, fructify abundantly the days of prayer and study of the Assembly your Eminence so graciously sponsors. Fraternally in Christ,

Arturo Cardinal Tabera Araoz, C.M.F.
Cardinal Prefect—SCRSI

SCRSI DECREE: RELIGIONUM LAICALIUM

Lay religious institutes both of men and of women have made well thought out petitions to be allowed to use some of the faculties (insofar as they are not related to the clerical state) which were delegated to superiors general of clerical institutes by the pontifical rescript of November 6, 1964. The Sacred Congregation of Religious reported the matter to the supreme pontiff, Paul VI, and was commissioned by the same supreme pontiff to give to the aforementioned institutes a fitting indication of his esteem for them and at the same time to make the exercise of their internal government more expeditious. By reason of this commission, the Congregation has decided to decree the following points.

I. *The superiors general of pontifical lay institutes both of men and of women are granted the following faculties:*

1. With the consent of their council, of dispensing candidates to their institute from illegitimacy of birth provided the illegitimacy is not sacrilegious or adulterine.

2. With the consent of their council and for an adequate reason, of permitting property of their institute to be alienated, used as security, mortgaged, leased, placed in emphyteusis; and of granting permission to moral persons of their own institute to contract a debt up to the sum of money set down by the national or regional episcopal conference and approved by the Apostolic See.

3. Of obtaining for their subjects who ask for it a dispensation of temporary vows from the local ordinary of the house to which the petitioner is attached.

4. With the consent of their council and for an adequate reason, of permitting their subjects to be absent from a religious house for not more than a year. If this permission is given because of sickness, it can be granted for as long as the need lasts; if it is granted for the purpose of performing works of the apostolate, for an adequate reason it can be given for even beyond a year provided that the apostolic works to be performed are related to the purposes of the institute and that the norms of both common and particular law are observed.

With the consent of their council, they can subdelegate this faculty to other major superiors who, however, cannot use it except with the consent of their own council.

5. With the consent of their council, of granting their subjects who are professed of simple perpetual vows and who ask for it the faculty of ceding their patrimonial property for an adequate reason and in accord with the norms of prudence.

With the consent of their council they can subdelegate this faculty to other major superiors who, however, cannot use it except with the consent of their own council.

6. Of allowing their subjects to change their will. With the consent of their council they can subdelegate this faculty to other major superiors of the same institute.

7. With the consent of their council, of transferring either for a time or perpetually the location of an already lawfully established novitiate to another house of the same institute, the local ordinary where the novitiate house is located being foreadvised and all matters prescribed by law being observed.

8. With the consent of their council, of confirming local superiors for a third triennium after previous consultations with the local ordinary.

9. To superioresses general of orders of nuns there is granted the faculty of dispensing for an adequate reason individual nuns from the obligation of reciting the Divine Office—if they are obliged to this by common law—when they are absent from choir; or of commuting this obligation to other prayers. With the consent of the council, this faculty can be subdelegated to the superioresses of individual houses.

The same faculty is likewise granted to all superioresses of Independent monasteries of nuns.

II. *Declarations concerning the extension, subject, and use of these faculties:*

1. The aforementioned faculties pertain to pontifical non-clerical institutes.

2. The aforementioned faculties should also be considered as being granted to superiors general of pontifical societies living in common without public vows (see Book II, Chapter XVII of the Code of Canon Law); the faculties given under numbers 2 and 3

are given also to superiors general of pontifical ˜secular institutes in a proportionately applicable way.

3. The subject of these faculties is the person of the superior general or of the superioress general or the person who, when these are lacking, succeeds to them in governing for the meantime in accord with the approved constitutions; in the case of the faculty mentioned at the end of number 9, the subject is that of the superioress of the independent monastery and, when she is lacking, the person who succeeds her in governing in the meantime.

4. If the superior general or the superioress general is impeded in their office, they can subdelegate these same faculties, either in whole or in part, to a member of the same institute who acts as their vicar and who therefore can use the faculties personally and can subdelegate them again to others in individual cases, according to the limitations and conditions laid down above.

5. The matters decreed here take effect immediately and do not require any so-called formula of execution.

From the offices of the Sacred Congregation of Religious, May 31, 1966.

I. Card. ANTONIUTTI
Prefect

SCRSI DECREE:
CUM SUPERIORES GENERALES

Concerning faculties delegated to Major Superiors of Religious for granting secularization of members in temporary vows.

Since Superiors General of Religious experience some difficulties concerning the use of faculty no. 3 of the DECREE, "Secularization of Religious," dated May 31, 1966, on the secularization of religious members from temporary vows, the Congregation for Religious and Secular Institutes, after the question had been submitted to the study of the consultants and after the mind of Superiors and General Superiors had been ascertained, undertook to examine the matter in recent Plenary Session, October 8 and 9.

The Fathers considered the bond of temporary vows of men and women in lay institutes, when they freely request it, could return to the secular state, and the vows, *ipso facto*, be dissolved.

The Supreme Pontiff in an audience with the undersigned Cardinal Prefect, on November 13, 1969, approved the recommendation of the Plenary Congregation and ordered that it become a matter of public law.

Wherefore, in accord with the present DECREE the faculty of laicizing men and women is granted to Major Superiors of Religious with the consent of the proper council. Members professed in temporary vows who seek it may be returned to secular life. In which case, the temporary vows, *ipso facto*, will cease.

Everything contrary notwithstanding.

Given at Rome, November 27, 1969

I. Card. ANTONIUTTI
Prefect

SCRSI DECREE—AD INSTITUENDA

By which some faculties are granted to religious communities.

For purposes of experimentation in accordance with the Motu Proprio, ECCLESIAE SANCTAE, frequent dispensations from common law have been earnestly requested from the Sacred Congregation for Religious and Secular Institutes.

However, in fact, since the reasons are common to certain petitions and are rightly adaptable to all Institutes in general, the Sacred Congregation in Ordinary Session, on April 24, 1970, expressed the fittingness of suspending or changing several canons. Having considered duly all matters, it seemed fitting to the Fathers to state the following:

1. A Pontifical Religious Institute will be obliged to have recourse to the Holy See, in accordance with particular law, with regard to combining provinces already established or otherwise redefining their limits, founding new provinces or suppressing those established, or the total suppression of the same. Let a General Chapter establish the norms to be observed in the establishment or innovation of Provinces, inserting them into the Constitution.

2. The obligation of seeking the approval of the Apostolic See of erecting an exempt religious house, or suppressing it in virtue of Canon 497, no. 1 and 498 is suspended, except for Monialium Monasteriis *sui juris* (cf. Perf. Carit. no. 7), except for those which are under the jurisdiction of local ordinaries (cf. C. 497, no. 1 and M.P., ECCLESIAE SANCTAE 1, 34, no. 1).

3. Observing the Constitutions of a particular religious institute, which may demand a greater age or some other greater requirement, those persons who have not made their perpetual profession or who have not completed their 35th year are not eligible for the office of Superior General. For other major superiors (cf. C. 488, no. 8) besides perpetual profession, 30 years of age suffices. But for all other offices the particular law is competent to determine the required age, except for the Master of Novices in which case at least the age of 30 is required.

4. The rule by which testimonial letters for male aspirants are sought in accordance with Canons 544 no. 2 and 545 is suspended, except for the obligation arising out of the nature of the case, always to seek useful information concerning the candidate to be admitted.

5. The determination of the time of spiritual formation is left to the particular rules of the Institute before the candidates begin the novitiate or the novices take temporary vows (cf. Canons 541 and 571, no. 3), caution being taken, however, that at least 5 whole days be observed and the same spiritual exercises be performed in a fitting and proper manner.

6. The obligation of making a will which Canon 569, no. 3 established concerning novices in a religious congregation before profession of temporary vows, may be transferred to a time which immediately precedes perpetual vows.

7. The obligation of exploring willingness (cf. Canon 552) is suspended.

8. The prescription of Canon 607, whereby superiors and local ordinary are seriously bound to be on guard lest religious women decide apart from cases of necessity to leave the house alone, is suspended; the burden, however, of being on guard lest troubles arise, remains.

The Supreme Pontiff, Pope Paul VI, in audience with the undersigned Cardinal Prefect, June 1, 1970, saw fit to approve these judgments in Ordinary Session.

For this reason, the Sacred Congregation for Religious and Secular Institutes determined to make the aforementioned deliberations a matter of public law at the time of the present Decree.

The items here decreed take effect immediately and do not need any particular formula for their execution.

These matters remain in effect until such time as revised Canon Law takes effect.

Everything to the contrary notwithstanding.

I. Card. ANTONIUTTI
Prefect

June 4, 1970

THE FORMULA FOR RELIGIOUS PROFESSION[1]

The Sacred Congregation for Religious and Secular Institutes was asked if each person making religious profession might freely compose a formula for religious profession, and to describe the elements which must always be present in that formula. A reply was given by the Congregation on February 14, 1973 (Prot. n. 16935/72).

(1) The "Order of Religious Profession" published by the Sacred Congregation for Worship, prescribes that the formula for profession must be submitted for approval to the Sacred Congregation for Religious and Secular Institutes. However, it cannot be claimed that the composition of the formula for religious profession can be left to individual candidates for profession. It ought rather to be substantially the same for each institute, granted the identity of duties and rights deriving from profession.

(2) Further, it is sufficiently clear that no formula can ever omit certain elements which are of the nature of the profession of public vows (can. 1308, par. 1). These are: that the vows, made

---

1. Published in *Notitiae*, the organ of the Congregation for Divine Worship, July-August, 1973, p. 283.

to God, comprise chastity, poverty and obedience; that the obligations in question be understood to be undertaken 'according to the rule and constitutions'; that mention be made of the name or office of the person who receives the profession in the name of the Church; that the time for which profession is made be specified.

Provided these essential requirements are met, each institute may compose its own formula for profession, adapted to its needs and its specific spirituality.

(3) Granted what has been said above, there is nothing to prevent individual aspirants to profession from adding, at the beginning or at the end of the approved formula, their own sentiments of willingness or devotion. These must however be expressed soberly and sensibly and must be in keeping with the gravity and the solemnity of what they are about to do.

> ✠ A. MAYER, Archbishop of Satriano
> *Secretary*

COMMENT

The *Order for Religious Profession, Ordo Professionis Religiosae,* was published in 1970 by the Sacred Congregation for Divine Worship. An interim English translation "for study and comment by the bishops and major superiors of religious communities in the member countries of the International Committee on English in the Liturgy, Inc. (I.C.E.L.), Toronto, Canada" was published by I.C.E.L. in 1971, U.S.C.C. 1330 Massachusetts Avenue, N.W., Washington, D.C., 20005.

On page 111 of the *Ordo Professionis Religiosae* it is stated that each religious family may compose its own formula for profession, submitting it for approval to the Congregation for Religious and Secular Institutes. On the same page a sample formula for profession is offered as a help to religious institutes.

The person making profession says:

For the honor of God, impelled by a firm resolve to consecrate myself more deeply to him and to follow Christ more closely throughout my life, I, N.N. do hereby, in the presence of my brothers (sisters), profess before you, N.N.,[2] my vows of perpetual[3] chastity, poverty and obedience in accordance with the (Rule and) Constitutions of N.[4]

I give myself to this family with all my heart so that by the grace of the Holy Spirit and with the help of the Virgin Mary, I may try to achieve perfect charity in the service of God and the Church.

The person who accepts the vows may say as follows:

And I by virtue of the power given to me in the name of the Church accept the vows made by you in N.[5] I earnestly commend you to God, so that you may perfect your offering, linked with the sacrifice of the Eucharist.

DECREE ON THE FORM OF ORDINARY GOVERNMENT AND ON THE ACCESS OF SECULARIZED OFFICES AND BENEFICES

Experimentations on the form of government have given rise to a certain number of problems and questions, particularly with regard to what concerns the personal authority of a superior. In addition, it has been judged opportune to review carefully, in the present circumstances, the restrictions of canon 642, relative to secularized religious.

After study by consultants, the Fathers of this Sacred Congregation, in the Plenary Assembly of September 24 and 25, 1971, considered carefully the following questions:

1. May one, contrary to canon 516 of the code of canon law, admit a collegial government, ordinary and exclusive, for an institute, for a province or for a house, in such a way that the superior, if there is one, would be simply an executive?

2. May one suspend canon 642 of the code of canon law and authorize religious regularly dispensed from their vows to obtain

---

2. Add the name and office of the superior who accepts the profession.

3. Or state the length of time for which profession is made.

4. Mention the name of the religious family.

5. Mention the name of the religious family.

offices, benefices or ecclesiastical charges whatsoever, without a special permission of the Holy See?

Everything well considered, the Fathers of the Assembly above mentioned unanimously agreed to the answer that follows:

1. To the first question: *Negatively.* According to the spirit of the second Vatican Council (Decree, "Perfectae Caritatis," n. 14 and of the apostolic Exhortation "Evangelica Testificatio," p. 25) account taken of legitimate consultation as well as of the limits established by common law as well as by particular law, superiors must be invested with a personal authority.

2. To the second: *Affirmatively.*

At the time of the Audience according to the Secretary of the Sacred Congregation on November 18, 1971, the Sovereign Pontiff, Paul VI, approved these decisions. Consequently, the Sacred Congregation has decided to publish the decisions by means of the present decree. These become effective immediately, without further statement. They will remain valid until the new code of canon law has legal force. Given at Rome, February 2, 1972.

Hildebrand, Cardinal Antoniutti
Prefect

Canon 516 states: The Superior-General of every Institute or monastic Congregation, also every Provincial Superior and local Superior at least of every formal house, shall have their Councillors whose consent or counsel they must seek according to the terms of the constitutions and the sacred canons.

Canon 642 is suspended with the promulgation of this decree.

Decree, DUM CANONICARUM, AAS (2) 63 (1971) 3182

The final clause of Canon 637 is to be understood in the following sense: when a religious in temporary vows is found to have contracted a physical or mental illness which would render him incapable of living the religious life without harm to himself or the institute, he may be refused admission to the renewal of temporary vows or to final profession. The decision is to be made by the competent superior, with the consent of his council, on the basis of examinations by physicians or other experts. The decision can be made, even if the illness has been contracted after profession.

(3) However, the laws of charity and equity must be observed. His Holiness, Pope Paul VI, in the audience granted to the Secretary of this Sacred Congregation on November 20, approved these dispositions and directed that they be put into effect immediately, without any formula or execution, until such time as the revised Canon Law becomes effective.

All things to the contrary notwithstanding.

Given at Rome, on the eighth day of December, 1970

H. Cardinal Antoniutti, Perfect

(2) The text of Canon 637 reads as follows: "When his vows have expired, a temporarily professed religious may freely leave his institute. At the same time, the institute may decide not to admit him to the renewal of his temporary vows, or to perpetual profession, provided there be just and reasonable motives for this. HOWEVER, IT IS NOT PERMISSIBLE TO DO SO ON GROUNDS THAT AN ILLNESS HAS BEEN DIAGNOSED, UNLESS IT BE ESTABLISHED THAT HE HAD CONCEALED THE ILLNESS BEFORE PROFESSION". The provision which follows is a commentary on the last part of Canon 637 and it changes the legislalation in the sense indicated.

(3) This sentence marks the departure from the legislation enshrined in Canon 637. Note, however, that it does not refer to all illnesses but only to illnesses which would harm him or the institute if he remained a member of it.

PRINCIPLE DOCUMENTS ON RELIGIOUS LIFE
PUBLISHED SINCE 1965

1. Documents of Vatican II especially:
   Decree: Perfectae Caritatis, October 28, 1965
   Constitution: Lumen Gentium, Ch. 5 and 6, November 21, 1964

2. Pope Paul VI
   Motu Proprio: Ecclesiae Sanctae, August 6, 1966
   Exhortation: Evangelica testificatio, June 29, 1971

3. *Decree: Religionum laicalium,* May 5, 1966
   Broader faculties given to Major Superiors:
   a) Dispensation of candidates from impediment of illegitimacy
   b) Alienation of goods of the Institute
   c) Permission to live outside a house of the community
   d) Permission for subjects in simple perpetual vows to give away goods belonging to their patrimony
   e) Permission to change a will
   f) Permission to transfer the location of the novitiate
   g) Permission for a third term for Local Superiors

4. *Decree:* Cum Superiores Generales, Nov. 27, 1969
   For Institutes of Pontifical Right it is no longer necessary to apply to the Holy See for an indult of secularization for a Sister of temporary vows.

5. *Decree:* Ad instituenda, June 4, 1970
   a) Only the first division or total suppression of provinces is still reserved to the Holy See
   b) In exempt institutes seeking approval of the Holy See for erection or suppression of houses is suspended
   c) Requirements for the office of Superior General
   d) Testimonial letters
   e) Length of time for retreat prior to entrance into Novitiate and also to temporary vows
   f) Making of a will before perpetual profession instead of before temporary commitment
   g) Canonical examination suspended
   h) Religious women going out without a companion

6. *Decree:* Dum canonicarum, December 8, 1970
   a) Regarding the Sacrament of Penance
   b) Regarding refusal of admission to renewal of temporary vows or to final profession because of illness

7. *Decree:* Experimenta circa regiminis rationem, February 2, 1972

   Concerning the necessity of the personal authority of the Superior, without prejudice to the practice of legitimate consultation and to the limits placed by common or particular law.

8. *Instruction:* Renovationis causam, January 7, 1969

   The entire law on the novitiate, with the possibility of promises, is revised. Each institute should have its Formation Program based on this instruction with approval by the General Chapter.

These documents, in English, will usually be found in:
   Assisting Those Who Leave Religious Institutes, Jan. 30, 1974; Cf. RR vol. 33, no. 4, July 1974, p. 769.
   Canon Law for Religious after Vatican II, cf. RR, vol. 31, no. 6, Nov., 1972, pp. 949-966; vol. 32, no 6, Nov. , 1973, pp. 1273-87; vol. 34, no. 1, Jan., 1975, pp. 50-70.
   Recent Documents Concerning Religious, cf. RR, vol 33, no. 1, Jan., 1974, pp. 3-19.

ANALYTICAL INDEX

PAPAL AND ECCLESIAL DOCUMENTS

Cum Sanctissimus, Aloysius Cardinal Lavitrano, Prefect, SCRSI, 1948, pp. 251-257

Pope Paul VI's *Allocution on Secular Institutes*, September 20, 1972, pp. 257-263

Pope Paul VI, *Mysterium Fidei*, 1966, pp. 49-71

Immensae Caritatis, Sacred Congregation for the Discipline of the Sacraments, 1973, p. 71

Pope Pius XII, *Primo Feliciter*, 1948, pp. 247-251

Pope Pius XII, *Provido Mater Ecclesia*, 1947, pp. 236-247

Ordo Paenitentiae, 1974, U.S.C.C., p. 71

Renovationis Causam, I. Cardinal Antoniutti, Prefect, SCRSI, 1969, pp. 132-151

Pope Paul VI, *Sacram Unctionem Infirmorum*, 1972, p. 71

Sacramentum Paenitentiae, Sacred Congregation for the Doctrine of the Faith, 1972, p. 71

Venite Seorsum, I. Cardinal Antoniutti, Prefect of SCRSI, 1969, pp. 157-165

Norms Regulating Papal Enclosure of Nuns, I Cardinal Antoniutti, Prefect, SCRSI, 1969, pp. 166-170

Formal Reply to *Dubia Concerning Venite Seorsum*, I Cardinal Antoniutti, January 2, 1972, pp. 170

Pope Paul VI, *Ecclesiae Sanctae*, p. 188 ff.

Pope Paul VI, *Marialis Cultus*, 1974, p. 100

Behold Your Mother, U.S.C.C., 1973, p. 100

To Teach as Jesus Did, U.S.C.C., 1972, p. 100

Basic Teachings for Catholic Religious Education, U.S.C.C., 1973, p. 100

General Catholic Directory, Sacred Congregation for the Clergy, 1971, p. 100

Mysterium Ecclesiae, Congregation of the Faith, June 24, 1973

Indulgentiarum, Apostolic Constitution, January 1, 1967

Pope Paul VI *Allocutions on Renewal*
    August 6, 1964, p. 208
    October 28, 1966, p. 207
    December 22, 1967, p. 206
    August 26, 1967, p. 208
    January 22, 1968, p. 207

April 25, 1968, p. 207
November 22, 1969, p. 207
December 8, 1970, p. 206
January 12, 1972, p. 206
September 20, 1972, p. 257
October 19, 1972, p. 207

DECREES

RELIGIONUM LAICALIUM, SCRSI, May 31, 1966, pp. 266-269

CUM SUPERIORES GENERALES, SCRSI, November 27, 1969, pp. 269-270

AD INSTITUENDA, SCRSI, June 4, 1970, pp. 270-272

REVISION OF LAW ON SACRAMENTAL CONFESSION, 1970, pp. 72-73

FORM OF ORDINARY GOVERNMENT AND ON ACCESS OF SECULARIZED OFFICES AND BENEFICES, SCRSI, February 2, 1971, pp. 274; 46-47

DUM CANONICARUM, SCRSI, 1971, pp. 275

FORMULA FOR RELIGIOUS PROFESSION, Congregation of Divine Worship, August, 1973, pp. 272-73

LETTERS

Most Reverend Luigi Raimondi, on Religious Habit, January 28, 1972, pp. 124-125

John Cardinal Krol to Sisters, on Religious Habit, December 20, 1973, pp. 125-127

I. Cardinal Antoniutti to Most Reverend Leo Pursley, on Religious Habit, pp. 128-129

Most Reverend Luigi Raimondi, Re. Permissions for leaving cloister, April 21, 1967, pp. 155-6

John Joseph Cardinal Carberry, Re. *Venite Seorsum*, May 6, 1970, pp. 172-173

Most Reverend Edward Heston, C.S.C., to Cardinal Carberry, Re. *Venite Seorsum*, June 13, 1970, pp. 174-175

John Joseph Cardinal Carberry to Contemplative Nuns, Re. *Venite Seorsum*, August 3, 1970, 175-176

TOPICAL INDEX

I. The Mystery of Religious Life

1. The Church in the Mystery of Christ
   Cf. LG, 1; 2; 3; 4; 5; 6; 7
   Mysterium Ecclesiae; Indulgentiarum

2. The Mystery of Holiness; Holiness of the Trinity, the Source, Cause and End of the One Same Holiness in Christ's Body, the Church
   Cf. LG, 39; 40; 41; 42; 48

3. Religious Life Rooted in the Baptismal Consecration in the Mystery of Christ
   Cf. LG, 43; ET, 1; 2; 3; 4; 7; 37

4. Religious Life—Total Surrender to God in Love
   Cf. LG, 43; 44; 13; ET, 7; 4; 30

5. Religious Life—Publically Vowed Perpetual Commitment to the Evangelical Counsels in Pursuit of Perfect Charity
   A. Consecrated Chastity
      Cf. LG, 44; PC, 12; ET, 13; 14; 15
      SCRSI, July 10, 1972
   B. Consecrated Poverty
      Cf. LG, 44; PC, 13; ET, 16; 21; 17; 19; 20; 18
      SCRSI, July 10, 1972
   C. Consecrated Obedience
      Cf. LG, 44; 46; PC, 14; ET, 23; 24; 25; 26; 27;
      28; 29; 55; PC, 5; 6.
      SCRSI, August, 1971; December, 1971; July 10, 1972
   D. Authority in Religious Institutes
      Cf. L.G., 22; 23; 43; 45; CD, 2-6, 8; ESI, 22-40; PC,
      14; ET, 25; 23; 28; 24; Canons 501-502

6. Religious Life in Sacramental Encounter with Christ
   A. *Mysterium Fidei:* Mystery of Faith; Mystery of Eucharist Verified in Sacrifice of the Mass; Christ Sacramentally Present; Sacramental Presence Effected through Transsubstantiation; Exhortation
   B. *Immensae Caritatis*
   C. *Sacramentum Paenitentiae*
   D. *Ordo Paenitentiae*
   E. *Sacram Unctionem Infirmorum*
   F. *Revision of Law on Sacramental Confession and Canon 637*

7. Mystery of Religious Life in Christ's Body, the Church
   Cf. LG, 44; 46; 48; 31; PC, 2, 6, 8, 20; ET, 50; 9; CD, 33; 34; 35; ESI, 22-40

8. Religious Life in the Mission of the Church
   Cf. LG, 46; 31; 44; AG, 1; 18; 33; 34; 40; CD, 33; 34; 35; ET, 56; 20; ESI, 28, SCRSI, April, 1968; March 31, 1971; July 10, 1972; *Marialis Cultus; Behold Your Mother; To Teach us Jesus Did; Basic Teachings for Catholic Religious Education; General Catechetical Directory.*

9. Religious Dynamically Faithful to Charism of Founder
   Cf. LG, 45; PC, 2; ET, 11, 32

II. Renewal of Religious Life
   1. Necessary for Renewal of the Church
      Cf. LG, 48; ET, 52; 10; 31; 53

   2. Basic Principles for Authentic Renewal in the Radical Following of Christ
      Cf. LG, 46; 7; PC, 2; 6; 7; ET, 2; 49; 47; 48.
      ORDO PROFESSIONIS RELIGIOSAE

   3. Prayer, Primary Orientation of Religious Life
      Cf. PC, 6; 7; ET, 45; 46; 42; 43; 44; 35; SCRSI, August, 1971

   4. Communal Life Renewed
      Cf. PC, 15; ET, 34; 33; 39; 38; 40; 41; 54; SCRSI, April, 1968; August, 1971

5. Sign of Consecration, The Religious Habit
   Cf. LG, 44; PC, 17; ET, 22; SCRSI, August, 1971; January 22, 1972; July 10, 1972; February 25, 1972; Letters from Cardinal Antoniutti; Most Reverend Luigi Raimondi; Cardinal Krol.

6. Authentic Renewal of Formation
   Cf. PC, 18; ES II-II, 33-38
   SCRSI, *Renovationis Causam;* Instruction on Formation Renewal; Guidelines and Principles, RC, 1-9; Special Norms, RC, 10-38

7. Renewal of Cloistered and Monastic Religious Life
   Cf. PC, 9; 16; ET, 8; ES II-II, 30; 31; SCRSI, *Venite Seorsum;* Instruction on the Contemplative Life and on the Enclosure of Nuns; Norms Regulating Papal Enclosure of Nuns (1-17); Letter from Cardinal Antoniutti, August, 1969; Letter from Reverend Edward Heston, C.S.C., June, 1970; and Letters from Cardinal Carberry, August, 1970; March, 1972 and Appointment of Special Commission of Bishops for Contemplative Nuns in U.S.

III. Appropriate Adaptation in Religious Life: Expression and Effect of Authentic Renewal of Consecrated Vowed Life
   Cf. 43; PC, 3; 4; ET, 51; 12; 36; ES II-I, 15; 16; 17

1. General Norms for Adaptation
   A. Adaptation of Various Forms
      Cf. PC, 7-11
   B. Basic Elements
      Cf. PC, 12-15
   C. Other Elements
      Cf. PC, 7-17
   D. Formation
      Cf. PC, 18
   E. Apostolic works
      Cf. PC 20

2. Adaptations should be made appropriately in
   A. Mode of Living
      Cf. ET, 5; 12; 51

B. Ancient traditions
   Cf. PC, 9; ET, 36; ES II-I, 17
C. Prayer Life
   Cf. P.C., 6; 7; 8; ET, 8; 49; PC, 3; ES II-II, 20; 21
D. Perspective of Founder
   Cf. PC, 2; ET, 11; 32; ES II-I 15: 16
E. Apostolic Service to the Church
   Cf. PC, 8; 9; 10; 18; 20; CD, 33; 34; 35; ES III,
   12; AG, 5; 6
F. Mode of Government
   Cf. PC, 3; 14; CD, 35; ES II-I, 2; 6; 7; 18; SCRSI,
   February 2, 1972; January 17, 1970; April 16, 1970;
   January 11, 1972
G. Demands of Culture and Social and Economic Conditions
   Cf. PC, 19; AG, 10; 11; 18; 23; 24; 25; 27; 42; GS, 58
H. Mental and Physical Health
   Cf. PC 12; ET 33; Allocutions of Pope Paul VI relative
   to Renewal

3. Appropriate Adaptation and Renewal are Obligatory for
   Religious by the Very Nature of Religious Life and the Right
   of the Holy See to Interpret Its Norms
   Cf. PC, 1; 2; 3; 25; ET, 56; 1; 2; 3; 52; LG 65; 68;
   69; SCRSI, April, 1968; December, 1971

4. Manner of Promoting Adaptation and Renewal
   Cf. Introduction to ES II; ES II-I, 1-11

5. Persons Bound to Promote
   Cf. ES II-I, 1-11

6. Revisions of Constitutions in the Light of Renewal and
   Adaptation
   Cf. ES II-I, 12-19; PC, 3
   A. Approval of Constitutions
      Cf. Canon 492 (Canon Law *in general* not abrogated or
      suspended); ES II-I, 8
   B. Principles to be included
      Cf. SCRSI, July 10, 1972

7. Adaptations and Renewal to be effected in
   A. Divine Office, Cf. ES II-II, 20; PC 3

B. Mental Prayer, Cf. PC, 6; ES II-II, 21
C. Mortification, Cf. PC. 5; 12; ES II-II, 22
D. Poverty, Cf. PC, 13; ES II-II, 23; 24
E. Common Life, Cf. PC, 15; ES II-II. 15; 26; 27; 28; 29

IV. Experiments
1. Nature, purpose, norms, Cf. SCRSI, August, 1971
2. Authority, Cf. PC, 4; 3; ES II-I, 1; 3; 4; 6; CD, 35; ET, 7; 25; 50
3. Scope and Limit: Experiments may not interfere with the purpose, nature, and character of the Institute, Cf. PC, 2; 20; 17; Limited by the general law specified for religious in the Code of Canon Law unless revised.
4. Limited by prudence: experiments which cannot be sanctioned by the Church for definitive approval of the Constitutions, should be avoided; Cf. further limitations indicated p. 222 of *Religious Life—A Mystery In Christ And The Church*
5. Reports of Chapters during Period of Experimentation to be submitted to the Sacred Congregation for Religious, Cf. SCRSI, July 10, 1972. Directives re. Government, (ibid)

V. Special Directives
A. Union of Institutes, or Federations, Cf. PC, 22; ES II-II, 39; 40
B. Supression of Institutes, Cf. ES II-II, 41
C. Conferences of Major Superiors, Cf. PC, 23; ES II-II, 42; 43
D. Establishment of New Communities, Cf. PC 19
E. Promotion of Vocations, Cf. PC, 24; ET, 3; 12; 45; 55; SCRSI, August, 1971

VI. Secular Institutes: Consecrated Secularity; Distinguished from Religious Life as Such
Cf. PC 11; Apostolic Constitution, *Provida Mater Ecclesia;* Special Laws Governing Secular Institutes; Motu Proprio *Primo Feliciter* (In Praise and Approbationof Secular Institutes); SCRSI, *Cum Sanctissimus* (Instruction on Secular Institutes); Pope Paul's *Allocution on Secular Institutes,* September 20, 1972

An Interesting Thought

The publication you have just finished reading is part of the apostolic efforts of the Society of St. Paul of the American Province. A small, unique group of priests and brothers, the members of the Society of St. Paul propose to bring the message of Christ to men through the communications media while living the religious life.

If you know of a young man who might be interested in learning more about our life and mission, ask him to contact the Vocation Office in care of ALBA HOUSE, at 2187 Victory Blvd., Staten Island, New York 10314. Full information will be sent without cost or obligation. You may be instrumental in helping a young man to find his vocation in life. *An interesting thought.*

NOTES

NOTES